MATHEMATICAL PUZZLES FOR BEGINNERS AND ENTHUSIASTS, Geoffrey Mott-Smith. 189 puzzles from easy to difficult—involving arithmetic, logic, algebra, properties of digits, probability, etc.—for enjoyment and mental stimulus. Explanation of mathematical principles behind the puzzles. 135 illustrations. viii + 248pp.
20198-8 Paperbound $2.00

PAPER FOLDING FOR BEGINNERS, William D. Murray and Francis J. Rigney. Easiest book on the market, clearest instructions on making interesting, beautiful origami. Sail boats, cups, roosters, frogs that move legs, bonbon boxes, standing birds, etc. 40 projects; more than 275 diagrams and photographs. 94pp.
20713-7 Paperbound $1.00

TRICKS AND GAMES ON THE POOL TABLE, Fred Herrmann. 79 tricks and games— some solitaires, some for two or more players, some competitive games—to entertain you between formal games. Mystifying shots and throws, unusual caroms, tricks involving such props as cork, coins, a hat, etc. Formerly *Fun on the Pool Table*. 77 figures. 95pp.
21814-7 Paperbound $1.25

HAND SHADOWS TO BE THROWN UPON THE WALL: A SERIES OF NOVEL AND AMUSING FIGURES FORMED BY THE HAND, Henry Bursill. Delightful picturebook from great-grandfather's day shows how to make 18 different hand shadows: a bird that flies, duck that quacks, dog that wags his tail, camel, goose, deer, boy, turtle, etc. Only book of its sort. vi + 33pp. 6½ x 9¼. 21779-5 Paperbound $1.00

WHITTLING AND WOODCARVING, E. J. Tangerman. 18th printing of best book on market. "If you can cut a potato you can carve" toys and puzzles, chains, chessmen, caricatures, masks, frames, woodcut blocks, surface patterns, much more. Information on tools, woods, techniques. Also goes into serious wood sculpture from Middle Ages to present, East and West. 464 photos, figures. x + 293pp.
20965-2 Paperbound $2.50

HISTORY OF PHILOSOPHY, Julián Marías. Possibly the clearest, most easily followed, best planned, most useful one-volume history of philosophy on the market; neither skimpy nor overfull. Full details on system of every major philosopher and dozens of less important thinkers from pre-Socratics up to Existentialism and later. Strong on many European figures usually omitted. Has gone through dozens of editions in Europe. 1966 edition, translated by Stanley Appelbaum and Clarence Strowbridge. xviii + 505pp. 21739-6 Paperbound $3.50

YOGA: A SCIENTIFIC EVALUATION, Kovoor T. Behanan. Scientific but non-technical study of physiological results of yoga exercises; done under auspices of Yale U. Relations to Indian thought, to psychoanalysis, etc. 16 photos. xxiii + 270pp.
20505-3 Paperbound $2.50

Prices subject to change without notice.
Available at your book dealer or write for free catalogue to Dept. GI, Dover Publications, Inc., 180 Varick St., N. Y., N. Y. 10014. Dover publishes more than 150 books each year on science, elementary and advanced mathematics, biology, music, art, literary history, social sciences and other areas.

THE INSTANT EPICURE COOKBOOK

The
INSTANT
EPICURE
Cookbook

GOURMET COOKING IN TWENTY MINUTES

LILLIAN LANGSETH-CHRISTENSEN

DOVER PUBLICATIONS, INC.
NEW YORK

International Standard Book Number: 0-486-23128-3
Library of Congress Catalog Card Number: 74-83767

Manufactured in the United States of America
Dover Publications, Inc.
180 Varick Street
New York, N. Y. 10014

To my husband, Ricardo

Contents

THE TOOLS FOR INSTANT EPICUREANISM   9

1. Hors d'Oeuvres   13

2. Soups   36

3. Fish   60

4. Cheeses and Eggs   87

5. Meat and Poultry   113

6. Vegetables   141

7. Pastas, Rice and Breads   168

8. Salads, Dressings and Relishes   190

9. Sauces   219

10. Desserts   237

11. Outdoor or Plug-in-Anywhere Cooking   261

12. Beverages   274

    Index   289

The Tools For Instant Epicureanism

THERE ARE only two steps needed to make us into Instant Epicures and the first of these is usually forced upon us. We find ourselves gradually, or suddenly, without time. The moment there is no time, or less than there used to be, we automatically change our eating habits. We no longer think in terms of fowl or pot roast, lentils or home-baked beans; we wouldn't dream of shelling peas or stringing beans. We discard the utensils for making soup stock and we put all thought of boiled beef and potato dumplings out of our minds forever. We turn, naturally, to prepared foods or quick-cooking foods. We still eat, but we cut down on the time that used to be spent in preparing and cooking the food. At first this goes very well; all soups come out of cans, all vegetables are canned or frozen, the main dishes are quickly fried or heated and desserts are out of the freezer (straight or via the oven).

It works, but after a while we are forced into the second step: to make our new way of eating more interesting, to learn an entire repertoire of dishes and menus that can be prepared out of combinations of all the prepared foods with fresh foods and so give us the variety and delicacy we are accustomed to.

Instant Cookery is here for all of us, whether it is a chronic condition or an acute one. No one in this age can escape the necessity of producing meals in less time than it takes or the necessity of producing at least one or two of the courses for dinner in no time at all. Instant Epicureanism is an attempt to produce enjoyable foods or whole menus in minutes. Instant Eating of that food is the thing we must resist (ask your doctor). Running breakfasts, flying luncheons, snatched sandwiches and gulped Martinis are sins against our health—*ergo,* when there is very little or no time, the proper place to cut corners and reduce time is on preparation time, *never* on eating time.

In order to do this we need the necessary tools. You may no longer need that bulky potato ricer, since you are now using instant or frozen mashed potatoes, but you need a whole new set of hardware. It is impossible to limit your eating, for any length of time, to those dishes that need no cooking time and no preparation time either. Unfortunately it takes longer to cook something that is whole than something that is sliced or chopped. The quicker the cooking has to go, the smaller or thinner the object has to be. You cannot bake a fat onion in less than twenty minutes, but you can broil onion slices, spread with cheese and butter, in less than two minutes . . . so . . . you need a slicer, you need a mincer, a chopper and a grater. You need, in fact, the tools of your new trade, Instant Epicureanism.

You may already own, or be able to invest in, one or two electric appliances. A good electric beater with attachments for grinding is excellent. An electric blender will really blend, mix, mash, mince and, if you turn it off fast enough, it will chop. In some ways the two appliances overlap, but in many ways their functions are totally different. If your problem is *time* only and not space or money, then the electric mixer, the blender, the broiler and skillet will serve your fast-preparing, fast-cooking program well.

If you cannot lay in such luxuries then there are wonderful un-electric kitchen gadgets, utensils and tools that will cut preparation time down to a minimum. On second thought, these are tools you should own even if you have all the latest plug-in equipment. Let the blender do a blender's work, but grind your single sprig of parsley through the Mouli mincer and grind that little piece of Parmesan through the Mouli grater.

Let's face it, to lift the ordinary quickly prepared recipes from dullness to interest, to make them look attractive and tempting, we have to be able to chop a shallot, crush a garlic clove, mince parsley, slice a lemon and do just about one hundred and one other little tricks. These very things are what take time, and still we cannot abandon them and retain our Epicurean status. Necessary tool number one, then, is the indispensable Mouli.

THE "MOULI" ROTARY MINCER. Mouli is a French trade name for *moulin*—the mill. (Remember that great red windmill in Paris, the Moulin Rouge?) A Mouli costs $3.00 and comes to you, via any good kitchen hardware department or store, direct from France. It chops your parsley—just put in the sprigs, turn the handle and your quickly broiled fish steak is buried under freshly chopped, aromatic parsley. Grind or mill any fresh herb through it. Mince chives over your canned Vichyssoise, chop mint over your broiled lamb chop or oregano over your salad. Your Mouli will be practically your best friend.

THE "MOULI" ROTARY GRATER. Sister or brother of the above, it grates nuts and cheese, bread crumbs and crackers. It, too, costs $3.00 and it is as indispensable as the Parmesan cheese it grates freshly over your pastas or vegetables, over your soups and casseroles.

THE GARLIC PRESS. It costs about $1.45 and crushes your garlic clove without perfuming your hands for hours. It just might happen that you would get your hand kissed immediately after mincing garlic without a garlic press. It also prevents you from giving one of your guests a piece of pure garlic (and indigestion) while your other guests get only a whiff. You can mix your crushed garlic with salt and use it to great advantage on meats, you can crush it into your vinegar or salad dressing bottle and you can add it to your favorite barbecue sauce. If you have gotten along without a garlic press up to now, go out with your dollar and change your way of life.

SALAD BASKET. The French call it their *panier à salade* and it speeds the drying of your salad greens without bruising the leaves. It costs about $3.25 and there is a collapsible one that takes very little storage space. It can also be used for deep frying or parboiling.

VEGETABLE MASTER. This is a three-legged gadget with four interchangeable grills that slices, chops, grates and cuts julienne. There are similar pieces of equipment with other names that answer the same purpose. The Vegetable Master costs $3.95 complete and it will also grate cheese or bread. As these things go, it is very inexpensive and extremely useful. It is also easy to wash.

MOULINEX SALAD MAKER AND MEAT GRINDER ELECTRIC COMBINATION. The makers of the Mouli products make an electric do-all appliance which shreds, slices, juliennes, chops, grates and minces. It grinds meat, nuts, chocolate and cheese and there is nothing you can do to a vegetable that the Moulinex will not do. It runs on AC and DC and it is extremely compact. It costs $42.50 and if you want a single aid, trust the French to design something that is perfect for the purpose.

BATIREX. This is a six-wheeled gadget that chops or minces vegetables, herbs or fruit. There is a German one on the market called the Schneidermeister, which has a plastic housing. The French Batirex is all metal and costs $7.00. You slice your onion or potato and then you wheel your Batirex over the slices and in a moment you have chopped or minced onion.

VEGETABLE SLICER. These come in combinations of metal and wood, or they can be found in all-metal. The all-metal slicer with adjustable blade at about $2.25 is excellent. You run cucumbers, onions, beets or potatoes over its adjustable cutting surface and you come up with the neatest, evenest slices you ever saw. Cucumber salad in seconds, coleslaw, paper-thin pickled beets.

All these recommended aids to fast preparation can be bought in kitchenware departments or specialty shops. If you cannot obtain them in your neighborhood, all you have to do is remember the number six and write to the Bazar Française, 666 6th Avenue, New York, N.Y. 10010; Chelsea 3-6660. They will be glad to fill your order.

CHAPTER I

Hors d'Oeuvres

Guests are, although they do not know it, very difficult to please and sometimes I wonder why we keep on inviting them. If you prepare elaborate hors d'oeuvres, in minutes of course, they are embarrassed and invariably say, "But you shouldn't have gone to so much trouble." The maddening thing is that they say this while they eat, with gusto, the very hors d'oeuvres they maintain you shouldn't have taken the trouble to prepare. What hostesses really want to hear is that it tastes good and that any trouble they may have taken is appreciated.

During dinner the same guests take on a reproachful attitude. They are apt to refuse a second helping on the grounds that they ate so many appetizers they spoiled their appetites. This is always done with accusation and sometimes even with an accompanying pat on the general region where hors d'oeuvres are supposed to repose. If the hostess goes to the other extreme and tries to solve the whole thing by tearing open a bag of potato chips or by opening a can of salted peanuts, the guests feel neglected and approach dinner with understandable doubts and depression. All this teaches the hostess to try to find a golden middle course . . . never serve too many hors d'oeuvres and never serve too few.

The too-elaborate hors d'oeuvre can, however, be turned into a virtue. A clever hostess, with little effort and expense, can produce appetizers and hors d'oeuvres that will so completely fill her guests that dinner can be a meager main course with fruit and coffee to follow.

There are hostesses (substitute host for hostess wherever necessary; Instant Epicures can be either male or female) who affect serving a glass of sherry or an apéritif with a dry biscuit before dinner. This may be very continental and very healthful but the hors d'oeuvre is actually the Instant Hostess's greatest blessing. If she comes in from work a few minutes ahead of her guests or if she gets her children fed and to bed a few minutes before her husband comes home, she can take her first few moments of leisure to prepare one or two of the following quick appetizers which, when combined with a good drink, will hold the average guest and/or husband content and happy while dinner is being prepared. This does not mean that the Instant Hostess has to miss the cocktail hour, or half hour as the case may be; she should be able to make her dinner preparations without pressure and rejoin her guests long before the second drink is served.

Hors d'oeuvres should always be prepared according to established rules. They should be good because they are the opening move and in a sense they give the cue for dinner. They should stimulate the appetite rather than appease it and they should arouse interest in the dinner that is to follow. A guest who is given pâté wtih cold grapes and an icy Martini knows perfectly well that dinner isn't going to be an upside-down cake of ham paste and pineapple. A meal is a progressive pleasure and the hors d'oeuvres should always lead up to the first course, or the main course, depending on the menu. Don't serve curried shrimp before a Sénégalaise or cheese puffs before a Fondue Neufchâteloise.

The hors d'oeuvre, besides its pleasurable functions, should also produce a sort of blanket for the first drink. The guest or husband who comes straight from a day of meetings, no lunch, several canceled orders and a jibe from his immediate superior should never put an ice-cold drink into an empty stomach which has spent the day preparing itself for an ulcer—or, for that matter, into a stomach that has enjoyed three coffee breaks, a heavy chocolate-coated doughnut and a tax return all on the same day. The same holds good for ladies' stomachs which have been confronted with an unbalanced checkbook, tight shoes, suddenly straight hair and a rival in a single afternoon. The hors d'oeuvres in these cases have to have spongelike action and absorb part of the alcoholic content of the first drink and leave you with a relaxed guest or husband or boy friend who has gradually laid aside tension for that nice feeling of warmth and appetite which should by rights be every man's and woman's approach to dinner.

TOMATO JUICE COCKTAIL

1 14-ounce can tomato juice
2 onion slices, ¼ inch thick
2 thin lemon slices, seeded
½ teaspoon sugar

½ teaspoon salt
¼ teaspoon Worcestershire sauce
½ cup vodka
1 dash Tabasco sauce
black pepper

Combine all ingredients except black pepper in blender and blend until onion and lemon slices are finely chopped. Correct seasoning. Serve chilled or poured over ice cubes. Sprinkle top with coarsely ground black pepper.

If no blender is available, use 2 teaspoons grated lemon rind and ¼ cup frozen chopped onion, thawed.

CLAM JUICE COCKTAIL

3 cups clam juice
½ cup tomato juice
½ cup ketchup

½ lemon, juice only
1 dash Tabasco sauce
celery salt

Shake all ingredients with ice in a cocktail shaker. Serve in wide glasses dusted with celery salt.

For the hostess who comes home just before, or sometimes with, her guests—or for the hostess who was not planning to be one until the doorbell rang—here are four open-the-tin-and-combine-and-serve hors d'oeuvres that are so good they should be in every hostess's repertoire. Whether she has fifteen minutes to prepare dinner or no minutes at all, she can always open four cans. Stir the contents of three with bottled French or Italian dressing and one with mayonnaise and serve them up with cocktails. You can also mix these four instant concoctions, put them in four suitable dishes and serve them as a first-course hors d'oeuvre at the table. If you add 2 sliced tomatoes in French dressing and a tin of sardines you can have *du vrai hors-d'oeuvre français* at the drop of a *chapeau.*

ITALIAN MUSHROOMS

1 12½-ounce can button mush-
    rooms, drained
2–3 tablespoons bottled Italian
    dressing, to taste

2 sprigs parsley ground through a
    Mouli
salt and pepper

Combine mushrooms and dressing and season if necessary. Sprinkle with parsley and serve. These can be served with forks or cocktail picks.

KIDNEY BEANS

1 12-ounce can kidney beans,
    drained
2–3 tablespoons bottled French
    dressing, to taste

1 small onion, sliced
salt and pepper

Mix beans and dressing and garnish with onion slices. Season if necessary and serve.

CHICKEN LIVER PÂTÉ

2 4-ounce cans chicken liver pâté
sherry to taste
onion salt and pepper

1 box salty crackers
    or
1 package potato chips or Fritos

Stir pâté and sherry together until smooth. Season to taste and serve as a spread with crackers. Or, if you prefer, you can thin pâté to dipping consistency with sherry and serve with potato chips or Fritos.

ITALIAN ARTICHOKE HEARTS

1 No. 303 can artichoke hearts, drained	¼ cup mayonnaise
	2 tablespoons bottled Italian dressing
2 tablespoons capers	

Beat mayonnaise and dressing. Pour over artichokes, sprinkle with capers and serve with picks as an appetizer or as part of a first-course hors d'oeuvre tray.

Many of the following fruit and meat combinations can be arranged on picks to be served with cocktails. By increasing the quantities, they can also be served as a first course at dinner or luncheon.

MELON AND PROSCIUTTO

1 large or 2 small cantaloupes ½ pound thin sliced prosciutto

(Prosciutto is smoked Italian ham. It can be sliced paper thin and is obtainable at Italian markets and delicatessen stores. Many supermarkets are also stocking it.)

Cut melon in half, scrape out seeds and cut into thin wedges, allowing about 4 to a serving. Arrange on a platter with sliced ham and serve as cold as possible. Pass salt and pepper separately. When used as an hors d'oeuvre with cocktails, cut the melon into cubes, wrap each cube with a strip of the ham and secure with picks. Chill until needed.

FIGS AND SALAMI

12 fresh figs 12 thin slices imported salami

Arrange figs and salami on a serving plate and chill until needed.

HAM AND PINEAPPLE APPETIZERS

1 1-pound slice smoked ham,   1 can pineapple chunks, cut in
   cut into cubes   half

Serve ham and pineapple chunks in cocktail glasses on lettuce leaves. Pour over a mustard-flavored mayonnaise, thinned with a little pineapple juice.

For cocktails, impale a cube of ham and half a pineapple chunk on each cocktail pick and serve the mustard-flavored mayonnaise separately.

LIVER SAUSAGE AND GRAPES

8 slices liver sausage, skinned   8 small bunches green grapes

Arrange sausage and grapes on a platter and chill until needed.

For cocktails, impale a cube of liver sausage and a grape on each cocktail pick.

PEPERONI AND BANANAS

8 slices peperoni   4 bananas, peeled and cut in half
                              lengthwise

Arrange peperoni and bananas on a platter and chill until needed.

For cocktails, cut peeled bananas across into thick slices. Wrap each slice with a strip of peperoni and secure with a cocktail pick.

LIVER PÂTÉ I AND II

Variation I

Take a few minutes to make this pâté, or a double quantity of it, fill it into a crock and store in the refrigerator. It will keep several days. At cocktail time, place the cold crock on a tray and surround it with salty crackers.

1 4-inch section liver sausage, skinned and cut into chunks	1 3-ounce can sliced mushrooms, drained
mayonnaise	½ envelope pecans or walnuts
2 onion slices	

salt and freshly ground black pepper

Blend sausage chunks with just enough mayonnaise to make a thick paste. Add onion and mushrooms and blend just long enough to chop them medium fine. Break nuts by crushing with rolling pin or wooden spoon, add nuts and season well.

If no blender is available put sausage through meat grinder with onion and mushrooms and add mayonnaise, nuts and seasonings after sausage is ground.

Variation II

½ pound liver sausage, skinned and cut into chunks	½ cup stuffed olives or 1 jar chopped olives
½ cup chilled sour cream, whipped	salt and pepper
6 parsley sprigs ground through Mouli	

Mash or blend liver sausage. Add whipped sour cream (sour cream will not get stiff but it will thicken when whipped), add chopped olives and season well. If a blender is used the whole olives can be roughly sliced and blended with the sausage. The whipped sour cream should be added gradually to make mixing or blending easier. Place pâté in a bowl, cover with chopped parsley and chill until needed.

The next four recipes are suggested as first-course seafood cocktails. If you want to serve them as a main course at luncheon or dinner, increase the quantities and arrange them in a single serving dish or salad bowl, surrounded by lettuce leaves.

If you want to serve them with cocktails, arrange them in a bowl and provide cocktail picks. When they are served in this way there is always the hazard of dripping the sauce on one's chin or clothes. To avoid this, decrease the quantity of sauce so that there is just enough to bind the shrimp or lobster but not enough to run or drip. The sauces can be served separately as "dips" if this method is preferred.

SHRIMP COCKTAIL I AND II

Variation I

1½ pounds frozen peeled and
    cooked shrimp, thawed
¼ cup mayonnaise
2 tablespoons heavy cream
2 tablespoons ketchup

2 tablespoons orange juice
2 tablespoons Madeira
salt and pepper to taste
4 lettuce leaves
1 lemon, quartered
    parsley, for garnish

Arrange chilled shrimp on lettuce leaves in 4 cocktail glasses. Stir all other ingredients into a smooth sauce and pour over the shrimp. Garnish with parsley and lemon quarters.

Variation II

HOT SHRIMP COCKTAIL

2 1-pound boxes frozen peeled
    shrimp, thawed
½ teaspoon salt
½ teaspoon sugar
1 teaspoon each dried red and green
    bell peppers

2 tablespoons creole mustard
4 tablespoons heavy cream or sour
    cream
1 clove garlic, crushed

Bring 2 cups water to a boil, add salt, sugar and dried peppers and add the shrimp gradually so that the water does not stop boiling. Cover and boil 2–4 minutes longer, or until shrimp are opaque; do not overboil. In the meantime stir mustard into cream and add garlic. When shrimp are done, drain well and bind with the mustard sauce. Increase cream or mustard to taste and season well. Serve the shrimp in the sauce with cocktail picks or divide them into four heated dishes and serve as a first course.

CHAD'S SHRIMP COCKTAIL

24 frozen peeled and cooked shrimp,
 thawed
½ cup mayonnaise
2 tablespoons chili sauce
2 tablespoons sweet pickle
 relish, drained

salt and pepper to taste
8 lettuce leaves
1 lemon, quartered
4 sprigs parsley

Arrange shrimp on lettuce leaves in 4 cocktail glasses. Mix mayonnaise, chili sauce, relish and seasoning and pour over shrimp. Add a lemon wedge to each glass and serve garnished with parsley.

LOBSTER AUGUSTE

1 can grapefruit sections, drained
1 pound frozen lobster, thawed
¼ cup mayonnaise

¼ cup tomato ketchup
1 tablespoon chopped chives or
 parsley

salt and pepper

Arrange grapefruit and lobster in 4 cocktail glasses. Mix remaining ingredients and thin with syrup from grapefruit can. Pass sauce separately.

This is a lobster cocktail that cannot be served after a long cocktail hour, or, for that matter, after a short one. Serve it instead of cocktails at a Sunday luncheon, or serve it as a first course at an after-the-theatre supper. If you cannot afford theatre tickets and lobster and champagne all on the same evening, serve it after the movies or TV.

LOBSTER COCKTAIL

1 2-pound box frozen lobster,
 thawed and drained

8 pitted green cocktail olives, sliced
4 splits of champagne or 1 quart

8 sections lemon peel

Divide lobster into 4 cocktail glasses, sprinkle with olives, fill glasses with champagne to height of lobster and crush a lemon peel over each glass to obtain a spraying of oil as over a Martini. Refill with champagne and squeeze of lemon as lobster is eaten.

ARTICHOKE AND LOBSTER

1 pound frozen lobster meat, thawed

1 10-ounce can hearts of artichoke, drained

¼ cup diced mustard pickle

2 tablespoons bottled French dressing

3 tablespoons mayonnaise

1 tablespoon mild mustard

salt and pepper

Combine first three ingredients, season and set aside. Combine dressing, mustard and mayonnaise and stir until smooth. Use just enough of this mixture to bind the lobster mixture. Chill until needed and serve with salty crackers, as a fork hors d'oeuvre or in cocktail glasses as a first course at the table.

CRAB MEAT WITH AVOCADO SAUCE

1 4-ounce can crab meat

1 avocado

2 teaspoons brown mustard

½ teaspoon Worcestershire sauce

1 lemon, juice only

2 tablespoons heavy cream or sour cream

salt and pepper to taste

Drain and pick crab meat. Mash or blend all other ingredients and add the crab meat. Serve with pumpernickel rounds or salty crackers.

SHERRIED AVOCADO

2 avocados

1 lemon, cut into 5 wedges

½ cup sherry

Cut avocados in half, remove stone and sprinkle cavity with lemon juice. Pour 2 tablespoons sherry into each avocado half and serve with lemon wedges.

AVOCADO HABANA

1 large or 2 small avocados
½ teaspoon salt
½ teaspoon chili powder
¼ teaspoon black pepper
1 lime, quartered

2 teaspoons lemon juice
½ garlic clove, crushed
2 slices onion
mayonnaise

Cut avocados in half, remove stone and scoop out meat. Mash or blend with next 6 ingredients and add just enough mayonnaise to make a smooth dip. Refill the dip into 1 or 2 of the empty half shells and serve with lime wedges and potato chips.

AVOCADO COCKTAIL

2 avocados
2 limes for garnish

1 teaspoon confectioners' sugar
½–¾ cup heavy dark rum

Cut chilled avocados in half. Remove stone and sprinkle cavity with sugar. Fill with rum and eat. This is an excellent first course after a Daiquiri, whiskey sour or whiskey on the rocks. It is not the right first course after Martinis, obviously. You can also serve it instead of cocktails and follow with a light wine with the next course.

SLICED TOMATOES AND CAVIAR

2 small tomatoes
1 small cream cheese, at room temperature

1 2½-ounce jar black caviar
sour cream

If there is time, peel the tomatoes by dipping in boiling water for a few seconds and drawing off the skins. Slice peeled or unpeeled tomatoes thinly. Drain by laying the slices on a paper towel. Beat cream cheese with caviar. Add just enough sour cream to make a soft paste. Divide the caviar-cheese over the tomato slices. Sprinkle with fresh-cut chives when they are obtainable.

HERRING IN MUSTARD SAUCE

1 jar herring bits in white wine
  (or marinated dressing)
2 tablespoons brown mustard
2 tablespoons sour cream
1 tablespoon minced dill

½ slice onion
1 pinch sugar
salt and pepper
1 package frozen pumpernickel
  rounds, thawed

Drain marinade from herring. Blend it with remaining ingredients and season to taste. Arrange herring pieces on a serving plate, pour over the sauce and serve with pumpernickel rounds.

If no blender is available, chop onion—or use frozen chopped onion, thawed—and mix ingredients well.

TOULON ANCHOVIES

2 cans rolled anchovy fillets
2 tablespoons French mustard
  (Dijon if possible, otherwise
  use prepared mustard)
freshly ground pepper
1 tablespoon tarragon vinegar

8 parsley sprigs chopped
  through Mouli
1 garlic clove, crushed
2 teaspoons dried or fresh chopped
  chervil
buttered black bread cut into fingers

Drain oil from anchovies, add mustard, vinegar and pepper and stir into a dressing. Add remaining ingredients, pour over anchovies and serve with buttered black bread.

NORWEGIAN SHRIMP

4 slices brown bread, cut into
  12 rounds
4 tablespoons butter
2 lemons, sliced paper thin
1 can tiny Norwegian shrimp,
  drained

1 1-ounce jar black caviar
4 scallions, minced
1 tablespoon smallest capers
mayonnaise

Cut rounds of brown bread the same size as the lemon slices, discarding the small end slices from the lemons. Butter the bread rounds, lay a lemon slice on each and top with a mixture of the next 4 ingredients stirred with just enough mayonnaise to bind.

SARDINE SPREAD

There is no time or trouble lost in mashing sardines. They are usually pretty well mashed before I even get them out of the can. Pour off some of the oil if you want the spread to be dry.

2 3½-ounce cans boneless and
    skinless sardines
2 tablespoons soft butter

2 teaspoons brown mustard,
    or to taste
2 teaspoons lemon juice
    salt and pepper

Mash sardines with a fork and stir in all other ingredients, increasing the mustard to taste. Season well and serve with Melba toast rounds or crackers.

SARDINE PUFFS

2 egg whites, beaten stiff
1 cup mayonnaise
1 cup mashed sardines
    (2 3½-ounce cans)

salt, pepper and paprika
4 slices toast or white bread

Fold stiff egg whites into mayonnaise and sardines. Season and pile on bread or toast slices. Cut each slice into 4 pieces and sprinkle with paprika. Push under the broiler until puffed and brown, about 3 minutes.

The following hot cheese puffs sound more complicated than they are. They puff and brown in seconds and mixtures are quickly prepared. Turn to the chapter on cheeses for many more recipes that can be cut in half and served with cocktails—for a medium-large cocktail party a fondue can be kept hot for guests to dip from as they choose. The hostess has to remember to stir it now and then and to add a little kirsch—after all it is a cocktail party and even the fondue can go too dry.

CHEESE PUFFS I AND II

Variation I

½ cup mayonnaise
¼ cup grated Parmesan cheese
1 teaspoon minced onion
½ teaspoon brown mustard

salt and pepper
1 egg white, beaten stiff
20 Melba rounds
paprika

Combine mayonnaise, cheese, onion and mustard and season to taste. Fold in egg white and mound the mixture on Melba toast rounds. Sprinkle with paprika and push under broiler until puffed and brown. Watch carefully as this happens very quickly!

Variation II

1 8-ounce package pimento
    cream cheese

1 egg, beaten
salt, pepper and paprika
36 Melba toast rounds

Mix cheese and well beaten egg, season to taste and spread on toast rounds. Sprinkle top with paprika and push under broiler until puffed and golden.

CHEESE AND HAM PUFFS

1 8-ounce package cream cheese
1 2-ounce can deviled ham
2 tablespoons drained pickle relish

¼ garlic clove, crushed
salt, pepper and paprika
Melba toast or bread rounds

Mix all ingredients, season to taste, spread on toast or bread and push under broiler until brown.

"THE FARM" PUFFS

4 small white onions
    (evenly sized)
16 Melba toast rounds

½ cup mayonnaise
½ cup grated Parmesan cheese
salt, pepper and paprika

Peel onions and slice across as thin as possible, using only the center slices; each onion should yield at least 4 evenly sized center slices. Lay onion slices on Melba toast rounds. Mix mayonnaise and

Parmesan cheese, adding more Parmesan if necessary to make a thick paste. Season and mound mixture on the onion rings. Sprinkle with paprika and push under the broiler until brown.

PARMESAN CHEESE DROPS

These can be mixed and baked in less than 10 minutes. They are better made in small batches (this recipe yields just enough for one baking sheet) and eaten while hot.

¼ cup sifted flour	2-3 tablespoons grated
½ cup heavy cream	Parmesan cheese
½ teaspoon salt	butter for baking sheet

Stir flour, cream and salt until smooth. Drop small spoonfuls on a buttered baking sheet, sprinkle heavily with cheese and bake in a 450° F. oven for 6 minutes. Leave room for spreading. Makes approximately 16 drops.

MELTED CHEESE

1 roll hickory-smoked or garlic- flavored cheese	Triscuits paprika

Cut thin rounds from cheese roll. Lay rounds on Triscuits, sprinkle with paprika and push under the broiler until cheese starts to melt and is lightly browned (about 1 minute).

CHEESE-STUFFED ENDIVE

3 spears Belgian endive	2 tablespoons sherry
1 container Roquefort cheese spread	salt

Cut endive across just over the root end so that leaves will separate without breaking. Stir cheese with just enough sherry so it will spread easily. Season if necessary. Fill cheese into lower part of leaves and lay in a star design on a large platter. The endive has a bitter taste that is lovely with the Roquefort and the stalks

stay crisp for quite a long time. Select nice fat endive stalks—if they
are thin you may need 4 instead of 3.

CREAM CHEESE AND RED CAVIAR

2 8-ounce packages cream cheese
2 3-ounce jars red caviar
2 tablespoons fresh or frozen
　　chopped chives

1 lemon, quartered
salty crackers

Place the two cheeses next to each other lengthwise on a
serving plate or cheese board. With a knife, smooth the sides so
that it will appear as one slab of cheese. Scoop out a square in the
center, going down about ½ inch and coming to within an inch of
the edges. Spread the cheese gained in this way onto the edges to
heighten them. Do this with a knife dipped in hot water.

Fill the indentation in the top of the cheese slab with the
caviar and sprinkle with chopped fresh or frozen chives. Surround
the cheese with salty crackers and arrange 2 or 4 spreaders on the
platter.

STUFFED MUSHROOMS I THROUGH III

Variation I

1 pound medium-sized mushrooms
1 wedge chive cream cheese, at
　　room temperature

2 tablespoons sour cream
salt and pepper
paprika

Wipe or peel mushrooms and cut out stems. Blend cheese
and sour cream until smooth, add mushroom stems and blend only
long enough to chop them medium fine. Season cheese to taste, fill
into mushroom caps and mound high in center. Sprinkle with
paprika or chopped chives.

If no blender is available, chop mushroom stems with mincer
and mix with cheese and sour cream.

Variation II

1 pound medium-sized mushrooms
1 4-ounce can liver pâté
2 tablespoons sherry, or to taste

salt and pepper
3 sprigs parsley, chopped through
　　a Mouli

Wipe mushrooms and cut out stems. Blend liver pâté and sherry, add mushroom stems and blend long enough to chop them medium fine. Season and fill pâté into mushroom caps, mounding the filling high in the center. Sprinkle with parsley.

If no blender is available, chop mushroom stems with a mincer and mix with liver pâté softened with the sherry.

Variation III

1 pound medium mushrooms
1 4-ounce can liver paste, at room
  temperature

1 tablespoon mayonnaise
1 tablespoon sherry, or to taste
frozen chopped chives, thawed
salt and pepper

Wipe mushrooms and cut out stems. Blend liver paste and mayonnaise until smooth, add the stems and just enough sherry to make a stiff paste. Season to taste and fill into mushroom caps, mound filling high in the center. Sprinkle with frozen chopped chives, thawed.

If no blender is available, chop mushroom stems with a mincer and mix with liver paste, mayonnaise and sherry.

COCKTAIL FRANKFURTERS IN HOT SAUCES I AND II

1 1-pound package cocktail frankfurters

Heat frankfurters according to package directions and serve with one of the following sauces. Frankfurters can be impaled on picks with the sauce poured over, or the sauce can be served separately as a "dip."

Variation I

2 tablespoons spiced mustard,
  "Mister Mustard" or
  Bahamian mustard
2 tablespoons mild brown mustard

½ teaspoon dry yellow mustard
1 teaspoon vinegar
2/3 cup sour cream
salt, pepper and 1 pinch sugar

Stir first two mustards together. Moisten dry mustard with vinegar and combine. Add sour cream and season to taste.

Variation II

1/3 cup dry yellow mustard
1/3 cup ketchup
1/3 cup drained horseradish

3 tablespoons frozen chopped
onion, thawed

Combine all ingredients and serve.

Dips

The two major faults of the "dip" are, first, its name and, second, its aptitude to drip on its way from the bowl to the mouth. You can change a "dip" into a "dunk" but that's even worse, so you at least improve the dripping by making them just soft but not runny. You serve them with good crisp crackers, raw vegetables or fresh potato chips. A limp celery stalk and a drippy dunk are the sort of things that give cocktail parties a bad name.

Raw vegetables are low in calories, easy to prepare and a colorful addition to the hors d'oeuvre table. With a potato peeler it is easy to scrape strings from celery. Divide one head into stalks. Scrape 2 carrots (they scrape and cut more quickly when they are cold) and cut them into sticks. Cut 2 unpeeled cucumbers into sticks. Cut the root end off 2 stalks of Belgian endive and separate the leaves. Divide 1 small cauliflower into flowerettes. If you can find cleaned radishes you can use them in the collection and crisp watercress stalks are a great addition.

If you like, you can prepare the raw vegetables and store them in the refrigerator in sugared water (1/2 teaspoon to 2 cups). Mix the following vegetable dips in larger quantities and have them available in the refrigerator. This will prove to be a welcome foresight, indeed, if guests should show up unexpectedly. Just before serving, drain the raw vegetables and arrange them in a salad bowl or dish with a few ice cubes and pass the dips separately. (If you want to isolate yourself from your fellow man you can add scallions, spring onions and Bermuda onion rings to the collection of raw vegetables.)

Cauliflower is especially good with the mustard sauce, cucumber is good with either and carrot sticks are good with the ketchup sauce. The mustard sauce can also be served with wedges of unpeeled sweet apples. (Do not cut the apples until just before serving or they will turn brown.)

RAW VEGETABLE MUSTARD DIP

4 tablespoons mayonnaise | 1 teaspoon Worcestershire sauce
2 tablespoons heavy cream | 2 teaspoons brandy
2 tablespoons brown mustard | 2 teaspoons lemon juice
salt, pepper and cayenne

Mix and serve.

RAW VEGETABLE KETCHUP DIP

2 tablespoons ketchup | 1 teaspoon Worcestershire sauce
4 tablespoons mayonnaise | 2 teaspoons gin
2 tablespoons heavy cream | 2 teaspoons lemon juice
salt, pepper and cayenne

Mix and serve.

Either sauce can have ½ teaspoon curry powder added.

All dips can be made in the blender or viva voce. If preferred, softened cheeses can be pressed through a strainer and mixed with other ingredients into any of the following dips. Cream and Roquefort cheeses will be soft if taken from the refrigerator at least one hour before they are used.

CREAM CHEESE DIP

Probably the simplest of the dips, but one of the nicest.

1 8-ounce package cream cheese | 2 tablespoons sour cream
½ onion, grated | mayonnaise
salt to taste

Mix first 3 ingredients and add only enough mayonnaise to make a smooth paste. Serve with crackers or potato chips.

To make this dip a little more unusual, use pimento or chive cream cheese, or add a tablespoon of minced chives.

CARNIVAL DIP

1 package onion soup mix
1 cup sour cream
1 small cream cheese, quartered
6 thick slices cucumber

4 stuffed olives, roughly sliced
2 slices green pepper
3 sprigs parsley
salt and pepper

Combine soup mix, sour cream and cream cheese and blend until smooth. Add cucumber, olives, green pepper and parsley and blend until olives and pepper are chopped medium fine. Season to taste and serve with crackers.

If no blender is available, the cucumber and green pepper can be chopped with a mincer. Use chopped olives and put the parsley through a Mouli.

CHIVE CHEESE DIP

1 8-ounce package chive cream
      cheese
sour cream

4 stuffed olives, halved
¼ envelope chopped walnuts
salt, pepper and cayenne

Soften cheese in blender, adding only enough sour cream to bring cheese to proper consistency. Add olives and blend until they are medium fine. Add walnuts, correct seasoning and serve.

If prepared without a blender, stir cheese with cream and chop the olives before adding them. Add nuts, season and serve with crisp crackers.

WATERCRESS DIP

This is a recipe which combines watercress and horseradish, the two words of which one never knows whether they should be four.

If you have a blender and all the time in the world, like about 4 minutes, break the coarsest stems from ½ bunch of watercress and discard. Blend the remaining leaves and tender stems with the cheese and horseradish.

If no blender is available, the watercress can be finely chopped, or put through a Mouli.

½ bunch crisp watercress
1 8-ounce package cream cheese
2 tablespoons grated horseradish,
    drained

sour cream
salt and pepper

Moisten with just enough sour cream to bring to dipping consistency. Season and serve with crisp crackers.

A N C H O V Y   D I P

1 8-ounce package cream cheese
4 inches anchovy paste out of a
    tube, or to taste

sour cream
¼ envelope pecans,
    broken (optional)

If you don't dispense your anchovy paste like tooth paste, substitute 1 to 2 tablespoons anchovy paste out of a jar and mix it with cream cheese and enough sour cream to moisten. Add pecans if desired. Do not serve this dip with salty potato chips or crackers. It is best with rye Melba toast or sesame-seed crackers.

B L U E   C H E E S E   D I P

1 3-ounce package cream cheese
2 1½-ounce wedges Blue cheese or
    Roquefort

beer
½ teaspoon Worcestershire sauce
salt and pepper

Keep cheeses at room temperature so that they can be stirred quickly and easily into a smooth paste. Mash cheeses with a fork, add a little beer and stir until smooth. Add just enough beer to reach the desired consistency. Season and add Worcestershire sauce to taste.

To prepare this dip in the blender, place about one-third of the Roquefort in the blender with 2 tablespoons beer, blend until smooth and add cheeses in small pieces until more beer is required. Add beer very carefully, as dips become too liquid before one realizes it. If the dip is prepared long before it is to be served, during that minute before you go to the office, it can be made with a little more beer, as refrigeration hardens the cheeses. There are Roquefort and Blue cheeses available in the markets which are packed in plastic containers and are of spreading consistency. The recipe can be made with this type of Roquefort or Blue cheese, in which case the cream cheese should be omitted and only enough beer should be stirred into the cheese to change the spread into a dip.

HOT CHEESE DIP

1 8-ounce package sliced cheese,
    cut into quarters
1 tablespoon butter
1 tablespoon tarragon vinegar

1 teaspoon brown mustard
1–2 teaspoons anchovy paste,
    to taste
salt and pepper

Heat first four ingredients over low heat or in a double boiler until cheese is melted, add anchovy paste and season to taste. Pour into a bowl and serve with crackers or toast that can be dipped directly into the hot cheese.

AVOCADO DIP

1 4-ounce jar pimento, chopped
2 avocados, peeled, stoned and
    crushed, or 1 cup crushed
    avocado

1 3-ounce package cream cheese
1 2-ounce package Blue cheese
1 lemon, juice and grated rind
2 tablespoons horseradish

¼ cup mayonnaise or to taste

Mix all ingredients except mayonnaise with softened cheeses and add just enough mayonnaise to bring dip to desired consistency. Serve with potato chips, crackers, or raw carrot sticks.

Frozen Hors d'Oeuvres

One final word about hors d'oeuvres. Instant Epicures should know that the frozen food department of your market carries breaded scallops, shrimp and clams. It also stocks fish cakes, fish sticks and Chinese egg rolls, fried onion rings and fried potatoes.

All these frozen foods make excellent hors d'oeuvres. Thaw and/or heat them according to package directions and serve them hot with cocktail picks. Up to this point the procedure is fast and simple; after this it is up to you to concoct a sauce or dip that will enhance and improve them. The Chinese egg rolls come packaged with a little envelope of strong yellow mustard. Mix the mustard, put it into a little dish on a tray and surround it with the egg rolls cut into bite-size sections. It is sometimes good to cut the egg roll while it is still frozen, but some brands are so tightly rolled that they can be cut with a sharp knife after heating.

For fish cakes or sticks, shrimp, clams and scallops turn to the sauce chapter and prepare tartar sauce, chutney, mayonnaise, mustard mayonnaise or any sauce recommended for fish. For the onions or potatoes prepare ketchup mixed with mustard in half-and-half proportions. Try any of these combinations, or reverse them or invent a hot sauce of your own. If it is a large cocktail party, heat only a package at a time. Cold breaded scallops are discouraging.

CHAPTER II   *Soups*

N o COOK can possibly prepare a soup stock or any of the bases
needed for the average soup when she or he has only a few minutes
to do it in. All the prescribed processes of simmering, de-spuming,
reducing and clarifying—not to say terrifying—are now being left,
and very successfully too, to the Messrs. Campbell, Knorr, Lipton,
Maggi and many others who have made a fine art of producing
soups. The manufacturers of condensed, concentrated, dehydrated,
canned, frozen and packaged soups have excelled themselves for us
and we would be foolish not to avail ourselves of the products of
their study and labors. We can serve them as they come or we can
improve them and combine them according to our tastes.

Almost all soups (and many other things) take well to a generous
addition of sherry. Garnishes can turn soups from Drug-Store-
Lunch-Counter regulars into Haute Cuisine. Accompaniments can
turn them from a first course into a meal. Combinations can turn
them into wonderful additions to your repertoire. Try a five-minute
egg, an Oeuf Mollet (*see* page 101), in the next bouillon you serve
and accompany it with a slice of toasted cheese bread sprinkled with
a little julienne of ham (slivers of ham, when we are on less inspired

subjects), and so the dreary luncheon of a boiled egg and cold ham becomes a pleasant occasion to which you can invite guests. The whole thing will take no longer than the five minutes the egg must boil.

Matchmaking among the soups is an old epicurean sport. You can combine your own concoctions or you can make the most of the classic combinations that have made restaurants and even cities and countries famous. A can of cream of green pea soup and a can of turtle soup heated together with a little (or a lot of) sherry added just before serving makes the Boula that we used to go to the Plaza for. Add whipped cream (pressed from a can), dust with Parmesan, push it under the broiler and you have Boula Gratinée—and who could ask for more in minutes? Plain chicken consommé heated with blanched almonds and shredded or dried chervil is otherwise known as Consommé des Épicuriens.

There may be some thousands of soups and only fifty that come in cans, but any mathematician will tell you what a frightening number of combinations can be made out of one deck of cards . . . so fifty soups should make it possible for us to go on indefinitely with new and interesting inventions. You may buy very ordinary-sounding soups, but never forget that when the French combine cream of chicken soup with cream of asparagus they come up with Crème Reine Hortense. A cream of tomato soup garnished with strips of green pepper (and truffles if you can afford them) is really just a simple little Purée St. Sébastien.

A package of Knorr's potato soup and a can of Campbell's tomato soup may sound commonplace, but add a few slivers of green pepper and a little leftover diced chicken (or you can always buy a slice of cold chicken at the corner delicatessen) and suddenly you have Potage Sigurd, Paris in your dinette.

With all these possibilities and our now firmly established complete lack of time, we cannot simply say, "I don't like soup." You have to learn to like it—serve it hot, serve it cold, but serve it. The greatest problem is that most of us gave away our mothers' soup plates long ago or we don't have any of those lovely big soup spoons. We lack the equipment, but it can be replaced. Soups are essential to instant cookery; they are, or should be, gay, good-looking, interesting and inexpensive—something you cannot always say for your wife—and from the lowliest bouillon cube to the most beautiful of the bisques from Paris, they just take heating or chilling and a goodly swish of sherry and *voilà*, you have a meal or a course that will change a meal into a dinner.

If you think of soups as fattening, and that is a word that shouldn't appear between these covers, dissolve a bouillon cube in a cup of boiling water, stir in one envelope of plain gelatin and sprinkle it with parsley or chives or chervil (where diets are concerned we give you complete leeway). Eat it or drink it for lunch each day, and if you do it long enough you will not only be thin but you'll have strong fingernails. Needless to say, you don't get anything else for lunch.

If hors d'oeuvres give the Instant Cook time to prepare dinner, a well-tempered soup gives her time to add the final touches to a dinner which should have been on the broiler while the soup was going down.

COLD CUCUMBER SHRIMP SOUP

(In Blender)

1 package frozen peeled and cooked shrimp, thawed	1 teaspoon sugar
3 cups cold buttermilk	½ teaspoon salt
1 cucumber, roughly sliced	¼ teaspoon each dry mustard and curry powder
1 slice onion	1 tablespoon dill

Divide shrimp in half. Blend half the shrimp, buttermilk, cucumber, onion, spices and seasoning until smooth. Include dried dill in blender, but if fresh dill is obtainable, add it only during last few seconds of blending. Correct seasoning and serve in iced cups garnished with remaining shrimp.

OYSTER AND MUSHROOM STEW

1 10-ounce can frozen oyster stew	1 3-ounce can sliced mushrooms
2 cups milk	1/3 cup heavy cream, whipped
2 sprigs parsley	4 scallions, sliced (include some of the greens)
1 chicken bouillon cube	salt and pepper
1 cup boiling water	

Heat oyster stew in milk until melted. Remove oysters with slotted spoon and chop roughly. Add parsley and return to saucepan. Add bouillon cube dissolved in boiling water, add mushrooms and season to taste. Heat to boiling, pour into cups and garnish with a topping of whipped cream sprinkled with scallions.

OYSTER STEW

2 dozen oysters and their liquid	3 tablespoons chopped filberts or
2 cups milk	cashews
2 cups cream	2 tablespoons freshly grated
2 tablespoons butter	horseradish
salt and pepper	2 tablespoons chopped spring
	onions or scallions

Cook oysters in their own liquid over low heat. Heat milk and cream but do not boil. When oysters are puffed and edges curl add them to milk and cream, add butter, season to taste and heat but do not allow to boil. Serve sprinkled with nuts, horseradish and onion (all toppings are optional).

LOBSTER SOUP

1 can Newburg sauce	brandy or sherry to taste
1 can cream of mushroom soup	1 small can lobster meat
1 cup cream	1 pimento cut into strips
	salt and pepper

Heat soups and cream to boiling, stir in brandy or sherry to taste and season with salt and pepper. Garnish with pieces of heated lobster meat and strips of pimento.

CLAM BISQUE

3 cups milk	2 tablespoons chopped celery
1 can minced clams	1 pinch basil, mace, marjoram
1 onion, sliced or chopped	and rosemary
2 tablespoons chopped parsley	salt and pepper

Heat milk, clams and their juice and onion to boiling. Add parsley, celery and herbs, heat for a moment longer and serve.

CLAM COMBINE

1 can chile con carne
4 cups bottled clam juice

½ cup heavy cream, whipped, or whipped cream topping

salt and pepper

Heat chile con carne and juice to boiling. Serve in cups, topped with salted whipped cream or whipped cream topping dusted with a little salt. Garnish with any of the following toppings:

shaved hazel nuts or almonds
chopped green onions

cucumber slices
paprika

BISQUE ANITA

6 ounces frozen or canned crab meat
(1 cup)
1 10½-ounce can cream of
tomato soup
1 10½-ounce can cream of
pea soup

1 cup heavy cream
¼ cup sherry, or to taste
¼ cup sour cream
1 teaspoon fresh minced or
dried dill
salt and pepper

Thaw or drain crab meat and remove all cartilage. Heat soups and cream to just under boiling. Stir in crab meat and sherry and reheat but do not boil. Season and serve at once topped with sour cream whisked until light with salt and dill.

A good dinner for Sunday evening would be bowl-sized portions of Bisque Anita, served with Ricardo's Salad (*see* page 199), Broiled Italian Bread (*see* page 183) and red wine. Serve cheese and grapes with the remaining wine for dessert.

CLAM JUICE MARINARA

3 cups clam juice
1 cup tomato juice
1/3 cup cream, whipped

4 thin onion slices
4 thin lemon slices
salt and pepper

Combine juices, season and serve in chilled cups. If juices are not cold, place an ice cube in each cup. Top with salted whipped cream and lay a slice of onion and lemon on each serving.

SHRIMP OR CRAB BISQUE

2 cans cream of tomato soup
1 can cream of green pea soup
1 pound frozen cooked shrimp
   or crab meat, or 1 can
   shrimp or crab meat

½ cup sherry or to taste
½ cup heavy cream, whipped
salt and pepper

Combine soups and shrimp or crab meat and heat to boiling. Add sherry, correct seasoning and serve in cups or soup plates with a topping of salted whipped cream.

There is a legend in Italy about a village priest who was so concerned about his parish that he literally stuck his nose into everything. He was right there at all times and nothing could be done without him. They called him Father Pomodoro—Father Tomato—because, in Italy, there is nothing that can be cooked without a tomato.

Here are soups for Instant Epicures which are based on tomatoes. They all rely on that ever dependable and wonderful cream of tomato soup for, like Father Pomodoro, there is practically nothing in the line of tomato soups that can be done without it.

Just in case you have never tried it, chill cream of tomato soup ice cold, put a gob of salted whipped cream on top and sprinkle the cream with chopped parsley (using a Mouli, of course) or chives. Serve as a summer luncheon with a green salad and some Bel Paese or Gorgonzola. You can get the cream out of a pressure can and you can drop ice cubes into the soup if there is no time to chill it.

BULGARIAN CHEESE SOUP

2 cans cream of tomato soup
1 peeled tomato, sliced
1 3-ounce package cream cheese
   with chives

½ ripe avocado, sliced thin
salt and pepper

Heat soup to boiling, add tomato slices and reduce heat to simmer for 3 minutes. Season and serve soup in cups or plates. Rice the cheese over the soup through a coarse sieve and garnish with avocado slices.

ICED TOMATO SOUP

2 cans cream of tomato soup
1/3 cup heavy cream, whipped

2 tablespoons chutney, chopped
salt to taste

Top chilled soup with seasoned whipped cream and top cream with chutney. Although this is traditionally a cold soup, it can also be served hot.

HOT TOMATO JUICE

1 No. 3 can tomato juice
1/4 cup frozen chopped onion,
    thawed
1 teaspoon Worcestershire sauce

1/2 cup whipped cream topping
salt and pepper
2 tablespoons dehydrated parsley or
    chives

Heat juice with onion and Worcestershire sauce to boiling. Serve topped with whipped cream seasoned with salt and pepper. Sprinkle with parsley or chives.

BULGARIAN YOGURT SOUP

1 package Knorr's leek soup
1 container yogurt
1/2 3-ounce package cream cheese

3 tablespoons fresh or frozen
    chopped chives
salt and pepper

Prepare soup according to package directions. Add yogurt, reheat and season. Sprinkle with cream cheese riced through a coarse sieve. Add chives and serve hot or cold.

LEEK AND CLAM SOUP

1 envelope Knorr's leek soup
1 can minced clams
salt and pepper

1/4 cup frozen chopped onion,
    thawed
1 tablespoon dehydrated parsley

Prepare leek soup according to package instructions. Add clams and their juice and heat to boiling. Season and serve garnished with chopped onion and parsley.

LEEK SOUP

1 package Knorr's leek soup
2 slices buttered toast cut into
    8 rounds with cookie cutter

4 tablespoons grated cheese
salt and pepper

Prepare soup according to package directions and season. Divide into four cups or bowls. Float 2 toast rounds spread with cheese and browned under broiler on each cup and serve.

ABJY L'AMID

1 package Knorr's cream of leek
    soup
1 cup heavy cream, chilled

1 tablespoon lemon juice, or to
    taste
8 thin lemon slices

Prepare leek soup as directed using only enough milk to make 2 cups soup. Add cream and lemon juice and chill a few minutes. Serve cold garnished with lemon slices.

LEEK SOUP GRATINÉE

1 package Knorr's leek soup   1 or 2 onions, sliced paper thin
¼ cup grated Parmesan cheese

Prepare soup according to package directions. Pour into a casserole or bowl and cover surface with onion slices. Sprinkle Parmesan cheese over onion and brown under the broiler or in a very hot oven.

POTAGE AFRICAINE

2 cans or envelopes cream of potato
    soup
½ tablespoon curry powder,
    or to taste

1 15-ounce can artichoke hearts
salt and pepper

Prepare soup according to package directions. Stir a little hot soup into curry powder in a cup and when it is smooth, stir into the soup. Add artichokes and cook gently until they are heated through, season and serve.

CONSOMMÉ AFRICAINE

4 cups consommé   2 teaspoons curry powder, or to taste
                    4 artichoke bottoms, diced

Heat consommé. Stir in curry powder as for Potage Africaine, add artichokes, cook until they are heated through and serve.

PRAGUE SOUP

Very good potato soup can be made out of a combination of frozen mashed potatoes, bouillon and cream. Since tomato slices do not float very well, the little raft with its topping of cream sinks if the soup bowls are too deep. It looks best when it is served in open, shallow soup plates—the kind everybody's mother had but no one has any more.

1 package, or 2 cans, cream of   ¼ cup sour cream
        potato soup   2 tablespoons frozen chopped
2 slices bacon   onion, thawed
1 tomato, peeled and sliced   salt, pepper and paprika

Prepare potato soup according to package directions and heat to boiling. In the meantime fry bacon crisp, drain and crumble. Season and divide soup over four plates or bowls. Float a tomato slice on each serving and top tomato with sour cream. Sprinkle onion and bacon on the cream and sprinkle a little paprika over the top.

RUSSIAN PEA SOUP

2 packages split pea soup   4 paper-thin lemon slices
2 cups cream   salt and pepper
4 knockwurst, skinned and cut
    in thick slices

Prepare soup according to package directions, substituting cream for the milk. Heat knockwurst slices in the soup, season to taste and serve each plate or cup with a lemon slice.

BORSCH
(In Blender)

1 can shredded beets
1 can bouillon
1 tablespoon sugar
¼ cup sour cream
½ cup lemon juice

4 ice cubes
salt and pepper
¼ cup sour cream for topping
1 lime or lemon, quartered
4 sprigs dill or parsley

Blend beets and their juice, bouillon, sugar, half the cream, lemon and ice until smooth. Season to taste. Serve in chilled cups topped with remaining cream and garnished with dill and lime quarters.

BORSCH I THROUGH VI

Variation I

1 quart jar borsch, chilled
½ pint sour cream

½ bunch watercress
salt and pepper

Beat sour cream with seasonings until it is light and smooth. Remove coarse stems from watercress and chop leaves through Mouli or mincer.

Divide soup over 4 chilled bowls. Top with seasoned cream and sprinkle generously with watercress.

Variation II

1 quart jar borsch, chilled
½ pint sour cream

2 tablespoons minced fresh dill
1 lime, thinly sliced

Follow above recipe, substituting minced fresh dill for the watercress. Garnish each serving with lime slices.

Variation III

1 quart jar borsch, chilled
½ pint sour cream, whipped

1 smallest jar black caviar
1 lemon, sliced thin
salt

Prepare as above, whipping cream with salt. Divide the caviar into 4 parts and center cream with caviar on each cup. Serve with thin lemon slices.

Variation IV

1 quart jar borsch, chilled
½ pint sour cream, whipped

1 orange, slices and grated rind
salt

Top 4 cups of borsch with sour cream whipped with salt to taste and the grated rind of the orange. Cover each serving with thin slices of the orange with rind trimmed off.

Variation V

1 quart jar borsch
½ pint sour cream

1 16-ounce can small whole white
potatoes, heated
salt and pepper

Heat borsch. Place hot potatoes in each soup bowl, pour over the hot borsch and pass seasoned sour cream separately.

Variation VI

1 quart jar borsch
¼ pint sour cream
1 thick slice boiled ham, cubed

1 garlic clove, split
salt
1 teaspoon minced dill

Heat soup. Rub ham cubes with garlic clove and add to borsch. As soon as ham is heated through serve soup with a topping of sour cream beaten with salt and dill.

The Instant Epicure has to be short of time, long on love of food, medium long on budget and endlessly long on wisdom. He has to know that it is no longer stylish to consider soups unstylish. They are an essential part of good healthy living. They are one of the foundations of instant cookery and with wisdom they can be turned into really lovely new menus. And if by chance you are short of time and fat besides, then take to the bouillon and you'll solve both your problems.

AGNELLOTTI

4 cups bouillon (canned or from
    bouillon cubes)
1 1-pound jar ravioli

1 small onion, sliced and divided
    into rings
4 tablespoons Parmesan cheese

Heat soup to boiling with ravioli and onion rings. Divide over 4 soup bowls, sprinkle with cheese and serve.

BOUILLON

4 cups beef bouillon
1 envelope gelatin
¼ cup sherry

2 egg yolks
2/3 cup heavy cream
1 tablespoon minced parsley

salt and pepper to taste

Place gelatin in cup, add sherry, stir and set aside. Heat bouillon in top of double boiler, take from stove and stir in gelatin until dissolved. Stir yolks into cream until smooth and gradually add soup, stirring until smooth. Season and reheat in top of double boiler. Serve hot sprinkled with parsley.

COLD ORANGE SOUP

3 cans beef bouillon
1 orange, grated rind and juice
salt and pepper

1 orange, sliced
½ cup finely chopped green pepper
¼ cup finely chopped onion

2 tablespoons minced mint leaves

Combine bouillon with orange juice and rind and season well. Serve over orange slices placed in cups and topped with mounds of green pepper, onion and mint mixed together. You can save time by chopping the pepper, onion and mint leaves in the blender. You can also dribble a little Cointreau over the oranges.

MALTESE SOUP

2 10½-ounce cans beef bouillon   ¼ green pepper, shredded
2 oranges   pepper
                4 sprigs parsley put through a Mouli

Heat bouillon. Cut two large curls of orange rind from the top and bottom of each orange with a potato peeler and slice the center part of the oranges into 4–6 thin slices each. With kitchen scissors, cut peel into long slivers. Add peel and shredded pepper to hot soup. Take from heat and serve garnished with orange slices and sprinkled with parsley. Spoon a little green pepper and orange rind onto the orange slices if you are serving the soup in a shallow plate. This is very pretty and refreshing. You can add orange rind and shredded peppers to a jellied bouillon in summer.

CAMERANI

1 1-pound jar spinach ravioli   salt and pepper
3 cups strong beef bouillon   ½ cup grated Parmesan cheese

Simmer ravioli in bouillon until heated through. Season to taste and serve sprinkled with Parmesan cheese.

STRONG SOUP

1 1½-pound can beef stew   ½ cup Madeira
1 bouillon cube   salt and pepper
1 can beef bouillon   4 slices smoked tongue, cut into
1 3-ounce can button mushrooms   julienne strips

Dissolve bouillon cube in bouillon, add stew and mushrooms and simmer until meat is heated through. Add Madeira, season with salt and pepper if necessary and serve in soup plates or bowls, garnished with tongue.

ZUPPA PAVESE

If you have some of those individual earthen casseroles it makes serving Zuppa Pavese more authentic and easier. If not, prepare the entire recipe in a casserole shallow enough to go under the broiler.

8 thick slices stale or toasted Italian bread
4 eggs, beaten

¾ cup grated Parmesan cheese
2 cans beef bouillon

Break bread into 4 individual earthen casseroles, pour 1 beaten egg over each portion, sprinkle generously with Parmesan cheese and fill casseroles with beef bouillon. Sprinkle with more cheese and broil quickly under high heat.

NEWBURG CONSOMMÉ

2 cans consommé
¼ cup sherry

½ can Newburg sauce

Blend or stir together, heat to boiling and serve.

SPINACH SOUP

2 No. 1 cans consommé
1 package frozen chopped spinach, thawed
1 slice onion

salt and pepper
1 hard-cooked egg, sliced (optional)
2 tablespoons sherry, or to taste

Whirl consommé, spinach and onion in blender until smooth. Season and boil 3 minutes. Add sherry and serve topped with hard-cooked egg slices (optional).

If no blender is available, the spinach can be chopped finer with a vegetable mincer. Use the mincer for the onion too, and then combine with the consommé.

CONSOMMÉ MIKADO

2 10½-ounce cans chicken consommé
1 cup tomato juice
1 peeled tomato, sliced

2 slices cold meat (ham, tongue, chicken or turkey) cut into julienne strips

Heat consommé and tomato juice, add tomato slices and serve garnished with a julienne of meat. The meat may be leftovers, or sliced meat gotten from a delicatessen or market.

CONSOMMÉ AGNÈS SORREL

1 can chicken consommé
1 can cream of mushroom soup
3 slices tongue, cut into julienne
strips

2 slices cold cooked chicken, cut into
julienne strips

Heat soups according to can directions. Serve garnished with strips of tongue and chicken—tongue and chicken can be bought at any delicatessen.

CONSOMMÉ NESSELRODE

2 No. 1 cans chicken consommé
4 tablespoons chopped canned
mushrooms, drained

1 tablespoon parsley, chopped
through Mouli
salt and pepper

Heat consommé, add mushrooms and boil 2 minutes. Season and serve in cups. Sprinkle with parsley. Pass a decanter of sherry for anyone who likes to add a little to this soup.

CONSOMMÉ ZEPHYR

4 cups chicken consommé
1 8-ounce section liver sausage

salt and pepper
1 package shelled pistachio nuts

Skin liverwurst, slice thickly and cut into cubes. Roll the cubes into little balls or dumplings and drop into simmering consommé. Serve soup hot with sprinkling of pistachio nuts.

BULGARIAN CHICKEN AND YOGURT SOUP

2 cans chicken consommé
1 chicken bouillon cube
1 cup yogurt
2 eggs
2 egg yolks

2 teaspoons sweet marjoram
¼ teaspoon basil
salt and pepper
2 slices pressed chicken cut into
julienne strips, optional

Simmer consommé and bouillon cube until cube is dissolved, reduce heat. Beat eggs and yolks into yogurt until light and add a little of the hot consommé, beating constantly. Gradually beat yogurt mixture back into the consommé. Do not allow it to boil after eggs have been added. Correct seasoning and serve in hot cups sprinkled with herbs and julienne of chicken.

MONTE CARLO SOUP

1 can chicken consommé
2 cans cream of mushroom soup
1 egg yolk
½ cup heavy cream

salt and pepper
1 small cucumber, sliced very thin
    on metal slicer
½ cup dry bread crumbs

¼ cup grated Parmesan cheese

Combine and heat soups. Beat yolk into cream, reduce heat under soup and stir in cream. Never allow soup to boil after adding yolk. Season to taste and pour into a casserole or baking dish. Arrange cucumber slices on top of soup. Spread with crumbs, sprinkle with cheese and push under the broiler until the cheese is browned.

COLD CHICKEN CONSOMMÉ

2 cans jellied chicken consommé
1 4-ounce jar red caviar

2/3 cup sour cream, whipped
2 teaspoons curry powder

salt and pepper

Fill four soup cups half full of cold jellied soup. Divide caviar over the 4 cups and fill with remaining soup. Top with curried cream.

COLD MADRILÈNE

2 No. 1 cans jellied madrilène
1 package frozen melon balls,
    thawed and drained well

salt and pepper
1 lime, quartered
1 tablespoon dill, preferably fresh

Divide melon balls into four large soup cups and season to taste. Add soup, which should be cold and semijellied, not chilled into a stiff jelly. Garnish each cup with a piece of lime and sprinkle with chopped dill.

HOT MADRILÈNE

2 No. 1 cans madrilène
1 tablespoon tomato paste

½ cup sherry
2 stuffed olives, sliced

salt and pepper

Heat all ingredients to boiling, season to taste and serve in cups.

MADRILÈNE COSTA BRAVA

2 cans jellied madrilène
4 thin orange slices

¼ cup sour cream
1 teaspoon Worcestershire sauce

1 tablespoon chopped mint leaves

Serve madrilène cold, but not chilled into a stiff jelly. Divide into 4 bouillon cups. Top with quartered orange slices and garnish with sour cream mixed with Worcestershire sauce and sprinkled with mint.

PURÉE MALAKOFF

1 can vichyssoise
1 can tomato soup
6 raw spinach or lettuce leaves,
    cut julienne

2 tablespoons butter, melted
salt and pepper

Heat soups separately to boiling. Smother spinach or lettuce julienne in butter and season. Pour soups into plates or cups and stir once to make a red and white spiral swirl. Garnish with the julienne.

CHICKEN AND COCONUT SOUP

2 cans cream of chicken soup   1 cup grated coconut
1 cup cream   salt and pepper to taste

Combine all ingredients and simmer 4 minutes.

EGG SOUP

If you live in the country you can probably buy pullet eggs, which are especially good in this soup. The French suggest pigeon or quail eggs, poached, an undertaking which only a Frenchman would or could undertake with ease. In any case, boil your eggs 5 minutes or poach them for about 3 minutes. Peel 5-minute eggs carefully and put one into each serving of soup. If you use poached eggs, trim them neatly. Sprinkle with paprika and parsley and after you break the yolk the soup will be colorful as well as good.

2 cans cream of chicken soup   4 sprigs parsley, chopped through
1 cup cream   Mouli
4 5-minute eggs   salt, pepper and paprika

Heat soup with cream while boiling or poaching eggs. Serve one egg in each cup of seasoned soup and sprinkle with parsley and paprika.

CRÈME MIRANDA

1 can concentrated cream of chicken   salt and pepper
    soup   1 2½-ounce can goose liver purée
1 chicken bouillon cube   4 parsley sprigs, ground through a
1 cup cream   Mouli
1 3-ounce can sliced mushrooms   8 Melba toast rounds
½–1 cup water to thin to desired
    thickness

Dissolve bouillon cube in boiling chicken soup. Reduce heat, add cream, mushrooms and water. Season and divide soup over 4 hot soup plates or cups and rice a tablespoon of goose liver purée over each cup. Garnish with parsley. Spread remaining purée on toast rounds, sprinkle with more parsley and serve with the soup.

HAM SOUP

2 cans cream of chicken soup
1 cup frozen chopped onion, thawed

2–3 slices ham, minced
2 egg yolks

Heat soup. In the meantime mix onion and ham with the egg yolks into a smooth paste. Add ham gradually and increase or decrease the amount so that the paste does not become too dry. Add this mixture to the hot soup, stir, season and serve.

Do not boil after the egg yolk mixture is added. The soup can be garnished with strips of chicken meat if desired.

BULGARIAN CHICKEN SOUP

2 cans cream of chicken soup
½ cup Minute Rice
2 egg yolks
½ lemon, juice only

1 cup yogurt
salt and pepper
2 sprigs parsley ground through Mouli

Prepare rice according to package directions while soup is heating. Beat yolks with lemon juice and yogurt. Reduce heat under soup, stir the egg mixture into the soup and add rice. Do not boil after egg yolks are added. Season to taste and serve sprinkled with parsley.

POTAGE CZARINA

2 10½-ounce cans cream of chicken soup
1 cup light cream
2 tablespoons raisins
1 teaspoon shredded or dried tarragon leaves

4 mushrooms, sliced thin
4 thin slices ham, cut julienne
4 stuffed olives, sliced thin
salt and pepper

Heat soup to boiling with cream, raisins, tarragon and mushrooms. Stir well and season to taste. Serve garnished with julienne of ham and olives.

CRÈME GERMINAL

2 10½-ounce cans cream of chicken 1 can white asparagus tips, or
    soup, combined with 1 package frozen asparagus
1 cup cream spears
       1 teaspoon fresh chopped or dried tarragon

Heat asparagus tips in the soup with the dried tarragon. If fresh tarragon is available use it as a garnish, sprinkling it on the soup just before serving. Fresh frozen asparagus may be substituted. Frozen asparagus should be boiled according to package directions, reducing the cooking time to half and letting the drained asparagus cook in the soup for 3 or 4 more minutes.

APPLE SOUP

1 jar apple sauce ¼ teaspoon cinnamon
1 lemon, juice and rind wine to taste
1 tablespoon currant jelly sugar to taste

Heat apple sauce with lemon rind and jelly in the top of a double boiler over boiling water until jelly is dissolved. Beat in cinnamon, wine, lemon juice and sugar to taste. Serve cold with toasted grated coconut and bread crumbs.

RUSSIAN SPINACH SOUP

1 package frozen spinach ½ small cucumber, roughly sliced
4 scallions or spring onions salt, sugar and pepper
4 sprigs each parsley and fresh 2 slices smoked salmon or sturgeon,
    dill or 1 teaspoon each dried   cut into strips
½ teaspoon dried chervil

Cook spinach according to package directions. Transfer cooked spinach and the water in which it cooked to blender and blend into a smooth purée. Add enough cold water to make four servings. Season well and add the remaining ingredients. Blend only long enough to chop the cucumber, not to purée it. Serve in large bowls or plates, garnished with smoked salmon or sturgeon and with ice cubes in each plate.

If no blender is available, the greens can easily be pressed through a sieve or vegetable mincer.

BATWINJA

Although the Batwinja is a medium-thin soup it should be served with attractive side dishes, like a curry. The guests help themselves according to their tastes. Serve the soup in large bowls or soup plates and add any other side dishes you can think of. Needless to say, a really well-filled Batwinja is a meal in itself. The quantity given is for four. If preferred, you can substitute frozen greens for the fresh ones. Prepare according to package directions and use the water in which the greens cooked, decreasing the quantity of bouillon accordingly.

1½ pounds spinach
½ pound sorrel, beet tops, chard or
    turnip tops
2 cups bouillon or 1 cup each
    bouillon and white wine

2 tablespoons butter
¼ teaspoon sugar, or to taste
salt and pepper

Wash greens well and cook, covered, over low heat without water. Press the leaves down with a wooden spoon after they have cooked about 2 minutes. Continue to cook about 2 minutes longer or until leaves are wilted and tender. Stir in butter until melted, season and pour into blender with all liquid. Blend into a smooth purée, add cold bouillon (and wine) and blend a moment longer. Correct seasoning and serve. Each guest adds ice cubes to the soup and any or all of the side dishes. The soup should be well seasoned, as the ice cubes melt and thin the soup.

If no blender is available, the greens can easily be pressed through a sieve or vegetable mincer.

Side Dishes

¼ cup smallest pearl onions
¼ cup pine nuts
¼ cup grated horseradish
½ cup drained pickle relish
½ cup sliced dill pickle

1 cup peeled, cooked shrimp or any
    leftover cold fish
6 parsley sprigs ground through the
    Mouli
bowl of small ice cubes

POTÉE BOURGUIGNONNE

In Burgundy this soup is supposed to simmer—they call it "smile"—for at least eight hours, with the potatoes added during the last half hour. We leave the cooking to Messrs. Campbell, Libby, Nestlé, etc., and end up with a hearty soup entirely lacking any great traditions.

1 1-pound can beef and vegetable soup
1 cup water
1 bouillon cube
1 can mixed vegetables or any leftover cooked vegetables

1 can onion soup
½ package frozen small white potatoes, thawed
salt and pepper
8–12 thick slices French bread, toasted and buttered

Combine soups and vegetables and simmer potatoes in the soup for 5–7 minutes before serving. Season and serve in bowls with the toasted bread on each portion. In France the bread is spread with chicken fat instead of butter.

SOPA DE AJO I THROUGH IV

The Spanish are very peninsular about their food and also very instant about some of their soups. Here are four ways of getting a garlic breath, which is never a problem in Spain where everyone eats Spanish food.

The bread can be fresh, stale, toasted or oven-dried.

Variation I

4 cups water
8 thick slices Italian or French bread
4–8 garlic cloves, minced
¼ cup frozen chopped onion
salt and pepper

1 teaspoon paprika
1 tablespoon fresh or dehydrated parsley
3 tablespoons olive oil

In a soup kettle, pour water over bread and bring to a boil. Fry garlic, onion, parsley and paprika in oil and add the mixture to the bread as soon as the garlic is brown. Stir well, season and bake in a 450° F. oven for a few minutes before serving.

Variation II

Add 4 hot 5-minute eggs (*see* page 100) to the soup as it comes out of the oven. You can also use poached eggs if you prefer.

Variation III

Add 1 small can sliced mushrooms to garlic while it is frying.

Variation IV

Fry 2 slices bacon, cut into small squares with kitchen scissors, with the garlic and omit the olive oil.

And speaking of Spanish soups, this Gazpacho Andaluz has become instant with the invention of the blender. All you have to do is peel the onions and tomatoes. Needless to say, you can change the quantities to your taste.

GAZPACHO ANDALUZ

2 onions, peeled and roughly sliced	pepper, salt, oil and vinegar to taste
1 large cucumber, roughly sliced	or
¼ sweet red pepper, roughly sliced	¼ cup well seasoned herbed Italian
½ green pepper, roughly sliced	or French dressing
4 tomatoes, peeled and sliced	½ cup garlic croutons,
¼ head lettuce	crisped in butter

1 pimento, diced

Blend first 6 ingredients and season to taste with French dressing. Chill soup until needed and serve with small pieces of ice or an ice cube in each cup. Garnish with diced pimento and fried garlic croutons. Add ice or water if the soup is too thick.

Gazpacho can also be made as Sopa de Ajo with the addition of bread and water and garlic. In this case cut recipe for Garlic Soup (Sopa de Ajo, Variation I) in half and add it to half the quantity of Gazpacho.

GULYAS SOUP

1 1-pound can beef stew	1 1-pound can small white onions
1 teaspoon paprika	2 bouillon cubes dissolved in 2 cups
1 1-pound can small white potatoes	boiling tomato juice

salt and pepper

Stir paprika into a little gravy from the beef stew, return it to the stew and add potatoes and onions. Stir together over low heat and add more paprika if desired. Add boiling bouillon-tomato juice mixture and season to taste. Heat the soup to boiling, stirring several times, and thin with more tomato juice if desired.

And while we are advising on matters of Gulyas Soup—and Gulyas was a soup long before it was a stew—reduce the liquid to a quantity that will give you enough sauce to dunk your bread into and serve it as a main course. The bread should be the crusty Italian kind and if you swoosh it around on the end of a fork you are no more vulgar than the Swiss with his fondue; if you swoosh it around with your hand and fly it into your mouth before it dribbles you are no more vulgar than half the people in Hungary. It is not only important to know what's good, it's important to know what's a good way of eating it. Certain refinements at the table are as passé as a curled pinky or a letter that avoids starting with "I." All this doesn't mean you throw bones over your shoulder or push your plate back when you are through. And don't leave anything on the plate for Miss Manners. Miss Manners was one of the casualties of the First World War.

CHAPTER III   *Fish*

Fᴵꜱʜ ᴇɴᴊᴏʏ an element in which we cannot exist for long and they, in turn, do not do well out of water. When a man is a misfit he is always told that he is like "a fish out of water" and presumably fish say the same sort of thing about their misfits, "Just like a man in water." This leaves us with a great deal in common with the average fish, besides the fact that most people like to eat fish and some fish even like to eat people.

This interesting reciprocity does not exist anywhere else in our diet. There never has been a man-eating lamb, in spite of the fact that we eat thousands of sheep a year. Our relationship with our meats is entirely one-sided, but with fish we stand on a much more sporting basis. Fish are, in a sense, our equals. Men spend a great deal of time devising ways of catching fish, while fish spend a great deal of time, especially some of the large old canny ones, devising ways of not being caught. Fish are fun to catch (which cannot be said of calves or chickens) and if you are not a complete angler then they are fun to select and buy.

Here again Instant Epicuremanship comes into play. If your town boasts a nice old-fashioned fish market, one with a propeller in the ceiling, you can go and select your own favorite. There will be rows of lovely glistening fish, half buried in chopped ice, a tank full of glossy black lobsters, and bins and barrels of clams and herrings. Just looking at a frog's leg can suggest brilliant dinner ideas and inspirations. All this comes to you in an atmosphere of combined art and taxidermy. You can interrupt your menu contemplations by looking at the faded prints of large burbots and bowfins. They always hang crookedly above eye level and here and there you will find further inspiration in a stuffed burfish or a terrapin. On the whole, the taste of fish market decorators runs rather to the horrors than the flowers of the sea. They are given to dried brachiopods and stuffed urchins. They seem to think that a dusty limulus or a really fine sting ray is going to make you want Saumon à l'Épicurienne for dinner.

When your selections are made the fishman, who always wears an ancient fedora, will do them up nicely in little wooden trays. Along with these purchases you will inevitably carry away some sawdust on your new suede shoes and a slight smell of the sea. If you were unwise enough to take a low-slung fuzzy dog or a child in a snowsuit, you can spend the rest of the day with your vacuum cleaner.

The packaged and frozen fish are excellent, but it is hard to look at a blue (for the sea) box of frozen fish at the supermarket while you lean on the handle of your cart (and hold up traffic) with visions of Sole Véronique and Truite à la Courtisane swimming before your eyes.

Fish are, on the whole, a fast-cooking delicacy and we deplore the fact that most epicures, Instant or otherwise, do not eat them as frequently as they should. Many cooks are afraid of fish, afraid of over- or undercooking them, and thereby rob themselves of a great taste pleasure and a great time saver. Cooking the fish that are quickly prepared is no problem. You are limited to fish steaks, filets and small fish and are not troubled with a great *darne de saumon* wrapped in cheesecloth or a whole cod. All fish-cooking difficulties come with the larger, more pretentious dishes; the quickly prepared fish are also the easily prepared ones and there is practically no place where you can go wrong on a broiled or boiled fish steak.

We say "that poor fish" of anyone who isn't wildly successful, but the comparison seems to stem only from the fish which are caught. The ones that get away are the lucky fish and there are lots of them. There are enough of them so that they can keep on multiplying faster than we can can or eat them. The day has not come when we speak of the extinct smelt or the sardine that is no more. We have never gotten ahead of the fishes and from all we hear they are happy in their element. The only person who comes out of the whole fish affair badly is the man who spends every leisure hour employing every wile he can contrive (not to mention the most expensive flies and lures) to land as many fish as possible —and then refuses to eat them. "I never eat fish," says he after a good day of sport, while he chews on his pork chop and muses over the rainbow trout he gave the man at the filling station. These blackguards have even been known to bury their catch—not even a Viking's funeral for a fighting, sporting adversary.

Fish, besides all their other attributes, can be made pets of. They may not leap about when you come home, but they never bark or disturb the neighbors. They can be hung (stuffed and glazed) on the wall, they can be eaten and they make subject matter for countless stories—fish stories, to be exact.

Shrimp

The French call them *crevettes,* the Germans call them *Krabben* and the Spanish call them *camarónes.* There is no choice between many shrimp without an "S," or many shrimps with an "S." You add it according to your humor.

No one buys, cooks, eats or even thinks about a single shrimp —they are far too popular in this country ever to be in the singular. Fortunately, they seem to multiply as happily and as rapidly as they are eaten. In regard to the name, it is derived from the habit they have of curling up or shrinking when caught. If this were really so, they should either be called shrinks (for shrink cocktails and shrink bisque) or we should mark our shirts "unshrimpable" and shrimp away from reality.

They cook in about four minutes and anyone who cooks them longer is making a terrible mistake. The short-cooked shrink is the crisp one and the long-cooked shrink is the tough one. There are fresh, frozen, peeled, unpeeled, cooked, breaded and fried frozen shrimp and every kind of canned ones on the market. Every restaurant menu suggests them as a first course and almost everyone orders them.

No one, short of a shrimp fisherman, has ever seen a shrimp with its head on (which attaches immediately to what we consider his tail). They are gray or green in life and turn pink in death, or at least in boiling water. Our shrimp, known by us as the common shrimp (Crago vulgaris), is not only consumed here in great quantities but it is shipped, or dried and shipped, to foreign countries. The Chinese dried shrimp comes from California, while the very small shrimp comes to us from Norway.

There are other recipes for shrimp in the hors d'oeuvre section. We give you sixteen ways of making them quickly here and suggest that you always keep some in the freezing compartment of your refrigerator. There are two broiled shrimp recipes that can be made under your kitchen broiler in the Outdoor or **Plug-in-Any-where** chapter farther along.

POOR SHRIMP

2 pounds frozen shelled and deveined shrimp, thawed	1 teaspoon curry powder
2 eggs, lightly beaten	salt and pepper
½ cup grated Parmesan cheese	2½ cups oil or vegetable oil for frying
1 cup bread crumbs	1½ cups chutney

Dip shrimp in egg and dredge with combined cheese, bread crumbs, curry and seasonings. Fry shrimp in hot oil or vegetable shortening until they are golden, about 4 minutes. Drain well and serve with chutney and any other curry accompaniments.

SHRIMP CASSEROLE

2 pounds frozen shelled and deveined shrimp, thawed	1 teaspoon each dried tarragon, chervil and chives
1 cup white wine	1 garlic clove, crushed
2 cups water	1 cup bread crumbs
1 bay leaf	1 lemon, juice only
¼ cup frozen chopped onion, thawed	¼ cup melted butter
	salt and pepper

Bring wine, salted water and bay leaf to a boil and add shrimp slowly so that water does not stop boiling. Simmer 4 minutes after last shrimp has been added. Remove shrimp and drain well. Raise heat, add onion to wine and water and boil quickly while arranging drained shrimp in a shallow buttered casserole. Mix herbs, garlic and seasonings with crumbs and spread over shrimp. Strain onions from broth and spread them over crumbs. Add a little of the broth to moisten slightly. Mix lemon juice and butter and pour over the casserole. Bake in a 450° F. oven until crumbs are brown.

FRIED GROUND SHRIMP

1 pound frozen shelled shrimp, thawed	½ teaspoon salt
	1 egg, lightly beaten
1 can water chestnuts (about 10)	sherry to taste
1 tablespoon cornstarch	2½ cups oil or vegetable shortening
paprika	

Grind shrimp and chestnuts through meat grinder, combine with cornstarch, salt and egg. Add just enough sherry to moisten. Sprinkle pastry board with paprika. Form shrimp paste into 12 small balls, roll in paprika and fry in hot oil until golden. The mixture can be made into balls and refrigerated until needed.

HOT SHRIMP IN RED SAUCE

2 pounds frozen shelled and deveined shrimp, thawed	2 lemons, grated rind and juice
	½ garlic clove, crushed
1 cup frozen chopped onion, thawed	3 tablespoons sugar
	3 tablespoons Worcestershire sauce
⅓ cup oil	2 teaspoons salt
1½ cups ketchup	½ teaspoon pepper
½ cup white wine	½ teaspoon paprika

In a skillet or electric skillet sauté shrimp and onion in oil until shrimp are pink, turning once. This will take about 4 minutes. Add all other ingredients, stir well and cook until bubbling. Serve with Minute Rice.

JAPANESE SPRING SHRIMP

⅓ cup cooking oil
2 pounds frozen shelled shrimp,
    thawed and drained
1 bunch scallions, diced
1 cup sliced celery
¼ cup soy sauce

2 chicken bouillon cubes
¾ cup boiling water
1 teaspoon sugar
1 5½-ounce can bamboo shoots
    (or 1 cup)
salt and pepper

Heat oil in pan, add shrimp and cook for 3 minutes, stirring once or twice. In the meantime—lay cleaned celery and scallions next to each other on a chopping board and slice across in ¼-inch slices. Add to pan with soy sauce, bouillon cubes, water and sugar and cook 2 minutes longer. Add bamboo shoots and cook until heated through. Season to taste.

SHRIMP AND CORN CASSEROLE

2 10-ounce cans corn, drained
1½ pounds cooked peeled shrimp,
    frozen or canned
3 tablespoons butter
½ teaspoon salt

pepper and cayenne
8 stuffed olives, sliced
¼ cup frozen chopped onion,
    thawed
1 cup cream

3 sprigs parsley put through Mouli

Fry shrimp in hot butter until pink and opaque, turning once, for about 3 minutes. Season, add onion and fry 1 minute longer. Add corn, olives and cream and continue to cook long enough to heat corn. Serve sprinkled with parsley.

SHRIMP SALAD VERTAIN

2 pounds shelled cooked shrimp,
    frozen or canned
½ head Boston lettuce
½ cup mayonnaise
1 tablespoon pickle relish, drained

1 tablespoon capers
½ cucumber, roughly sliced
1 slice onion
½ teaspoon dill
salt and pepper

1 tablespoon cut chives

Arrange drained shrimp on lettuce leaves in a salad bowl. Blend mayonnaise, relish, capers, cucumber, onion and dill until cucumber is roughly chopped. Season to taste, pour over shrimp and sprinkle with chives.

If no blender is available, chop cucumber and onion with mincer.

SHRIMP COCKTAIL OR SALAD

1½ pounds cooked shelled shrimp
   (if frozen shrimp are used,
   thaw and drain)
½ clove garlic
½ cup bottled French dressing
¼ green pepper, roughly sliced

½ onion, roughly sliced
4 sprigs parsley, stems removed
1 tablespoon Bahamian mustard
1 tablespoon lemon juice
1 curl lemon rind
salt and pepper to taste

Rub bowl with garlic and discard. Stir shrimp around bowl and set aside. Combine all remaining ingredients in the blender and blend until parsley and lemon rind are finely minced. Pour sauce over the shrimps and serve.

If no blender is available, use a vegetable mincer.

When you look at the menu in one of those fixed-price-dinner restaurants you'll find the price for the whole dinner next to the entrée. Don't be misled, look up at the appetizers and invariably you will find a parenthesis following the shrimp cocktails. It will enclose the discouraging information (50 cents extra).

SUMMER SHRIMP SALAD

1½ pounds canned or frozen
   cooked, shelled shrimp
1½ cups seedless grapes, stemmed

½ small cucumber, sliced thin
½ cup tart dressing
1 small head Boston lettuce

4 sprigs parsley

Combine shrimp, grapes, cucumber and dressing. Arrange on lettuce leaves in a salad bowl and sprinkle with parsley put through a Mouli.

SHRIMP BASIL

1½ pounds boiled peeled shrimp,
    frozen or canned
2 tablespoons butter
2 garlic cloves, crushed
1 large can Italian tomatoes

1 teaspoon dried basil
¼ teaspoon dried oregano
salt and pepper
2 sprigs fresh parsley, put
    through Mouli

½ cup heavy cream

Heat butter, fry garlic half a minute, add tomatoes, shrimp, herbs and seasoning and simmer until shrimp are heated through. Stir in cream. Reheat, sprinkle with parsley and serve.

SHRIMP DE JONGHE

1½ pounds cooked peeled shrimp,
    frozen or canned, heated
    in boiling water
¼ pound butter
½ garlic clove, crushed
½ cup frozen chopped onion,
    thawed

½ teaspoon each dried parsley,
    chervil and tarragon
½ teaspoon mace
salt and pepper
1 cup dry crumbs or crushed
    Holland rusks
grated cheese to taste

Melt butter, add garlic, onion, parsley, chervil and tarragon, mace and salt and pepper. Fry for 1 minute, stirring. Add crumbs and fry until they are brown. Add hot, drained shrimp to crumbs. Fill into 4 small Pyrex dishes, top with cheese and brown under a hot broiler.

SHRIMP AND MUSHROOM CASSEROLE

1 cup toasted garlic croutons (available at all markets)
2 tablespoons butter, for casserole
    and croutons
1 10½-ounce can cream of
    mushroom soup
1 10½-ounce can cream of chicken
    soup

1 can button mushrooms
2 pounds cooked, peeled shrimp,
    canned or frozen
¼ cup sherry
salt and pepper
Minute Rice, optional

Place croutons and butter in a pan in a 375° F. oven. Shake several times to toast croutons on all sides. Heat soups, mushrooms and shrimp to boiling in a buttered casserole. Add sherry and season to taste. Top with croutons and place in oven until ready to serve.

Serve with Minute Rice prepared according to package directions.

MARINATED SHRIMP

1½ pounds peeled uncooked shrimp, canned or frozen, thawed and drained
1 cup white wine
½ cup tarragon vinegar
¼ cup oil
1 teaspoon salt
2 teaspoons sugar

½ cup frozen chopped onion, thawed
1 bay leaf
¼ teaspoon dried thyme
salt, pepper and Tabasco sauce, to taste
½ garlic clove, crushed
¼ teaspoon ground cloves

Bring wine, vinegar and oil to a boil with remaining ingredients. Add shrimp and boil 3–5 minutes after water returns to a boil. Cool in the marinade, if there is time. Take out bay leaf and serve shrimp hot or cold in the marinade.

SHRIMP IN DILL SAUCE

2 pounds frozen peeled shrimp, thawed and drained
¼ pound butter
½ teaspoon Worcestershire sauce

½ teaspoon dried dill
1 lemon, juice and grated rind
salt and pepper
1 cup cream

Cook shrimp in butter for 4 minutes, turning once. Add Worcestershire sauce, dill and lemon juice and rind. Season to taste, add cream and boil for exactly 1 minute, stirring constantly.

Use fresh dill if it can be obtained. Serve with Minute Rice prepared according to package directions.

SHRIMP WIGGLE

1 pound frozen or canned cooked shrimp or peeled raw shrimp	¼ cup milk
	1 cup cooked, canned or frozen peas
1 tablespoon tarragon vinegar	½ cup pitted black olives
4 tablespoons butter	½ cup diced celery
4 tablespoons flour	¼ cup sherry
1 cup cream	salt and pepper

If raw shrimp are used, simmer 4 minutes in salted water, drain and sprinkle with vinegar. Melt butter in top of double boiler over boiling water, stir in flour and season. Add cream and milk and cook for 3 minutes. Stir well, add shrimp, peas, olives and celery and cook a few minutes longer. If not needed immediately, reduce heat to simmer and stir at intervals. Stir in sherry and serve on rice, with toast or in shells.

SHRIMP CURRY

1 pound shrimp, peeled and deveined	¼ cup chopped chutney
	2 tablespoons parsley, chopped through Mouli
¼ cup butter	
1 onion, chopped	2 pimentos, sliced
1 tablespoon curry powder, or to taste	½ green pepper, seeded and chopped
	salt and pepper

Chop onion and green pepper with quick chopper, vegetable mincer or in blender. Cut chutney and pimento into strips and cross strips with a knife. These two ingredients cut so quickly that they do not need to be chopped.

Melt butter in hot pan, add onions and stir until just transparent. Stir in curry powder until it is smooth, add shrimp and cook 2 minutes longer. Turn shrimp, cook 2 minutes. Add remaining ingredients, stir, and serve on toast. If there is time, this curry can be served on Minute Rice.

Oysters

The oyster, unless disturbed by storms or man or agencies beyond its control, grows, lives, loves, reproduces, eats, makes pearls and dies on a site or bed which it adopts when it is about three weeks old. If it doesn't like the climate or its neighbors that is too bad. Even the moment of adopting its place in life is largely chance of storms and tides. The whole thing is a little sad. There are no oyster migrations, they can't dance or visit, they can't ever get away if they settled in a poor neighborhood.

Oysters are bivalve mollusks, which sounds a little like a brand new sports car by Farina. They are our third largest fishing industry, right after the salmon and the tuna. Considering the people who have never eaten one and never plan to, it only goes to show how many oysters the oyster lovers eat.

Eating them has been an historic undertaking about which books have been written and adages coined. They were supposed to typify luxury and worldliness when cold oysters and champagne were the accepted midnight supper of emperors and millionaires. All the while the oyster stew made a good dish for the poor man and fried oysters were sold in newspaper cornucopias on street corners.

They cook quickly, lend themselves to wonderful combinations and you'd have to eat pounds of them to have as many calories as a slice of bread. They come small and tender, large as a gray pancake, and are best very cold or very hot. We bring you fifteen ways of making them, all fast and all worthy of the epicure you are, even though they are no longer millionaire fare.

BAKED OYSTERS

This is one of those recipes which is a snare. The oysters broil in less than 6 minutes, but the rock salt has to be hot before you put the shells on it. So, allow 10 minutes to get salt hot in a shallow pan. This does not take watching or care so you can leave it alone to get hot while you take a shower, vacuum the apartment or set the table. The only thing that is important is to put the oysters into the salt (shell side down, of course) exactly 6 minutes before you serve them. Allow one minute to put things on top of them and 5 minutes for broiling.

24 small oysters on half shell
¼ cup soft butter
1 tablespoon prepared horseradish, drained

3 tablespoons frozen chopped onion, thawed
2 dashes Worcestershire sauce
salt and pepper

rock salt

Heat salt in a shallow pan. Arrange oysters on hot salt, cover with a mixture of soft butter, onion, horseradish, Worcestershire and seasonings. Bake in a 400° F. oven for 5 minutes, or until sizzling. Serve at once.

OYSTERS CASINO

Arrange rock salt (buy ice cream salt) in 4 shallow pie plates. Heat in a 550° F. oven as above, place oysters on the hot salt and bake just long enough to crisp the bacon. Serve each guest with one plate of 6 oysters each.

24 oysters on the half shell
6 strips bacon cut into 4 equal
    pieces each
¼ cup soft butter
¼ cup frozen chopped onion,
    thawed

¼ cup chopped green pepper
salt and pepper
1 lemon cut into 5 pieces
1 bag rock salt

Mix butter, onion and peppers. Divide mixture over oysters. Squeeze a few drops of lemon juice from one section of lemon on each oyster. Season and top with a piece of bacon. Bake as described above and serve immediately (on heavy plates or place mats) with a section of lemon on each serving.

OYSTERS ROCKEFELLER

Always leave oyster in deep shell and discard the shallow top shell.

24 oysters on the half shell
½ package washed spinach put
    through mincer
½ cup bread crumbs
½ cup grated Parmesan cheese
½ cup butter, melted
1 dash Worcestershire sauce

2 tablespoons sherry
¼ cup frozen chopped onion,
    thawed
4 sprigs parsley, ground through
    Mouli
salt, pepper and cayenne
rock salt

Mix spinach (there should be ¾ cup), crumbs and cheese. Pour over melted butter. Add seasonings, onion and parsley and mix well. Spread mixture over oysters, lay oysters into hot salt as described above and bake in a 500° F. oven for about 8 minutes or until top is browned. Serve at once.

Oysters live in the Atlantic, the Pacific and the Gulf. We are, so to speak, surrounded by them and can buy them live and fresh from September to May. From May to September we can buy them canned. They are so fast cooking that if you are joining the ranks of the time-less you had better join the oyster lovers too.

ANGELS ON HORSEBACK

Les Anges à Cheval, or just bivalves on piggyback. Names are misleading, but oysters in bacon are good.

24 small oysters
12 slices bacon, cut in half
watercress or parsley

salt and pepper
1 lemon, quartered

Roll each dried and seasoned oyster in half a bacon strip and secure with cocktail picks. Lay in a shallow pan and bake in a 450° F. oven for 6 minutes, or until bacon is crisp. Serve 6 to a person with lemon wedges and garnish with sprigs of watercress or parsley.

OYSTER AND CORN CASSEROLE

1 quart oysters and their liquid
¼ cup butter
1 cup crumbs
1 1-pound can Golden Kernel corn
½ cup frozen chopped onion, thawed
1 pimento, minced
½ cup cream
salt, pepper and paprika

Butter baking dish well, add ¼ cup crumbs and shake to distribute crumbs evenly over butter. Add corn mixed with onion and pimento. Season and top with oysters. Combine cream and oyster liquid and pour over casserole. Cover with remaining crumbs, dot with remaining butter and bake in a 400° F. oven until browned, about 8–10 minutes.

OYSTERS POMPADOUR

1 quart oysters and their liquid
2 tablespoons butter
2 4-ounce jars hollandaise sauce
1 lemon, quartered
2 truffles, chopped, optional or
depending on finances
salt and pepper

Poach oysters with butter in their own liquid until edges curl. Drain, season and cover with hollandaise sauce. Sprinkle with truffles and serve with lemon wedges. A dish fit for a millionaire and only for a millionaire.

OYSTERS WLADIMIR

1 quart oysters and their liquid
2 cups Mornay Sauce
(*see* Cheese chapter)
¼ cup bread crumbs
¼ cup grated Parmesan cheese
2 tablespoons butter, for dotting
salt and pepper

Poach oysters in their own liquid until the edges curl. Drain, season and cover with Mornay Sauce. Sprinkle with crumbs and cheese, dot with butter and brown under the broiler.

OYSTERS ON ANCHOVY TOAST

1 quart oysters
flour for dredging
½ cup butter
2 teaspoons anchovy paste
4 slices toast
1 lemon, quartered
salt and pepper
1 cup tartar sauce

Dry oysters and roll in seasoned flour. Fry until brown on both sides in butter. Drain oysters and keep hot. Mix anchovy paste into butter in pan. Fry toast on one side only in anchovy butter in pan. Lay on 4 hot plates. Divide oysters over anchovy toast. Garnish with lemon wedges and pass tartar sauce separately.

PAN-FRIED OYSTERS

1 pint oysters, drained
½ tablespoon Worcestershire sauce
2 tablespoons butter
½ teaspoon celery salt
pepper and paprika

Sauté oysters in a heavy skillet in Worcestershire sauce, butter and celery salt, stirring constantly. Season to taste with pepper and add a dash of paprika for color. Serve hot on toast and accompany the oysters with coleslaw with Lemon Mayonnaise.

LIGHT FRIED OYSTERS

1 pint large oysters
2 small eggs
½ cup water

½ teaspoon salt
1 tablespoon baking powder
1½ cups cracker meal

fat for frying

Dredge oysters with half the cracker meal until well coated. Beat eggs with water and dip coated oysters into the mixture. Roll oysters in remaining cracker meal mixed with salt and baking powder. Fry 5 minutes in deep fat. Drain well and serve with crisp green salad, watercress or coleslaw.

OYSTER STEW ELMIRA

1 jar béarnaise sauce
2 cups light cream, warmed

1 cup oyster liquid
24 oysters

salt and pepper

Stir sauce into 1 cup cream. Heat remaining cream, add oysters and their liquid and cook until their edges curl. Take from heat, stir into the béarnaise cream, season and reheat but do not boil.

EGG AND OYSTER FRY

1 pint large oysters (about 12)
½ cup fine bread crumbs
½ teaspoon salt
pepper to taste

1 egg, lightly beaten
4 tablespoons butter
4 eggs
2 tomatoes, sliced

4 slices bread, toasted and buttered

Dip well-drained oysters in seasoned crumbs mixed with beaten egg and fry in butter for 4–5 minutes, turning once. Keep

oysters hot. Pour beaten seasoned eggs into saucepan and scramble
(*see* Scrambled Eggs) until creamy. Combine eggs and oysters and
serve on tomato slices arranged on toast.

OYSTER AND TOMATO CHOWDER

1 10½-ounce can cream of
    tomato soup
1 pint oysters and their liquid
¾ cup heavy cream

1 teaspoon Worcestershire sauce
1 teaspoon lemon juice
1 dash Tabasco sauce
salt, pepper and paprika

3 sprigs parsley, put through Mouli

Heat soup, oyster liquid, cream, lemon juice and seasonings
to boiling. Add oysters and cook only until they are puffed. Season
to taste, sprinkle with parsley and serve.

OYSTER STEW PASQUALE

1 pint oysters and their liquid
¼ cup butter
3 cups milk

1 cup cream
salt and pepper
4 pats butter

1 teaspoon paprika

Melt butter in a 2-quart casserole, add oysters and cook 3
minutes or until edges curl. Take from heat, add milk, cream and
seasonings. Reheat to just under boiling. Divide over 4 soup bowls,
put a pat of butter on each and sprinkle with paprika.

OYSTERS GRATINÉE

24 oysters
2 tablespoons butter
¼ cup frozen chopped onion
1 teaspoon dehydrated parsley

½ lemon, juice and grated rind
1 cup cream
¾ cup grated cheese
salt and pepper

Simmer oysters in butter with onion and parsley until edges
of oysters curl. Stir lemon juice and rind into cream, pour over
oysters. Cover with cheese and push under the broiler until cheese
melts.

Crab Meat

Four crab meat recipes that can be based on frozen or canned crab meat. If you have that nice old-fashioned fish market in your town you can buy fresh crab meat. Pick it well to remove all shells and cartilage and use for any of the following recipes. It will be nice in flavor and the chunks are usually large.

CREAMED CRAB MEAT

2 cups cooked crab meat
¼ cup chopped frozen onion,
    thawed
1 can button mushrooms
¼ cup butter
¼ cup dry sherry

2 tablespoons brandy
2 cups heavy cream
2 egg yolks
2 tablespoons parsley, put through
    Mouli
salt and pepper

Sauté onion and mushrooms in hot butter for 2 minutes. Add crab meat and cook for 3 minutes. Add sherry, brandy and 1½ cups cream and boil 3 minutes. Reduce heat, season and add ½ cup warmed cream into which egg yolks have been beaten. Stir into sauce over very low heat until smooth and thickened, do not boil. Sprinkle with parsley and serve with Minute Rice or with instant mashed potatoes.

CRAB MEAT AND ARTICHOKE HEARTS

1 pound cooked crab meat
1 7-ounce can hearts of artichoke,
    drained
½ cup mayonnaise
½ teaspoon dry mustard
½ lemon, juice only

2 tablespoons capers
2 tablespoons minced onion
salt and pepper
3 sprigs parsley, ground through
    Mouli

Pick crab meat to remove cartilage, combine with artichokes and arrange in a serving dish. Stir mustard into a little mayonnaise until smooth, add remaining mayonnaise, lemon juice, capers and onion. Pour over salad and garnish with parsley.

CRAB MEAT REMICK

1 pound frozen, canned or
    fresh crab meat
8 slices bacon, cut across into 4
    pieces each, fried and
    drained
¼ cup butter

24 to 32 clamshells
½ cup mayonnaise
2 tablespoons chili sauce
1 teaspoon dry mustard
½ teaspoon paprika
½ teaspoon celery salt
salt, pepper and 1 pinch sugar

Divide crab meat over 24 large or 32 small buttered clam-shells. Cover with 1 piece fried crisp bacon each. Pour sauce made of remaining ingredients over bacon. Push under broiler and broil until brown and sizzling. Serve 6 to 8 clamshells per person on large plates.

CRAB MEAT AND SHRIMP CASSEROLE

1 pound frozen or fresh crab meat
½ pound fresh-cooked shrimp or
    lobster meat
1 cup sour cream

1 teaspoon fresh chopped dill or
    tarragon (use parsley if
    fresh herbs are not available)
salt, pepper and cayenne

Arrange crab meat and shrimp or lobster in a shallow but-tered casserole. Pour over sour cream beaten with herbs and season-ings and bake in a 375° F. oven for 10 minutes or until just bub-bling. Casserole may be sprinkled with grated cheese if preferred.

SOFT-SHELL CRABS AMANDINE

12 small soft-shell crabs
2 eggs, well beaten
¼ cup water
1 teaspoon salt
1 cup bread crumbs

½ cup corn meal
oil for frying
1 3-ounce envelope shaved almonds
2 tablespoons butter
salt and pepper

Dry crabs, dip in eggs beaten with water and salt. Roll in combined bread crumbs and corn meal. Fry in hot oil, being sure that oil is deep enough so crabs do not touch bottom of pan. Fry 4 minutes, remove and drain. Serve with almonds, fried in butter for 1 minute, poured over the crabs.

FLOUNDER CASSEROLE

2 pounds flounder filets
    (4 filets)
1 4-ounce can sliced mushrooms
butter for pan
1 lemon, halved
1 can concentrated mushroom soup

½ cup heavy cream
2 tablespoons grated Parmesan
    cheese
4 sprigs parsley, ground through
    Mouli
salt, pepper and paprika

Arrange filets and mushrooms in a buttered, shallow casserole and sprinkle with seasonings and juice of half the lemon. Combine soup and cream and pour over fish. Sprinkle with cheese and bake in a 375° F. oven for 10 minutes or until bubbling and brown. Sprinkle with paprika and parsley and serve with lemon wedges.

GREEN FLOUNDER CASSEROLE

2 pounds filets of flounder
1 pound cooked spinach, frozen
    or fresh
2 tablespoons sherry

1 cup Medium Cream Sauce
    (*see* Sauces)
½ cup grated Parmesan cheese
salt and pepper

butter for casserole

Spread well drained and seasoned spinach in buttered casserole, add sherry and cover with fish filets. Season well and pour over cream sauce. Sprinkle with cheese and bake in a 450° F. oven until bubbling and golden.

CORN, CLAM AND SHRIMP CASSEROLE

2 cans whole kernel canned corn,
    drained
1 pound cooked shelled frozen
    shrimp, thawed
1 cup clams

½ cup clam juice
2 eggs, beaten
½ cup heavy cream
2 tablespoons butter, melted
salt, pepper and paprika

butter for casserole

Mix all ingredients and season well. Bake in a shallow buttered casserole in a 400° F. oven for about 10 minutes, or until bubbling. Be sure corn is hot through. Sprinkle with paprika and serve.

DIEPPE SOLE

1½ pounds filets of sole
1 cup white wine
1 can cream of mushroom soup
1 small can peeled shrimp
lemon slices and parsley for garnish

1 lemon, juice only
2 tablespoons grated Parmesan
cheese
salt and pepper

Poach sole for a few minutes in white wine, until the meat is no longer transparent. Drain well, retain the wine and arrange the sole in a shallow baking dish. Place dish in a 300° F. oven and heat mushroom soup with the wine, shrimp and lemon juice (use the lemon juice to taste). Season and pour over the fish, sprinkle, with cheese and brown under the broiler.

BROILED TROUT

2 packages frozen trout, thawed
8 tablespoons soft butter
2 tablespoons lemon juice

2 teaspoons minced onion
¼ teaspoon each salt and paprika
salt and pepper

Wash trout, dry well and salt cavity. Cream butter with next three ingredients. Spread a little of this mixture on each trout and place, buttered side up, on top broiler shelf. Broil until brown, turn, spread with more butter and brown on second side, about 4 minutes on each side. Divide remaining butter over the 4 trout and serve at once.

Scallops

Fresh and frozen scallops are available at all markets and can be used for luncheon or dinner menus. They are excellent for buffet suppers and casseroles. Always buy the small bay scallops—they are tenderer and sweeter than the large sea scallops.

COQUILLES ST. JACQUES DE BORDEAUX

1 pint scallops
1 tomato, peeled and chopped
½ cup frozen chopped onion,
    thawed
2 parsley sprigs, ground through
    Mouli

2 tablespoons butter
1 10-ounce can cream of mushroom
    soup
salt and pepper
sherry to taste, optional

Simmer scallops 5 minutes in salted water. Drain and mix with tomato, onion, parsley and butter. Simmer over low heat for 1 minute. Add soup, heat and divide over scallop shells. Push under broiler and brown lightly. Garnish with parsley and serve.

Scallops may be cut if they are large. Sherry should be added to taste with the soup.

SCALLOPS AMANDINE

1½ pounds scallops
3 slices bacon
¼ cup butter
½ cup flour for dredging

salt and pepper
4 parsley sprigs, ground through
    Mouli
1 envelope shaved almonds

Cut bacon into ½-inch squares with a kitchen scissors. Fry until transparent, add butter and scallops which have previously been washed, dried and well dredged with flour. Fry about 3 minutes, stirring until scallops are lightly browned. Add parsley and the shaved almonds. Continue to fry until almonds are golden, about 3 more minutes. Season and serve with brown butter or Parsley Sauce.

BROILED SCALLOPS

1 pound scallops
½ cup butter
½ cup bread crumbs
1 tablespoon capers

1 tablespoon dehydrated parsley
    flakes
salt and pepper
1 lemon, sliced thin

1 4-ounce jar tartar sauce

Butter a shallow baking dish and melt remaining butter. Dry scallops with a towel, dip them in butter and roll in well-seasoned crumbs. Arrange scallops in baking dish. Broil in pre-heated 450° F. broiler for 3 minutes. Add capers and parsley, shake to turn scallops, broil 3 minutes longer and serve at once, garnished with lemon slices. Serve with cold tartar sauce.

SCALLOPS IN WHITE WINE

1½ pounds scallops
1 cup white wine
1 4-ounce can sliced mushrooms, drained

1 can cream of mushroom soup
1 tablespoon dehydrated parsley flakes
salt and pepper

Dry scallops. Heat them to boiling with wine, reduce heat and simmer 4 minutes. Add drained mushrooms, soup and parsley and season to taste. Reheat and boil 4 minutes longer or until scallops are well heated and serve.

Fish Steaks

Broiling fish steaks is one of life's simplest occupations. The only trouble with it is that when you are through (about 6 to 10 minutes after you started) you have a broiled fish steak. This may be all very well for diets and Fridays and Lent and times when your mind should be on higher things, but at all other times a broiled fish steak is a dry and depressing thing. The answer, of course, lies in broiling it with more than plenty of butter, with herbs and other enchantments that make it palatable. After that there is only one other ingredient to change it and that is the sauce. We follow with a sort of chart for the steaks and suggestions for embellishing them.

If you do all these things you can have broiled fish steaks for a gala dinner or for the man you are planning to have cook for you for the rest of your life.

SALMON STEAKS

4 1-inch-thick salmon steaks
flour for dredging
¼ cup butter
4 sprigs parsley, ground through
    Mouli

salt and pepper
1 recipe Anchovy Sauce
    (*see* page 231)

Preheat broiler to hot, about 540–550° F. Dredge steaks lightly with flour, dot with butter and broil 2 inches from source of heat. Turn with a pancake turner after 3 minutes. Season with salt, pepper and put another pat of butter on each steak. Broil for 3 more minutes. Serve immediately with another pat of butter and a sprinkling of parsley. Pass anchovy sauce separately.

HALIBUT STEAKS

4 1-inch-thick halibut steaks
flour for dredging
1/3 cup butter

salt and pepper
1 recipe Swedish Cucumber Sauce
    (*see* page 230)

Prepare as Salmon Steaks, but increase broiling time to 4 minutes on each side and pass cucumber sauce separately.

SWORDFISH STEAKS

4 1-inch-thick swordfish steaks
flour for dredging
½ cup butter

salt, pepper and paprika
1 Horseradish Sauce
    (*see* page 226)

Prepare as Salmon Steaks, but increase broiling time to 4 minutes on each side. Sprinkle with paprika before serving and pass horseradish sauce separately.

CODFISH STEAKS

4 1-inch-thick codfish steaks
flour for dredging
4 sprigs parsley, ground through
    Mouli

salt, pepper and paprika
1 recipe Hollandaise Sauce
    (*see* page 232)

Prepare as Salmon Steaks, but increase broiling time to 5 minutes on each side. Sprinkle with parsley and paprika before serving and pass hollandaise separately.

LOBSTER SPREAD

1 container frozen cooked lobster, thawed and diced (1 pound)
½ cup stuffed olives
½ green pepper, seeded and sliced
5 parsley sprigs
1 curl of lemon rind
½ cup Lemon Mayonnaise
salt and freshly ground black pepper
buttered black bread rounds

Blend olives, green pepper, parsley, lemon rind and mayonnaise in blender until pepper and olives are roughly chopped. Arrange lobster on a serving platter, pour over the sauce and surround with black bread rounds.

If no blender is available, use a vegetable mincer.

LOBSTER LANDECK

1 pound frozen lobster meat
1 cup diced celery
4 lettuce leaves
2/3 cup mayonnaise
3 tablespoons chili sauce
2 tablespoons tomato paste
1 tablespoon Worcestershire sauce
1 tablespoon A-1 sauce
1 tablespoon chopped parsley
    or chives
salt and pepper

Arrange lobster and celery on lettuce leaves. Pour over a sauce made of all remaining ingredients.

LOBSTER CAROL

1 pound cooked lobster
½ teaspoon dry mustard
2/3 cup mayonnaise
2 tablespoons tomato ketchup
2 tablespoons clam juice
salt and pepper
1 teaspoon dried chervil
1 teaspoon each, chopped parsley
    and chives
½ head lettuce
1 teaspoon chopped mint
½ cup whipped cream topping

Stir dry mustard into a little mayonnaise until smooth, then combine with remaining mayonnaise, ketchup, clam juice, chervil, parsley and chives. Season to taste and pour sauce over the lobster meat. Arrange on lettuce leaves in 4 cocktail glasses or serve in a salad bowl, surrounded by lettuce. Stir mint into salted whipped cream and top the cocktail glasses or the lobster in the bowl with the minted cream. Sauce may be prepared in the electric blender. This is especially good when fresh herbs are available.

BRANDY LOBSTER COCKTAIL

2 cups canned or frozen lobster
    meat, thawed and drained
½ cup mayonnaise, cold
2 tablespoons chili sauce

2 tablespoons brandy
1 squeeze lemon juice
2 teaspoons each chopped parsley
    and chives

salt and pepper to taste

Combine mayonnaise with next 5 ingredients, fold in lobster meat and serve on crisp lettuce leaves.

BEEFEATER LOBSTER COCKTAIL

Don't pass this by, not until you've read the last ingredient. Or, read the end first and start from there.

2 cups cold lobster meat (frozen and
    thawed or canned)
¼ cup mayonnaise
¼ cup whipped cream

salt to taste
1 tablespoon **ketchup**
2 teaspoons lemon juice
½ teaspoon Worcestershire sauce

1 cup gin

Marinate the drained lobster in the gin as long as possible,* add the other ingredients and serve surrounded by ice.

This recipe is for 4 people, allowing ½ cup of lobster per person. The quantity of gin can be increased according to taste.

Serve with dry Martinis or champagne.

* As long as possible means—marinate while you are taking a shower and/or mixing a Martini. It doesn't mean for an hour or (God forbid) overnight.

LOBSTER CASSEROLE

2 pounds canned or frozen lobster
    meat, thawed and drained
1 10½-ounce can cream of celery
    soup, heated
1 10½-ounce can cream of tomato
    soup, heated

2 tablespoons sherry
1 tablespoon lemon juice
salt and pepper
½ cup bread crumbs
3 tablespoons butter for casserole
    and top

Combine lobster meat, soups, sherry, lemon juice and seasonings and pour into a wide, well buttered casserole. Top with bread crumbs, dot with remaining butter and brown in a 400° F. oven.

You can substitute mushroom soup for the tomato soup, and for further variety, a 7-ounce can of artichoke hearts can be added.

LOBSTER WITH HERBS

1 pound cooked lobster meat
¼ garlic clove
salt and pepper
½ cup butter
¼ cup white wine

1 tablespoon each chives and
    parsley, put through Mouli
1 teaspoon each dried tarragon,
    chervil and dill

Rub pan with garlic and discard. Cook seasoned lobster in hot butter for 3–4 minutes, shaking the pan or stirring so that meat is well coated. Add wine and herbs, stir and cook 2 minutes longer. Serve on buttered toast rounds.

LOBSTER THERMIDOR

1 pound frozen lobster meat,
    thawed and drained
½ cup butter

1½ cups heavy cream
6 tablespoons Madeira
6 tablespoons brandy
salt, pepper and cayenne

Heat lobster in salted water, drain well. Sauté in hot butter, turning to coat all pieces for 4 minutes. Add cream beaten lightly with Madeira and brandy. Season to taste and cook for 5 minutes before serving. Serve on rice.

FRIED FROGS' LEGS

24–28 pairs frogs' legs
1 tablespoon salt
flour for dredging
1 cup butter

1 clove garlic, crushed
1 lemon, juice only
1 lemon, quartered
salt and pepper

Lay frogs' legs in 2 quarts water with 1 tablespoon salt added. Melt butter, add crushed garlic, lemon juice and salt and pepper. Drain frogs' legs, dredge in seasoned flour. Increase heat under butter, add frogs' legs and fry until brown. Turn and brown other side, serve with butter poured over. Frying should take about 5 minutes to a side for small frogs' legs.

CHAPTER IV

Cheeses
and
Eggs

Cheeses

THE THING that makes epicureanism so pleasant, or call it connoisseurmanship if you prefer, is the tasting. Whether it is wine
tasting along the Rhone and the Rhine or whether it is cheese tasting in Roquefort and Edam or Jermyn Street or in that little cheese
shop on Third Avenue, it is always the best part of the game.

When you finally make your selection and carry your perfect
cheese home, you do so with pleasurable anticipation. You bring
out the proper wine, you invite a brother (or even a sister) appreci-
ator and the cheese warms your epicurean hearts. But the fact
remains that it never really tastes quite as good as it did at the
moment of discovery when the cheese man handed you the first
sliver of it across his counter on a long thin knife.

Sometimes he extends the cheese on a scoop, sometimes he hands
it with his fingers (cheese lovers are brothers under the skin). In a
little shop in Vienna there is a test Stilton standing out with a
silver scoop. You dig out some crumbly morsels, taste it and buy

yourself a Stilton, or you taste it and buy yourself the dill pickle you went there for. No matter what the purpose of your visit, you always taste the Stilton; in fact, now that we think about it, the purpose of the visit is to taste the Silton while the few grams of salami are only the excuse.

The connoisseur proceeds differently with different cheeses. He applies every sense to the game. He taps and listens to some cheeses, he feels and looks at others. Some have to be smelled and others have to be tasted. It is never more than a sliver, thoughtfully and slowly eaten, a savoring, an enjoyment. Certain expressions have to cross his face—connoisseurmanship requires that he explain himself along accepted lines. His degree of knowledge has to be established. He cannot just say "delicious" of a Roquefort or "not bad" of a Bel Paese and take it home; he has to say "not quite at the peak" or "an hour too late." He has to tap the Parmesan and say with authority, "Give it four more months." Since he says this to the cheese man he has to know what he is doing—the cheese man has a long slim knife in his hand. The rules of connoisseurmanship demand that he give a report on how his Stilton is doing at home. Here again he cannot say, "It is doing as well as can be expected," he has to give an accurate account of its ripeness, its temperature and a progress report on its, shall we say, smell. He has to be able to tell the cheese man that his Camembert will be ripe and right on Tuesday in order that the cheese man will continue to hand him little slivers. When other epicures are tasting at the same time it adds a note of rivalry and spices the game.

Taking your dog, provided he is also a connoisseur, is often very popular; he too is given slivers of cheese but the danger is always present that the dog will eat all of them with equal enthusiasm and be relegated to cheese rinds ever after.

There is, of course, the other side, the reverse of the medal, the one most of us belong on. For us, cheeses are arranged in pliofilm packages, foil packages, paper boxes or perforated containers. They are packaged in thin slices and the counter where they are displayed is refrigerated. You leave your dog outside and you wheel a cart along the counter. You help yourself to an 8-ounce package of cream cheese in silver foil for cocktails, a shaker-dispenser of grated cheese for the top of the casserole, a 1-pound package of sliced cheese for the children's lunch boxes, and a sausage of sharp cheese for emergencies. You wheel on to other counters without ever encountering a cheese man or anyone else except the check-out girl, and she doesn't care what cheeses you took provided she can distinguish the price which is stamped on each package, cold-bloodedly, with ink.

Connoisseurmanship must wait. The cheeses you bring home in this uninspired fashion are excellent, but the pleasures of the game are lost. The shades of Leicestershire and the Emmental, the Roque-fort caves and Limburg fade away. The Dutch villages and the steep Norwegian mountainsides, the sheep and goats and cows, the molds and the rennets, the wooden boxes and the baskets are all things of the past unless you can find a cheese shop or a "Gourmet Department" in a store that employs a cheese man.

Cheeses are, of course, one of man's oldest foods. They date back to a prehistoric period that coincided with man's discovery that he could obtain milk from an animal. After that nature took its course. Milk curdled and soured and became cheese, and man —the ever hungry and curious—tasted it and discovered it was good.

Cheeses are invented or discovered. A shepherd is said to have discovered Roquefort when he left his bread and sheep's cheese in a Roquefort cave while he went after his flock. When he remem-bered it some weeks later it had turned blue. He was either very hungry or very curious and ate it. He probably didn't say, "Ah, an excellent Roquefort!" but he did leave his cheese in the cave after that and enjoyed his discovery to the full. Madame Harel invented Camembert and there is a monument to her in Camembert. The American settlers invented something they called Pot Cheese and Liederkranz came originally from Canada.

To the Instant Epicure cheeses are infinitely important. Tastes have turned more and more toward unpretentious desserts. Meals are ended now, as they have ended for centuries along the Medi-terranean, with cheese and fruit. Try cold red grapes with a Lieder-kranz or green grapes with a Camembert, Stilton with port, Roque-fort with a bowl of fruit and nuts. Very simple, very quick; the cheese must be good, the fruit cold and everybody happy.

(See other cheese dishes in Hors d'Oeuvre chapter. Increase quan-tity and size and serve for lunch or supper.)

TWELVE MORNAY LUNCHEON DISHES

1 cup grated cheese, half Parmesan
    and half American, or
    any combination
4 tablespoons butter or margarine

4 tablespoons flour
1 cup consommé
½ cup cream, or more to taste
salt and pepper

Melt butter over low heat, stir in flour and gradually stir in consommé and cream. Add cheese and cook, stirring constantly, for about 4 minutes or until cheese is melted and sauce is smooth. Season and pour over any of the following ingredients:

1. Prepare 2 packages frozen asparagus according to package directions.

2. Heat 2 10-ounce cans hearts of artichoke; drain before pouring the sauce over the hearts.

3. Prepare 2 packages frozen spinach according to package directions. Drain and add 1 tablespoon sherry. Pour sauce over spinach and serve.

4. Pour Mornay Sauce over 4 poached eggs. Eggs can be on toasted English muffins.

5. Use sauce as above but place 1 slice ham, fried for a moment, between the egg and the muffin.

6. Pour Mornay Sauce over 4 5-minute eggs on a bed of sliced mushrooms. Heat 2 3-ounce cans sliced mushrooms. Sprinkle sauce with parsley ground through Mouli.

7. Peel and cube 2 large cucumbers. Sauté in a saucepan with 2 tablespoons butter for 1 minute. Season well and cover with Mornay Sauce.

8. Pour Mornay Sauce over 2 packages frozen cauliflower, prepared according to package directions.

9. Add ½ cup frozen chopped onion, thawed, to Mornay Sauce while it is cooking and use the sauce in any of the above ways.

10. Prepare 2 packages frozen corn according to package directions or heat 2 No. 2 cans corn, add minced red and green pepper according to taste and pour sauce over the corn. Stir and serve.

11. Pour Mornay Sauce over heated canned white onions. Use approximately half as much sauce as onions. Sprinkle with fresh or frozen chives.

12. Follow above directions, substituting heated canned white potatoes for the onions.

You are bound to find more rarebits and fondues here than usual. They cook quickly, and we have to leave the cheese puddings and soufflés to the people who have time. Quantities can be increased or decreased, to suit the purpose and the time of day.

If you are not always an instant cook, only when guests arrive unexpectedly or when guests stay longer than you had expected, then be sure to have cheeses in the house. They are lifesavers in emergencies.

FREIBURG FONDUE

¼ cup butter	2 tablespoons hot water
1 clove garlic, split	2 tablespoons white wine
2 pounds soft yellow cheese	(or 4 tablespoons water)

salt and pepper

Melt butter with garlic, remove garlic after butter is foamy. Add cheese (if an unsliced cheese is used it should be roughly diced), and stir over low heat until melted. Gradually stir in water and wine. Season and serve poured over toasted bread, sliced tomatoes, crisp bacon, 5-minute eggs, hot asparagus (frozen asparagus prepared according to package directions) or a combination of toast, tomatoes and bacon.

FONDUE AU VIN BLANC

1 pound Swiss cheese, coarsely grated	1 tablespoon kirsch, or to taste
	1 tablespoon flour
1 cup dry white wine	½ clove garlic

salt and pepper

Rub heavy pan with garlic and discard. Add wine and cheese and dust with flour. Stir with a wooden spoon over low heat until it boils, take from heat, stir in kirsch, season and serve at once with buttered toast cubes.

CHEESE QUICK

2 pounds grated American cheese
½ cup milk
1 envelope broken pecan meats

1 Bermuda onion, sliced
4 slices hot toast
salt and pepper

Heat cheese and milk in top of double boiler over boiling water until cheese is melted. Stir well, add pecans and season to taste. Pour over sliced Bermuda onion on toast.

CHEESE ENVELOPES

8 slices Gruyère or semisoft cheese,
    halved
4 thin slices ham
2 eggs

1 cup milk
1½ cups commercial bread crumbs
salt and pepper
¼ pound margarine

Make thin sandwiches of two slices cheese with 1 slice ham between. Cut into convenient shapes and dip into mixture of eggs beaten with milk. Dip into bread crumbs, turning to coat both sides. Dip back into egg and crumbs and fry in margarine until golden. Turn once to brown both sides.

FONDUE NEUFCHÂTELOISE

½ pound Swiss cheese, finely cut
1½ tablespoons flour
1 clove garlic, split
1 cup dry white wine
1 loaf French or Italian crusty white
    bread or 4 hard rolls

1 dash nutmeg, optional
salt and pepper
3 tablespoons kirsch, apple jack or
    brandy

Cut bread or rolls into bite-size pieces—each piece must have at least 1 side of crust.

Dredge cheese with flour. Rub a 1- to 1½-quart casserole or chafing dish well with garlic, add wine and set over very low heat. When bubbles rise to surface, add cheese gradually and stir after each addition until cheese is melted before adding more. Stir until mixture bubbles, season to taste and add nutmeg. Stir in kirsch, take from fire and set over heating unit at table and serve. The low heat is required to keep the fondue at proper consistency but not to cook it further.

Spear bread with fork, dunk bread into fondue, stir and eat. Each guest does this in turn. The stirring keeps the fondue soft and coats the bread thoroughly. Serve with kirsch and follow with tea or coffee.

This fondue is called Neufchâteloise as you should use Neufchâtel wine.

CHEESE EN BROCHETTE

½ pound Gruyère cheese or any
    semisoft cheese
4 thick slices bread, quartered
2 egg yolks

1 cup milk
salt, pepper and paprika
flour for dredging
fat for deep frying

Cut cheese into 12–16 thick wedges or slices. String on skewers alternately with bread slices. Beat yolks into milk and roll each skewer in the mixture. Dredge with flour and season well with salt and pepper. Sprinkle with paprika and fry in 375° F. fat for about 3 minutes. Fat should be just deep enough to cover.

CHEESE DEVIL

1 pound yellow store cheese,
    cut in chunks

1 can cream of tomato soup
1 teaspoon Worcestershire sauce
cayenne, salt and pepper

In the top of a double boiler over boiling water, melt the cheese in the soup. Add Worcestershire sauce and season to taste. Serve poured over toasted bread or over sliced tomatoes and toasted bread.

CHEESE MUFF

1 can Welsh rarebit

1 egg, beaten
¼ cup beer or ale

Heat rarebit in top of double boiler over boiling water. Beat in the egg and beer and continue to beat until light.

DEVILED CHEESE

1 cup grated American cheese
½ cup butter
¼ cup pickle relish

1 teaspoon brown mustard,
 or to taste
cayenne, salt and pepper
8 toasted bread rounds

Melt cheese with butter in a heavy skillet. Add drained pickle relish, mustard and a dash of cayenne. Salt and pepper to taste—stir until smooth and serve on hot toast rounds.

Cheese need not be something you give your children when they come home to lunch. Prepare any of these dishes and serve them with cold leftover meats or with simple broiled meats and fish. They stretch dinner and they need not stretch your waist measurement if you eat them instead of potatoes or pastas.

Although the cheese lover insists that cheese is man's oldest food, we know that if there was nothing else there were certainly apples before there was cheese. Combine them, eat apples and cheese and wash the whole thing down with red wine.

CROQUE-MONSIEUR

8 slices day-old thin-sliced bread,
 trimmed
½ cup soft butter

1 tablespoon anchovy paste
4 slices ham
4 slices Swiss cheese

Butter a baking sheet well, mix remaining butter with anchovy paste and spread on bread slices. Sandwich bread slices together with one slice of ham and one of cheese in each sandwich, trim, place on baking sheet and bake in a 400° F. oven until bread is golden and cheese begins to run. Serve very hot with green salad and cold beer. In France this is cut into fingers and served with tea. Mustard may be substituted for the anchovy paste and salami may be substituted for the ham.

CROQUE-MADAME

4 ¼-inch-thick slices Swiss cheese
flour for dredging
½ cup butter

pepper, coarsely ground through a
mill

Cut cheese into fingers and triangles, dredge in flour. Cheese should be at room temperature when it is dredged. Fry in butter until golden. Serve on toast slices and pepper well before eating.

HUNGARIAN TOAST

8 thin slices white bread
½ cup white wine
¼ cup butter
8 tablespoons tomato paste

4 large slices onion
4 slices yellow cheese
paprika
salt and pepper

Moisten bread with white wine and fry on both sides in butter, turn once and spread with salted tomato paste. Lay an onion slice on half the toast and a cheese slice on the other. Spread with paprika and seasonings and bake in a 400° F. oven until cheese is slightly melted and browned.

BAKED CHEESE AND TOMATO SANDWICHES

1 large or 2 small tomatoes,
    sliced thin
butter

4 slices bread
2/3 cup grated cheese
¼ cup chopped parsley

salt and pepper

Arrange tomato slices on generously buttered bread. Lay the slices on a well buttered baking sheet and sprinkle heavily with grated cheese and chopped parsley. Season well and dot with a little butter. Bake in a 375° F. oven until cheese is browned and edges of bread are toasted. Serve with a green salad.

BULGAR CHEESE BREADS

1-1/3 cups grated cheese
1 tablespoon flour
2 eggs
2 tablespoons milk
salt and pepper

4–6 slices white bread
butter or fat for frying
1 jar yogurt
2 tablespoons chopped fresh or
    frozen chives

Mix cheese, flour and eggs. Beat well with milk and seasonings. Dip bread into the mixture and fry in butter or fat until brown. Beat yogurt with chives and seasoning and serve as a sauce with the fried bread.

BRUSSELS SALAD

6 heads Belgian endive
6 ounces Gruyère cheese
1 tablespoon prepared mustard

1 lemon, juice and grated rind
3 tablespoons mayonnaise
¼ cup whipped cream

1 head Boston lettuce

Cut endive into quarters lengthwise and cut cheese into strips the same length as the endive. Arrange cheese and endive neatly, as if stacking logs, on lettuce leaves on 4 salad plates. Mix mustard and lemon juice with mayonnaise and fold in whipped cream. Pour dressing over the endive and cheese and dust with grated lemon rind.

CHEESE SLAW I AND II

Variation I

½ pound Swiss cheese,
    slivered or diced
½ cup French dressing
1 teaspoon prepared mustard

1 medium onion, chopped, or
    ½ cup frozen chopped onion,
    thawed
salt and pepper

½ head iceberg lettuce, shredded

Mix dressing, mustard, onion and seasonings in bowl, add cheese and lettuce and mix. Surround with sliced cold ham, rolled and secured with picks, and serve.

Variation II

½ pound Swiss cheese,
   slivered or diced
½ cup mayonnaise
1 diced celery stalk
3 sliced radishes

salt and pepper
4 sprigs parsley, ground through
   Mouli
½ 3-ounce envelope broken
   walnuts

½ head iceberg lettuce, shredded

Mix mayonnaise, celery, radishes, parsley and walnuts in bowl and season to taste. Add cheese and lettuce and mix. Serve as above.

SUNDAY CHEESE

2 packages snappy cheese
½ cup butter
¼ cup frozen chopped onion,
   thawed

1 teaspoon brown mustard, or
   to taste
cayenne, salt and pepper
8 slices toasted bread

Melt cheese with butter in a heavy skillet. Add onion and mustard and a dash of cayenne. Salt and pepper to taste—stir until smooth and serve on hot toasted bread.

CHEESE WAFFLES

3 cups sifted flour
3 tablespoons sugar
1½ tablespoons baking powder
1 teaspoon salt

1¼ cups grated cheese (6 ounces)
3 eggs, separated
2¼ cups milk
6 tablespoons melted butter

salt and pepper

Mix dry ingredients with egg yolks beaten with milk and butter. Season to taste, fold in stiffly beaten egg whites and bake in a hot waffle iron. Makes about 10 to 12 waffles.

Make Sunday supper of this with bacon, or creamed chicken.

CHEESE SCRAMBLE

¼ cup grated American cheese
1 tablespoon butter
1 tablespoon capers
2 tablespoons frozen chopped
    onion, thawed

8 tablespoons canned chopped
    mushrooms
2 tablespoons tomato purée
2 eggs
salt and pepper

4 slices buttered toast

Simmer cheese, butter, capers, onion, mushrooms and tomato purée for 2 minutes, stirring constantly. Add well-beaten eggs and stir until set. Serve on buttered toast.

For a tasty variation, add ¼ cup fresh cut chives when chives are in season.

Eggs

Where the purchase of eggs is concerned there is no connoisseurmanship and no epicureanism involved, and no tasting. A dozen eggs in America is a dozen eggs. They come in cartons, form-fitting cartons, that are shaped like twelve eggs. Sometimes they still come in divided cardboard boxes but no matter how they are packaged there is little danger, today, of getting a rotten egg among the fresh ones. All elements of chance and risk are removed. Buying a dozen eggs is just a matter of deciding whether they should be medium, large or extra large eggs, whether we want white or brown ones, and after we get them home we have to decide whether we are going to store them in the refrigerator or not.

Apparently refrigerator manufacturers expect us always to want ice-cold eggs, since they provide spaces to hold them, but we are under no compulsion to do so if we belong to the cook-with-eggs-at-room-temperature school of thought.

Eggs are, in other words, not interesting until we cook them. There is some agitation for dated eggs, but here again we will only buy the latest date instead of, as in wine, the earliest. The saddest thing about the egg today is the disappearance of the little feather that used to cling to an egg now and then to remind us of the hen that cackled and rejoiced over it. Now they might as well be made in a machine; the personal touch is gone.

When we open them the situation changes, the elements of

connoisseurmanship are immediately called into play. Do we really know how to open an egg? By the way a man opens an egg you can tell whether he is a chef or a short-order cook. By the way a woman opens an egg you can tell whether she is a housewife or a single working girl or a bride. How to separate an egg correctly is sheer virtuosity. The beating of the yolks and whites is the difference between the professional and the amateur. The cooking of the egg—we have gotten there at last—is the difference between night and day.

Since we are Instant Epicures we are not allowing a single hard-cooked egg to get into this book. It would take as long to boil and cool as we are proposing for the preparation of an entire meal. There are Oeuf Mollet (5-minute eggs), poached, scrambled and fried eggs. Omelets and pancakes, eggs for breakfast, lunch or dinner. Eggs in soups or omelets for dessert. They are so varied and valuable in Instant Cookery that no Instant Epicure should ever be without at least a dozen.

Tastes may have turned from the midnight supper of chafing-dish eggs to the joys of Lobster in Absinthe. But gone is the cook who made cooking for you her profession and gone with her are all the things that took all the hours you were out frivoling to prepare. When the host no longer employs his cook and when she is (usually) endowed with his name, he cannot leave her home stabbing lobsters. All late suppers are now based on the things you can cook after you get home and before you sit down to relax, a matter of ten or twelve minutes at best.

Obviously the egg fits into this scheme of things. Efficient, dated, streamlined and ovate, all we have to do is turn to some forgotten ways of preparing them. They say there is nothing new under the sun and considering that during the centuries there have been billions of eggs laid, prepared and eaten, we must be able to find some, to us, new ways of doing them. They couldn't all have been fried.

FRIED EGGS AU BEURRE NOIR

4 eggs	1 teaspoon drained capers
5 tablespoons butter	1 teaspoon malt vinegar
	salt and pepper

Fry eggs in half the butter and slide onto 4 hot plates. Add remaining butter to pan and brown, add capers and vinegar and pour over eggs. Season to taste and serve.

CURRIED EGGS

4 eggs	1 tablespoon flour
3 tablespoons butter	¾ cup bouillon
¼ cup chopped frozen onion, thawed	1 teaspoon tomato paste
	2 tablespoons cream
1 tablespoon curry powder	salt and pepper

Place eggs in boiling water and cook covered for 6 minutes. In the meantime melt butter in a skillet and fry onion until puffed and golden. Reduce heat, add curry powder and flour and stir until browned. Add bouillon and tomato paste and stir until smooth, add cream and correct seasoning. Carefully shell eggs, lay them in the sauce and cook gently for 1 minute longer. Correct seasoning and serve on toast.

You can substitute 2 cans button mushrooms, lobster, shrimp, crab meat or any cold leftover meat for the eggs.

SWISS EGGS

1 cup heavy cream	butter for pan
4 eggs	salt and pepper
	3 tablespoons grated Italian cheese

Pour cream into well buttered ovenware pan or pie pan. Break eggs into the pan, keeping yolks intact. Sprinkle with cheese, dot with butter and bake in a 350° F. oven for 5 minutes or until cheese is brown and eggs are set.

FIVE-MINUTE EGGS

What the Frenchman calls his *oeuf mollet* is, in fact, just a five-minute egg, shelled and served as, or in place of, a poached egg. Nothing is lost, the white does not have to be trimmed away and it can be kept warm without getting hard.

Lower eggs gently into boiling salted water. Boil exactly 5 minutes, pour off hot water and replace with cold water, or plunge the eggs into cold water; it does not matter if the shells crack at this point. Take out the eggs one by one and break the shells by tapping them carefully all around; the shells should be entirely crazed with little cracks. Peel off the cracked shells—they should come away very easily—and return the eggs gently to the cold water if they are to be used for cold dishes. Place them into warm water if they are to be kept warm for hot egg dishes.

OEUFS MOLLETS

4 5-minute eggs
¼ cup butter
4 slices smoked salmon

1 jar frozen hollandaise sauce, thawed
2 English muffins, split with a fork and toasted

Butter hot muffins, arrange a slice of salmon on each, put a warm egg on the salmon and serve with hollandaise sauce.

Use these 5-minute eggs on creamed frozen spinach, broccoli or asparagus. Try the asparagus and egg combinations with a slice of ham or Italian pepper ham and hollandaise sauce, or just melted butter and a little grated Parmesan cheese. Serve the eggs cold with herbed mayonnaise or cold tomato sauce.

SCALLION EGGS

4 5-minute eggs
4 lettuce leaves
4 scallions, minced (chives may be substituted)
1 tablespoon minced green pepper

1 teaspoon capers
1–2 tablespoons prepared French dressing
1 teaspoon paprika
salt and pepper
4 parsley curls

Arrange eggs on lettuce leaves. Combine scallions, green pepper and capers and moisten with dressing. Season and pour over eggs. Garnish with parsley and serve sprinkled with paprika.

GREEN EGGS

4 5-minute eggs
2 tomatoes, peeled and cut in half
1 cup watercress leaves

1 cup mayonnaise
2 tablespoons fresh grated or
    bottled horseradish

salt and pepper to taste

Arrange eggs on tomato slices. Mix mayonnaise with minced watercress leaves and horseradish. Season sauce to taste and pour it over the eggs. Set aside a few good sprigs of watercress to use as a garnish.

EGGS TERMINUS

Long before America established the coffee break, Europeans were interrupting their mornings with second or "fork" breakfasts. This second breakfast was more leisurely than the first breakfast— or lunch—and so the habit of "dropping in" to share it was established.

A well-educated guest could make a well-educated guess and time himself to arrive just when Eggs Terminus were being served up.

6 eggs
½ cup cream
1 tablespoon water
2 tablespoons minced chives
    or parsley
½ teaspoon salt

2 tablespoons butter
pepper, freshly ground through a
    mill
4 slices smoked salmon
4 slices buttered rye or
    pumpernickel bread

Beat eggs in top of double boiler with cream, water, salt and chives until they are smooth. Add butter, cover and set over rapidly boiling water in lower part of double boiler. Stir after 3 or 4 minutes, and serve as soon as eggs have reached preferred consistency. They should be soft, creamy and light. Divide eggs over four slices of bread covered with smoked salmon. Grind pepper over the open scrambled egg sandwiches and serve at once with hot instant coffee or tea. You can omit the chives in the eggs and sprinkle the finished eggs with chives after they are mounded on the salmon.

EGGS VIVEX

Follow recipe for Eggs Terminus, substituting ½ cup chopped thawed frozen onion for the chives. Serve on slices of cooked ham or tongue instead of smoked salmon.

EGGS TIVOLI

Follow recipe for Eggs Terminus, substituting ½ cup canned chopped mushrooms. Serve on paper-thin slices of onion instead of smoked salmon.

EGGS COPENHAGEN

Follow recipe for Eggs Terminus, adding ½ cup drained cottage cheese to the eggs and substituting crisp bacon for the smoked salmon.

Omelets

Omelets are important in Instant Cookery since they are ready to eat four minutes after being poured into the pan and the entire preparation is one continuous motion. Unfortunately, they also fall under the heading of "frightening recipes" along with soufflés and hollandaise sauce. Anyone who is short of time and likes to serve delicacies (or why read this book?) must know how to make an omelet. If you don't—this is the time to begin. First of all, don't be frightened and don't be led into one of those head-patting and tummy-massaging routines where hands go in opposite directions and all is confusion. The omelet does *not* have to be shaken while it is being stirred, filled, folded and rolled, with a single gesture and only two hands.

Beat the eggs, put butter into a hot pan, add the eggs, watch with sympathy and understanding, lift the edges a little. Fold over and slip onto a plate. Fillings can be poured over, or alongside of the omelet, and that is all. The Frenchman who loves his omelet says: *"L'omelette doit être dorée à l'extérieur, baveuse au centre."* *Baveuse* is a lovely word in any language to describe the soft, slightly runny, creamy interior of a perfect omelet. This is achieved by watching for the proper moment, but *not* by shaking and tilting. The reason for the shaking is to prevent the omelet from sticking to the pan. The proper amount of sizzling butter, a well-cared-for pan and rubbing oil over the pan before starting is all that is necessary. Shake it once to assure yourself the omelet is loose in the pan, but after that *restez tranquille*—and if the telephone rings, don't answer it. Don't answer it until after you have eaten the omelet. It is one of those things either you are supposed to burn your mouth with or, again like the Frenchman, you are supposed to blow on the first bite. You can make a single omelet of 6–8 eggs or you can make 2 or 4 smaller ones. Actually it depends on your pan. If you make individual ones, everybody has to start as soon as they are served (see above) so they can burn their mouths and so the last one—the hostess—eats hers entirely by herself, while everyone else pushes back chairs, sighs, lights cigarettes or munches salad. The large single omelet, when cut into sections, displays its interior and everyone can eat at once.

OMELETTE NORMANDE

5 eggs	salt
3 tablespoons butter	sugar or cinnamon sugar
1 jar sliced apples	
(pie filling)	

Beat eggs with salt to taste. Put butter into a hot pan—it should sizzle but not turn brown. Pour in two-thirds of eggs, cover with drained apple slices, pour in remaining eggs and allow to cook over low heat. Lift the edges now and then to allow the liquid egg to run under the cooked omelet. Fold omelet, slide onto hot plate and powder with sugar or cinnamon sugar.

SCRAMBLED SALMON

6 slices bacon	salt and pepper
2 tablespoons chopped onion	parsley sprigs, ground through
1 7-ounce can salmon	Mouli
4 eggs	paprika

Fry bacon until crisp, drain and keep hot. Add onion to fat and fry until transparent. Pour off most of the fat, retaining about 1 tablespoon fat and the onion in the pan. Add salmon, stir until coated and hot. Add beaten eggs and scramble as usual. Season and serve with bacon and freshly chopped parsley and sprinkle with a little paprika.

DOUBLE BOILER SPANISH EGGS

6 eggs
½ garlic clove
1 onion, chopped
1 tablespoon oil

1 tomato, peeled and chopped
1 green pepper, seeded and chopped
salt and pepper
4 slices buttered toast

Beat eggs. Crush garlic into upper section of double boiler, add onion and oil and fry over medium heat until onion is puffed and transparent. Add tomato and green pepper and stir well. Place upper section of double boiler over boiling water, add the eggs and season well. Cover and scramble, stirring once or twice, until eggs are creamy. Serve on buttered toast.

EGG SURPRISE

4 medium-large tomatoes
butter for casserole
4 teaspoons frozen chopped onion,
    thawed
4 teaspoons parsley, chopped
    through Mouli

4 eggs
¼ cup bread crumbs
2 tablespoons grated Parmesan
    cheese
4 teaspoons oil
salt and pepper

Cut top from tomatoes, scoop out centers and drain well. Season tomatoes and place them in a small buttered casserole or baking pan. Put a teaspoon onion and parsley in each tomato, break an egg into each and cover with crumbs and Parmesan. Pour a teaspoon of oil over each tomato and bake in a 375° F. oven until eggs are set, about 8 minutes. Serve at once with heated rolls.

POMODORO EGGS

4 medium-small tomatoes
4 eggs
1 tablespoon oil

½ teaspoon oregano
salt and pepper
butter for pan

Cut tops from tomatoes and scoop out pulp with a spoon. Season well, sprinkle with oil and oregano, and break 1 egg into each tomato. Set in a buttered pan and bake in 400° F. oven until eggs are set.

GENOESE EGGS

4 eggs
3 tablespoons oil

½ cup grated Parmesan cheese
salt and pepper

Heat oil in a heavy frying pan, break eggs into oil and fry until set. Sprinkle with cheese, transfer pan to a 400° F. oven and bake until cheese has melted, 1–2 minutes. Serve at once.

MARINER'S EGGS

4 poached eggs (3-minute)
4 slices buttered toast

4 anchovy filets
4 large stuffed olives, chopped fine

salt and pepper

Place well drained eggs on toast, split anchovies down the center and cross two strips over each egg. Sprinkle with olives, season and serve at once.

EGGS IN BLACK BUTTER
(Oeuf au Beurre Noir)

4 eggs
2 tablespoons butter

4 teaspoons lemon juice
1 teaspoon capers

salt and pepper

Brown butter in a cocotte or shallow pan, add lemon juice and capers. Break eggs into the pan and bake in a 375° F. oven for

5 minutes. If very well done eggs are preferred, the maximum time
can be 8 minutes.

TSCHIMBUR

4 poached eggs (or 4 five-minute   ½ garlic clove, crushed
     eggs)   salt and pepper
1 jar yogurt   3 tablespoons butter
           1 teaspoon paprika

While eggs are poaching or boiling, heat yogurt with garlic
and season well. Melt butter, stir in paprika and salt to taste. Serve
eggs covered with yogurt sauce and pour the paprika butter over the
yogurt at the last moment.

PARMESAN EGGS

4 eggs   2 teaspoons dry bread crumbs
4 tablespoons grated Parmesan   3 tablespoons butter
     cheese   salt, pepper and cayenne
2 teaspoons parsley, chopped
     through Mouli

Butter 4 small fireproof ramekins. Divide half the cheese
and parsley over them. Break an egg into each dish, sprinkle with
remaining cheese and parsley. Top with crumbs, season and place
a little butter on each. Bake in a 400° F. oven for 8 minutes, according to taste.

Pancakes

Thin pancakes are, of course, very fast-cooking affairs and if
you keep two pans going you can make enough pancakes for four
in a few minutes. If you measure the quantity of batter with a large
spoon (so that all the pancakes will be the same size) you can make
several at once in a large skillet or an electric skillet. There are also
Swedish pancake pans which are divided to make seven little pancakes at the same time. Pancakes can be kept hot in a very low oven,

they can be piled on a plate and set over hot water or they can be piled on a hot plate and covered with a warm napkin.

We do not give you recipes here for making any of the pancakes which are made from the wonderful ready mixes, griddle cakes, Swedish pancakes or potato pancakes. We give you only the basic batter for making the thin French pancakes which are known as *crêpes*. You can fill them with canned sliced mushrooms, heated with a little salted sour cream or any minced leftover meat. Fill them with red caviar and sour cream, or chives and salted cream cheese beaten with an egg yolk. They are the perfect containers for leftovers of any kind, fish, fowl or vegetable.

These pancakes are the basis for France's famous Crêpes Suzette and the many other versions that sprang from Hungary, Austria and Scandinavia. The fact that they are lightly sweetened does not necessarily limit them to desserts. The Hungarian Pallatchinken, filled with cottage cheese and lightly sugared, is still a popular main dish for luncheons or late breakfasts.

THIN PANCAKES, CRÊPES

Allow about 2 tablespoons batter per pancake. Melt about ½ teaspoon butter in the pan, then add the batter and tip the pan so that the batter is spread into a thin cake. Brown lightly on one side, turn and brown second side. Keep pancakes hot until all are completed.

4 eggs, well beaten	1 cup flour
1 cup milk	4 teaspoons sugar
1/3 cup melted butter	1 teaspoon salt

Beat eggs, milk and butter together with a rotary beater. Sift flour, sugar and salt and beat the liquid ingredients slowly into the dry ingredients. Let batter stand as long as possible (not over an hour). Heat pan as described above and add a little butter to the pan as necessary. One recipe of batter should make 12 to 16 pancakes, depending on their size. Add a little flour if they are too soft to handle or a little milk if they are too stiff. The quality of flour and the size of eggs differ, so we can only advise that the perfect batter for Crêpes should be the consistency of heavy cream.

FRUTTO DI MARE

1 recipe thin pancakes
1 1-pound container frozen crab
    meat, picked (substitute
    canned crab meat if
    necessary)

1 recipe Mornay Sauce or 1 can
    Newburg sauce
sherry to taste
½ cup grated Parmesan cheese

Heat crab meat in sauce and add sherry. Divide filling over hot pancakes and roll up. You can also set part of the sauce aside, fill the pancakes, roll them up, arrange them in a shallow baking dish and pour over the remaining sauce. Sprinkle with grated Parmesan cheese and heat in the oven or under the broiler until brown.

CRÊPES CANARINO

1 recipe thin pancakes
1 package frozen spinach, prepared
    according to package
    directions

1 recipe Mornay Sauce or 1 can
    cream of chicken soup,
    undiluted
½ cup grated Parmesan cheese

Combine drained hot spinach with hot sauce. Fill pancakes, roll up, sprinkle with Parmesan cheese and heat in oven or broiler until lightly browned.

FRUIT-FILLED CRÊPES FOR BREAKFAST OR LUNCHEON

1 recipe thin pancakes
2 cups warm apple sauce

½ cup lightly browned butter
12 slices crisp bacon

Fill pancakes with fruit filling, serve with a little brown butter poured over and arrange crisp bacon around pancake platter.

Substitute sausages, fried ham or fried Canadian bacon for the bacon. Substitute mashed bananas, sliced strawberries or whole cranberry sauce for the apple sauce.

CRÊPES SUZETTE

1 recipe thin pancakes	½ cup butter
10 lumps of sugar (not dots)	1 jigger Grand Marnier
2 oranges	1 jigger Curaçao or Cointreau
1 lemon	1 jigger brandy

Over a pan, rub half the sugar on the rind of the oranges and the other half on the lemon. Add the butter to the juices and crush the sugar. Set over low heat until the sauce bubbles, stir until smooth. Add half the liqueurs and the Crêpes, folded in quarters. When Crêpes are hot add remaining liqueurs and flame. Serve at once, adding part of the sauce to each portion.

PALLATCHINKEN

1 recipe thin pancakes	1 cup strawberry jam
	powdered sugar

Spread a tablespoon of jam on each pancake, roll up and arrange the rolled Pallatchinken on a long platter. Sprinkle evenly with powdered sugar, putting the sugar through a fine hair sieve to make an even sprinkling.

CHEESE PALLATCHINKEN

1 recipe thin pancakes	¼ cup raisins, mixed with
1 pound cottage cheese	¼ cup slivered almonds
1 egg yolk	powdered sugar

Mix cheese with egg yolk and raisins. Thin with cream or sour cream if mixture is too thick. Spread on pancakes, roll up and serve with sprinkling of powdered sugar as above.

TUNA PANCAKES

1 recipe thin pancakes	½ cup chopped frozen onion,
1 can tuna fish, mashed	thawed
¾ cup sour cream	½ teaspoon chopped dill
	salt and pepper

Spread mixture of heated tuna fish, cream, onion, dill and seasoning on pancakes, roll up and serve hot.

DANISH CRÊPES

1 recipe thin pancakes
1 cup thick apricot jam, heated

1 3-ounce envelope shaved almonds
¼ cup apricot brandy
powdered sugar

Mix jam, almonds and brandy, spread on pancakes, roll up and serve with sugar as Pallatchinken.

CRÊPES TROCADÉRO

1 recipe thin pancakes
2 cups vanilla ice cream

2 1-ounce squares semisweet
chocolate, grated

Fill hot pancakes quickly with ice cream and roll up. Arrange on plates and sprinkle with grated chocolate.

CRÊPES LEONARDO

1 recipe thin pancakes
1 cup heavy cream, whipped

1 tablespoon heavy rum
1 1-pint basket raspberries

Flavor stiffly whipped cream with rum, add half the raspberries and spread over the warm pancakes. Roll up and serve with the remaining raspberries spread over the pancakes. Sprinkle with powdered sugar if the berries are not sweet enough.

CRÊPES BLANCHETTE

1 recipe thin pancakes
1 can shredded pineapple, heated

1 jigger rum
powdered sugar

Fill pancakes with drained pineapple mixed with rum. Roll up and sprinkle with powdered sugar as Pallatchinken.

KÄTE'S PANCAKES

2 eggs

½ cup milk

¼ cup flour

2 tablespoons sugar

1 pinch salt

butter for pan

Beat eggs and milk. Combine dry ingredients gradually and stir the liquid ingredients into the dry. Fry a little batter at a time in buttered pans, spreading the batter to make very thin pancakes. Keep pancakes hot in a slow oven until all are completed. Serve with a filling of jam thinned with rum or orange marmalade thinned with Cointreau.

JONAS PANCAKES

2 eggs

2 tablespoons flour

2 tablespoons milk

Beat well, make paper-thin pancakes in a lightly buttered pan and keep hot until all are completed. Serve filled with:

1. sour cream and chives
2. sour cream and red caviar
3. strawberry jelly
4. cottage cheese, beaten with egg yolk and raisins

If the last filling is preferred, stir enough cottage cheese into 1 egg yolk to make a thick yellow cream. Add raisins to taste and spread on pancakes. Roll up and sprinkle with powdered sugar.

CHAPTER V

Meat
and
Poultry

Meat

B Y THE NATURAL laws of compensation our total loss of time and leisure should be offset by a substantial gain in money. Every hour we lose should represent lots of dollars earned. Any time that we take away from cooking should be used for making money, since it costs much more to cook Instantly that it costs to cook slowly.

A simple example of this is meat. The cook with all the time in the world on her hands and absolutely nothing to do can boil the cheapest cut of meat until it is tender, even if it takes all day. The cook with no time whatever has to buy more expensive cuts of meat, which by some natural order of things take much less time to cook than the cheap cuts. The filet at several dollars a pound as against the pot roast at less than a dollar a pound is an economic-gastronomic anachronism. There is no time for cooking the pot roast, ergo, there has to be money enough to buy the filet.

If you have neither time nor money then something is seriously wrong and your Instant Epicureanism is reduced to the few cuts of meat that satisfy both the ten-minute cooking limit and the low budget limit.

We give you fast-cooking kidneys, liver, chopped meat and frankfurters. We include recipes for quickly heated canned and smoked and frozen meats and then we come back to the filet steaks, which are the Instant Epicure's standby, his out. You can give your guests a Fondue Bourguignonne which they cook in exactly as long as it takes them to count to ten. It has the added advantage that they cook it while you sit by; all you do is provide the oil and light the flame. All you do besides that is to make enough money so you can buy great big beautiful chunks of filet of beef for your guests to spear idly and cook. The same law that makes most quick-cooking meats more expensive makes most guests eat more Fondue Bourguignonne than beef heart stew. A nice leisurely evening of spearing chunks of filet can lead up to a nice leisurely bankruptcy.

Another problem for the time-less man of today is the guest who likes his meat well done. Needless to say, the rare steak (not to say blue) takes three minutes on each side and so we satisfy the demands of epicureanism both aesthetically and horally. The well-done steak takes twice as long and the man who eats it may very well have no time for cooking, but he certainly falls short in his epicureanism. The epicure, in this book (if it weren't for what is said about sauces, it would be "in *my* book"), has to eat his lamb pink, his beef red and his veal white. Pork has to be well done, if only for the trichina's sake, and he has to enjoy minute steaks and Beef Steak Tartar. If he hasn't the whit or the wit to scrape it and if he thinks he is saving time by grinding it, we can only say, *"Epicius, wie hast Du Dich verändert!"**

FILET STEAKS

If you truly appreciate beef, you probably have discovered that the less you do to it, especially a filet steak, the better.

In the realm of how little to do to beef, you can scrape it and eat it raw, or broil it with nothing at all. The next step is a

---

* Epicius, how you have changed.

little salt and pepper. After that, one thing leads to another and we come up with a shadow of garlic and some brandy . . . but we stop right there.

4 1-inch-thick filet steaks
1 garlic clove, split
butter for sizzling

2 ponies brandy, warmed
coarse salt and pepper freshly
   ground through a mill

Do all this at the table, or in the living room, or wherever you eat.

First rub each filet with the split garlic clove and season with ground salt and pepper. Heat a heavy pan, add butter, sizzle it, and immediately put in the filets. Turn them as soon as they are brown (this should take seconds, not minutes), add more butter and one pony of brandy or two ponies, depending on size of the pan.

Flame the brandy, and when it dies down cook only for half a minute more before serving on very hot plates with the pan juices poured over.

Look at your watch. You should have taken less than 5 minutes for the entire operation.

FILET STEAKS DIANA

4 filet steaks, about 1 inch thick
1 tablespoon oil
½ cup butter

½ cup Madeira
2 tablespoons lemon juice
red currant jelly

salt and pepper

Oil and season filets and set aside until needed. Fry the filets in ½ the butter in a very hot pan approximately 1–2 minutes on each side. Set in a warm oven. Add Madeira to pan and quickly reduce by one third. Take from fire, beat in currant jelly, remaining butter and lemon juice. Correct seasoning. Pour over meat and serve.

FILETS MARSALA

4 1-inch-thick filet steaks
2 tablespoons butter for frying

¼ cup Marsala
¼ cup tomato butter

salt and pepper

Heat frying pan over high heat, add butter and 4 filet steaks. Brown, turn and season—fry on second side for about 3 minutes—season and arrange on 4 hot plates. Add Marsala to pan, swish around, season and pour over filets. Place 1 tablespoon tomato butter on each steak and serve.

TOMATO BUTTER: Mix 2 tablespoons tomato paste, 1 teaspoon lemon juice and salt and pepper to taste with 2 tablespoons soft butter. Chill in freezing compartment if there is time.

GRILLED FILET STEAKS WITH HERB BUTTER

4 filet steaks about 1 inch thick	1 teaspoon grated lemon rind
oil for brushing	3 tablespoons mixed chopped herbs
4 tablespoons soft butter	(use fresh herbs if possible)
salt and pepper	

Mix butter with lemon rind, herbs and seasonings. Form into 4 pats on waxed paper and put in freezer or ice compartment of refrigerator. Brush filets with oil, season well and grill under a hot broiler for 1–2 minutes on each side, according to taste. Serve on hot plates with a pat of the herb butter on each steak.

MADEIRA FILETS

4 1-inch-thick filet steaks	1/3 cup Madeira
3 tablespoons butter for frying	¼ cup parsley butter
salt and pepper	

Heat heavy frying pan over high heat, add butter and steaks. Fry until brown, about 2 minutes, turn and season. Fry on second side for about 3 minutes, season and arrange on 4 very hot plates. Add Madeira to pan, swirl around, season and pour over steaks. Serve with a piece of parsley butter on each steak.

PARSLEY BUTTER: Mix 1 tablespoon chopped parsley and 1 teaspoon lemon juice with ¼ teaspoon salt. Divide over 4 pats of cold butter, press down hard.

BEEF SAUTÉ

1½ pounds filet steaks, cut 1 inch
    thick
3 tablespoons butter
1 teaspoon flour

1 cup dry white wine
salt and pepper
3 parsley sprigs, ground
    through Mouli

Season meat well and lay it between two pieces of waxed paper. Pound it lightly with a mallet, turning it to pound both sides. The meat surface should be doubled in size. Cut the meat into pieces about 2–2½ inches square and fry them in a skillet over high heat in 2 tablespoons butter. Turn meat once, depending on your taste in these matters. It should fry from ½ minute to 1 minute on each side. Keep steaks hot in a slow oven, sprinkle pan with flour, stir until browned, add wine and cook quickly, stirring until smooth. Take from fire, add remaining butter and seasonings and stir until butter is dissolved. Pour sauce over hot meat, sprinkle with parsley and serve on hot plates.

MINUTE STEAKS

4 minute steaks
¾ cup butter
1 onion, sliced and divided into
    rings
1 tablespoon flour
½ cup bouillon

½ cup wine, red or white
    as preferred
1 tablespoon tarragon vinegar
1 tablespoon small capers
salt and freshly ground black
    pepper

Fry onion rings in ½ cup butter until transparent, dust with flour and stir until flour is browned. Moisten with bouillon and wine and as the sauce thickens add vinegar, capers and seasonings. Let sauce simmer for the minute during which you sauté the minute steaks in hot butter. Season steaks and serve with the onion sauce.

BEEF À LA RUSSE

½ pound filet of beef
½ cup frozen chopped onion,
    thawed
1 can sliced mushrooms

1 jar yogurt
1 package instant mashed potatoes
    or instant rice
¼ cup butter
salt and pepper

Have butcher cut meat into 2 thin slices and pound it thinner between 2 pieces of wax paper. Fry onion and mushrooms in half the butter. In the meantime cut the thin filet slices into finger-long slivers with a sharp knife and fry in a separate pan in remaining butter. Prepare mashed potatoes or rice according to package directions. Combine mushrooms and meat and add yogurt, season and heat. Serve surrounded by the potatoes or rice.

STEAK AU POIVRE

4 minute steaks, filet or rump
   steaks
1 tablespoon black peppercorns,
   roughly crushed with a
   rolling pin

2 tablespoons butter
½ cup dry white wine
2 tablespoons brandy
2 tablespoons heavy cream
salt

Coat both sides of steak with pepper, press down well in hot butter for 1 to 2 minutes on each side depending on thickness of steak. Arrange steaks on hot plates and keep warm. Pour off butter, leave pepper in pan, add wine, brandy and cream and stir well. Season and pour sauce over steaks.

STEAK AU POIVRE GRENOBLE

4 shell steaks or 4 slices filet
1 tablespoon Tellicherry black
   peppercorns, wrapped in
   cheesecloth

salt
¼ cup, or 1 bar butter
¼ cup brandy

Crush peppercorns with a mallet or hammer and press the crushed pepper into both sides of the steaks. Salt well and sauté the steaks in very hot butter for 3 to 5 minutes per side, depending on thickness of steaks. If steaks are 2 inches thick they should have about 6 minutes per side for medium rare. Actually, these pepper steaks are better when they are rare. Serve steaks on very hot plates. Pour brandy into pan, swish it well and pour over steaks.

Filet steaks are also filets mignon or tournedos. The tournedos are the center slices of the filet and are considered the best cut. However, even the tail end of the filet is good and we should be happy if we can afford any part of it.

Most butchers today sell 1-inch-thick slices of the filet with a nice piece of larding pork tied around the edge. The slices are so composed and designed that one of them makes a portion and you have to leave them intact; if you cut the strings it may turn out that you have several pieces of filet which were rolled together and tied to make a single roast from which the slices were later cut.

Judging by the number of well-known filet steak, filet mignon and tournedos recipes, one would gather that lots of people put their minds to inventing new combinations. Here are fifteen that have stood that famous test—time.

RARE PAN-BROILED FILET STEAKS

Pan-broil the filet steaks with butter in a very hot pan until well browned. Season and turn and broil other side until brown. Season and serve at once on very hot plates and add any of the following sauces or garnishes.

MEDIUM OR WELL DONE PAN-BROILED FILET STEAKS

Broil steaks as above; when both sides are brown, reduce heat, add a little butter and cook to desired doneness, turning once or twice. To test for doneness make a small cut in the meat (do this to the steak you are going to serve yourself) and continue to cook if meat is still too rare. Please note that all filet steaks are better rare or medium rare than well done.

BROILED FILET STEAKS

Broil steaks in a preheated very hot broiler or oven set at BROIL. Place broiler rack 3 inches from source of heat. When surface of steak is brown, season and turn. Season and continue broiling until desired doneness is reached. Allow about 3 minutes to a side for 1-inch-thick filet steaks to be served rare. Increase broiling time on each side to taste. Test for doneness as described above and serve at once on very hot plates with any of the following sauces or garnishes.

TOURNEDOS À L'AMÉRICAINE

Serve center slices of filet as described above. Place 1 fried egg on each tournedos and serve with hot tomato sauce.

TOURNEDOS ARGENTEUIL

Arrange broiled filet steaks on hot plates, garnish each with 6 frozen asparagus tips prepared according to package directions and pass 1 4-ounce jar hollandaise sauce separately. Heat hollandaise in top of double boiler.

TOURNEDOS BÉARNAISE

Serve tournedos on fried bread croutons and surround with béarnaise sauce. Béarnaise can now be purchased in jars at most frozen-food counters.

TOURNEDOS CHOISEUL

Serve broiled tournedos as described above with 1 can artichoke bottoms heated in their own liquid, drained and filled with 1 4-ounce can goose liver purée. Pass mushroom sauce separately. Heat 1 4-ounce can sliced mushrooms with ½ can cream of mushroom soup. Season to taste and thin with heavy cream. Stir until simmering, season and serve.

FILET STEAKS FLORENTINE

Arrange steaks on a bed of spinach. Use frozen spinach prepared according to package directions. Cover with Mornay Sauce (*see* page 90) and glaze for 1 minute under the broiler.

FILET STEAKS LYONNAISE

Serve broiled filet steaks with mashed potatoes and French-fried onion rings. Use frozen mashed potatoes and fried onion rings and prepare them according to package directions.

TOURNEDOS MAINTENON

Sprinkle finished tournedos heavily with grated Parmesan cheese mixed in equal parts with bread crumbs. Push under the broiler and broil until crumbs and cheese are brown.

FILET STEAKS MARSEILLAISE

Arrange tournedos on fried bread croutons, garnish top with rolled anchovy fillets and stuffed olives. Accompany with slices of peeled tomatoes and serve with Sauce Poivrade.

FILET STEAKS MIKADO

Serve broiled or pan-broiled tournedos with broiled tomatoes slightly scooped out and filled with Minute Rice. Serve Provençale Sauce separately.

FILET STEAKS NESSELRODE

Arrange tournedos on fried bread rounds, accompany with heated potato chips and canned purée of chestnuts.

FILET STEAKS ROSSINI

Arrange broiled filet steaks on fried bread rounds covered with a thin slice of canned goose liver. Garnish tops with truffle slices and pass Madeira Sauce separately.

TOURNEDOS VERT-PRÉ

Place 1 slice cold Maître-d'Hôtel Butter on each hot tournedos. Garnish with watercress and pass hot shoestring potatoes separately. Buy shoestring potatoes in cellophane bags like potato chips.

STEAK À LA STANLEY

1 thin sirloin steak
2 bananas, peeled and sliced
    lengthwise
2 tablespoons melted butter

½ teaspoon Worcestershire sauce
salt and pepper
½ cup freshly grated or bottled
    horseradish

Broil steak for 3 minutes on each side. Cover with banana slices, season and pour over butter mixed with Worcestershire sauce. Broil until bananas are lightly browned. Serve sprinkled with horseradish or pass horseradish separately.

SUKIYAKI

1½ pounds beef, filet or sirloin,
    cut into ½-inch dice
1 piece suet, big as a walnut
2 tablespoons butter
¼ cup sherry
1 4-ounce can sliced mushrooms
1 5-ounce can bamboo shoots

1 small green pepper, sliced thin
¼ cup bouillon
¼ cup soy sauce
2 tablespoons sugar
1 envelope slivered almonds
1 cup Minute Rice
salt and pepper

Prepare Minute Rice according to package directions. Place pan over heat, rub with suet, add butter and sauté beef until browned. Add remaining ingredients, cover and simmer for 5 minutes longer. Season to taste and serve with the rice.

ROSEMARY LAMB CHOPS

8 rib chops, trimmed
2 teaspoons rosemary
¼ clove garlic, crushed
1 tablespoon chopped chives or
    parsley (frozen or
    dehydrated)

¼ cup soft butter
¼ teaspoon Worcestershire sauce
salt and pepper

Stir rosemary and garlic together and rub well into chops. Broil 3 inches from broiler unit for about 4 minutes. In the meantime stir chives or parsley into butter, add Worcestershire sauce and season well with salt and pepper. Turn chops, divide chive butter over chops and broil 4 minutes longer. Serve at once.

CALF'S LIVER

1 pound calf's liver
1 large can button mushrooms
1 small can white onions
2 teaspoons flour

1½ teaspoons dry mustard
2 cups cream
½ cup sherry
salt and pepper

Simmer liver in salted water for 3 minutes. Remove all sinew and cut into half-inch strips, cut strips across into cubes and dredge with flour and mustard. Combine with mushrooms and onions, season well and cook in cream in the top of a double boiler over boiling water until onions are heated through, about 5 minutes. Add sherry, stir and serve.

CALF'S LIVER AND BACON

8 slices bacon
4 large or 8 small slices calf's liver,
    cut very thin

flour for dredging
salt and 1 pinch cinnamon
½ cup heavy cream

Beat salt and cinnamon into heavy cream. Fry bacon in heavy skillet until brown, drain well on absorbent paper. Pour off bacon fat, retaining only enough to fry liver. Dredge liver slices with flour, sauté quickly in hot bacon fat, turn once, and transfer immediately to very hot plates. Pour off all remaining fat. Reduce heat and swirl seasoned cream in hot pan. Pour over the liver and serve. Liver should cook only a moment on each side. Do not salt while cooking, bacon fat should give flavor.

RED WINE LIVER

1½ pounds sliced calf's liver
flour for dredging
3 tablespoons butter
1 cup frozen chopped onion, thawed
1 7-ounce can button mushrooms

½ cup red wine
½ teaspoon oregano
salt and pepper
¼ cup broken pecans, optional
¼ cup raisins, optional

Have liver cut into very thin slices. Trim and dredge lightly with flour. Melt butter in a large skillet, add onion and sauté 1 minute. Add liver and cook about 1 minute on each side. Add mushrooms, wine and oregano and season to taste. Cook, covered, until mushrooms are heated through. Sprinkle with pecans and raisins.

SOUR CREAM LIVER

1½ pounds calf's liver, sliced thin
3 tablespoons flour, for dredging
4 tablespoons butter
1–2 tablespoons tomato paste,
    to taste
1 can onion soup

1 cup sour cream
2 tablespoons sherry
salt and pepper
4 parsley sprigs, ground through
    Mouli

Dredge liver with flour and brown on both sides in butter. Add tomato paste and onion soup and cook until it starts to boil. Stir well, add sour cream and sherry, reduce heat and season well. Do not allow liver to boil after adding sour cream. Serve sprinkled with parsley.

KIDNEYS IN MUSTARD SAUCE I AND II

Variation I

4 veal kidneys
½ cup butter
1 tablespoon Dijon (or
    brown) mustard

salt and pepper
1/3 cup brandy, warmed
4 sprigs parsley, ground
    through Mouli

Skin and slice kidneys, removing all membranes. Sauté them in half the butter for about 3 minutes, shaking the pan to brown kidneys on all sides. Draw kidneys aside in the pan, stir in mustard, seasonings and remaining butter and stir 1 minute longer. Add the brandy and light it immediately. As soon as the flame dies down, grind the parsley over the kidneys, stir well and serve.

Variation II

4 kidneys
3 tablespoons butter
½ cup frozen chopped onion,
    thawed
1 teaspoon caraway seeds
3 tablespoons prepared mustard
3 tablespoons bouillon

1½ tablespoons flour
1 tablespoon lemon juice
salt and pepper
1 cup Minute Rice, prepared
    according to package
    directions

Plunge kidneys in boiling water, drain, draw off skins, remove membranes and slice. Sauté slices in hot butter with onion, stirring for about 4 minutes. Add caraway seeds and mustard and stir well. Add bouillon, dust lightly with flour and stir until smooth. Add lemon juice, season to taste and serve with rice.

RUSSIAN MEAT BALLS

½ pound ground beef
6 slices white bread
¾ cup milk
4 parsley sprigs, chopped
    through Mouli

1 large onion, sliced thin and
    divided into rings
3 tablespoons butter
¾ cup sour cream
salt, pepper and paprika

Soak bread in milk and press out well. Mix bread and parsley with meat and season to taste with salt and pepper. Fry onion rings in butter for a minute. In the meantime shape meat mixture into cakes and fry in butter with the onion until brown on both sides. If you sprinkle the meat with paprika it will brown faster on the outside and remain pinker on the inside. Add sour cream, cook until it bubbles, stir and serve immediately.

LUCERNE TOAST

4 slices hot toast, fried or toasted
3 shallots, chopped
2 teaspoons butter
¼ pound each ground beef and
    ground pork
salt, pepper, poultry seasoning and
    parsley

1 tablespoon tomato paste
2 tablespoons thick cream
1 tablespoon raisins
1 to 2 egg yolks
1 tomato, sliced thin
salt and pepper

Fry shallots in butter for 1 minute, stir in ground meats, seasonings, tomato paste, cream, raisins and parsley. Increase heat and stir for 2 minutes longer. Reduce heat to very low, add egg yolks and stir 1 minute longer or until mixture is well bound. Season well, spread on hot toast and cover with thin slices of tomato.

TONGUE WITH HORSERADISH SAUCE

1 1-pound can tongue
instant mashed potatoes
1 cup cream

¼ cup freshly grated or bottled
    horseradish
salt and pepper to taste

Tongue may be heated in jar or in a saucepan, according to directions on label. In the meantime prepare instant mashed potatoes. When both are hot, arrange tongue in the center of a fireproof baking dish and surround it with mashed potatoes. Pour over the cream, beaten with the horseradish, salt and pepper. Place in a 375° F. oven until sauce is hot.

GRILLED FRANKFURTERS WITH APPLE SAUERKRAUT

8 frankfurters, split
1 jar sliced apples (apple pie
    filling)

1 package sauerkraut
3 tablespoons brown sugar
1 tablespoon vinegar

1 teaspoon caraway seeds

Grill frankfurters under the broiler. Combine apples and sauerkraut and their juices with all other ingredients in a saucepan and bring to a boil. Reduce heat and simmer while frankfurters are grilling. Hot apple sauerkraut may be arranged in a shallow dish sprinkled with additional brown sugar and placed under the broiler until sugar is melted and browned. Watch carefully, as sugar burns easily.

HAM ASPARAGUS ROLLS

12 slices cold boiled ham
2 cans white or green asparagus
    spears
1 small onion, chopped

1 tablespoon brown mustard
2 tablespoons chopped capers
½ cup French Dressing
2 tablespoons chopped parsley

1 orange, sliced

Roll the ham around the asparagus spears and arrange on a platter. Mix onion, mustard and capers with French dressing and pour over the ham asparagus rolls just before serving. Surround with orange slices and sprinkle with chopped parsley.

HAM WITH ARTICHOKE HEARTS

1 1-pound can ham
1 can small white onions
1 can button mushrooms
1 can stewed tomatoes

1 teaspoon oregano
1 tablespoon dehydrated parsley
salt and pepper
1 10-ounce can hearts of artichoke

Cut ham in large cubes. Heat it in a casserole with the onions, mushrooms, tomatoes and herbs. When well heated, season to taste and add artichokes. Allow 1 to 2 minutes for artichokes to heat through but do not cook long enough for them to fall apart.

Veal Cutlets

Veal cutlets are not really very popular until we go to an Italian, French or German restaurant, or better still, until we travel in France, Italy or Central Europe. It is then that we discover veal and find that certain versions of thin scallopine or schnitzel can be browned in butter, turned and browned and served, all in about three minutes.

The côtelette de veau in France, the Italian scallopine and the German schnitzel are all veal cutlets which are pounded thin and are usually cut into small pieces before they are cooked. Your butcher will pound the meat for you—if he won't, divide a thin cutlet into its natural pieces, place the meat between two pieces of waxed paper and pound each piece with a kitchen mallet until it is a little more than 1/8 inch thick. You will then have large sheets of meat which should be cut into pieces about 2 inches by 2 inches. Cook the pieces in butter until they are brown, turn and brown the other side, season and serve. This is called *au naturel* and is very good with a fried egg and green salad. Traditionally, you should cross a pair of anchovy fillets over the fried egg.

SCALLOPINI À LA MARSALA

1 pound veal cutlet, pounded thin
    and cut into small pieces
1/4 cup flour for dredging

1/4 cup butter
1/4 cup Marsala
salt and pepper

Dredge veal with seasoned flour, sauté in half the butter until golden, turn and sauté until golden on second side. Transfer meat to a hot platter or plates and add remaining butter to pan. Scrape all brown matter into the butter, add the Marsala and swirl around pan. Stir well and pour over meat. Serve at once.

1 can sliced mushrooms may be heated and added to the sauce just before serving.

WIENER SCHNITZEL

1 pound veal cutlet, pounded thin
1/4 cup flour for dredging
2 eggs, well beaten

1 cup bread crumbs
1 cup butter
salt and pepper

1 lemon, quartered

Cut meat as for scallopini, dip in seasoned flour, beaten eggs and bread crumbs. Press crumbs well into meat, dip a second time into egg and crumbs if necessary. Fry in hot butter, turning once, until golden on both sides. Pan must be large enough so that butter is only deep enough to fry one side of meat at a time. Serve on hot plates with lemon wedges.

CÔTELETTE À LA FLORENTINE

1 pound veal cutlet, pounded thin
¼ cup flour for dredging
¼ cup oil
¼ cup butter

½ cup bouillon
4 sprigs parsley, ground through
    Mouli

Cut meat as for scallopini, dredge with seasoned flour, sauté in oil until golden on both sides, turning only once. Add butter to pan, boil up once and remove meat to a hot platter. Add bouillon to pan and scrape all the brown matter into the bouillon. Simmer for a minute and pour the sauce over the meat. Sprinkle with parsley and serve.

This type of cutlet can be sprinkled with Parmesan cheese and pushed under the broiler for just a moment before serving.

HERBED VEAL

1 pound veal cutlet, pounded to
    paper thinness and cut into
    small scallopini
¼ cup flour for dredging
¼ cup butter or oil, or half butter
    and half oil

salt and freshly ground black pepper
1/3 cup white wine
2 teaspoons each, fresh chopped or
    dried chervil, tarragon,
    oregano and parsley

Soak herbs in wine, dredge scallopini well with flour and sauté quickly in butter, or butter and oil, turning to brown both sides. Add seasonings, wine and herbs. Stir well, cover skillet and reduce heat. Cook a few minutes longer. Stir well before serving to incorporate all the pan brownings. Serve on hot plates with rice and Italian salad.

SCALLOPINI PALERMO

1½ pounds veal cutlet, sliced thin
1½ tablespoons flour
2 tablespoons butter

½ cup sherry
2 tablespoons bouillon
salt and pepper

Pound cutlets very thin between pieces of waxed paper and cut into 6-inch squares. Dredge lightly with seasoned flour. Melt butter in a skillet, add scallopini and brown on both sides over high heat. Add sherry and cook 1 minute longer. Arrange meat on hot platter, add bouillon to skillet, scrape well and pour over meat. Serve with Minute Rice prepared according to package directions, adding butter and chopped herbs to rice.

The Meat Fondues

If you own a French Meat Fondu unit you can prepare this at the table in great style. If you don't, you can do very well with a deep saucepan set over an electric unit or over an alcohol or Sterno flame. The only important thing is to have oil constantly boiling and to have a saucepan in which the oil will be deep enough to completely submerge the meat.

FONDUE BOURGUIGNONNE

2 pounds filet of beef cut into 1-inch cubes	1 pint cooking oil
	1 garlic clove, crushed
½ teaspoon salt	

Heat oil to boiling in saucepan or fondue kettle. Do this on the kitchen stove in order to save time. Add garlic and salt to oil and set it over fondue burner or electric unit and turn heat high enough to keep oil just boiling. Provide each guest with a fondue fork or bamboo spear (the metal fork becomes very hot and can easily burn your mouth; the wooden spear is actually preferable). Arrange the following 4 sauces in bowls and set the meat cubes before the guests. Each guest spears a cube of meat, puts it into the boiling oil and leaves it there until the desired doneness is reached. I always leave my beef cube in for about 10 seconds. The meat is then dipped into one of the sauces and eaten from the spear.

SAUCES: 1. 3 parts ketchup to 1 part each dry mustard powder and drained horseradish. Mix until smooth and serve.

          2. Curried mayonnaise. Curry powder stirred with a little mayonnaise and then beaten into more mayonnaise to taste.

3. Beat 1 jar frozen béarnaise sauce over warm water until smooth and warm.
4. Beat prepared mustard into sour cream, adding enough mustard to obtain a well-flavored sauce to your taste.

FONDUE DE VEAU

Substitute cubes of veal, calf's liver and calf's kidney for the beef. Brown as above and serve with the same sauces.

FONDUE ORIENTAL

Substitute cubes of lamb for beef and substitute boiling bouillon for the oil. Serve with curry sauce, Minute Rice and chutney.

Poultry

At one time it was necessary to know a great deal about buying a chicken. The feet had to be pale and limber, the breastbone had to be flexible and the expression had to be one of peaceful repose. The skin had to be pale, soft and unblemished. One learned to select the young and pretty and to reject the old and ugly. The whole thing resembled a beauty contest, the broader the breast and the narrower the hips, the better. The legs had to respond correctly to all sorts of reflex tests and the butcher's opinion had to be consulted.

When the bird was selected and carried home it had to be drawn, the feet were peeled for soup, the pin feathers were singed off over an open flame and the fat was rendered.

All that is over now, the average bird comes head- and footless, and its giblets are packed in a little separate envelope. It is labeled and numbered and has lost its personality. Chickens are tenderer than they used to be, broader in the breast and not a pin feather remains. They are all utterly and entirely alike, you can take the one nearest you and know that all the rest are the same. There is now a great equality, if not in all things, at least in broilers.

When we come to the various birds, there are very few we can just cook for a moment and eat. Wild duck are supposed to be rare but all other birds are supposed to be cooked until you can flex their knees and receive a soft and pliable response. Or you can just stick a fork into the fattest part of them—the thigh as in epicures—and if the life juices that flow out are white your bird is done, if they are pink you go on cooking it and cook yourself right out of inclusion here.

Since we cannot exclude the beloved birds, the poultry recipes included here are based on canned or frozen chicken meat. Instant Epicureanism is only possible when we include the freshly broiled or barbecued chickens that are obtainable at most food shops and markets today. We also include the turkey loaf that every delicatessen stocks and the chicken livers that cook so quickly.

All this is a little depressing but it is also a challenge. You may not be able to roast your chicken or boil your fowl since it cannot be done in the time we have at our disposal, but you can prepare some very good casseroles that require only the time it takes to heat them. There are good chafing-dish recipes—and we don't mean the chicken à la king with which Ma snared Pa—and there are things you can stir around in your skillet (whether in the kitchen or at the table) that may snare another generation if you play it, or cook it, right.

In some countries, when you order chicken at an inn, you hear a hideous squawk and presently you eat (if you can forget the squawk) the tenderest and juiciest of birds. The chickens here have had much more happen to them than that. They have been trimmed down to essentials. If your mother's cookbook gave recipes for using chicken feet in soup, you will have to buy them separately; they rarely come attached to the original chicken any more. You will have to rely on cooked frozen chicken meat, which can be bought in packages of dark meat, light meat, or both combined. There are a few recipes for chicken breasts, pounded out like a cutlet, which cook very quickly, and a few for using those hot broilers you can pick up on your way home from the office.

This is not the most lavish department of Instant Cookery but you need not swear off all chickens just because you swore off all leisure and all but ten minutes of what used to be your cooking time.

READY-COOKED BROILED CHICKENS

If your ready-cooked broiler is still hot from the shop when you get home with it, brush it with melted butter, using about ½ cup, and keep it hot in a low oven until needed. Repeat the brushing with butter and serve in any of the following ways:

1. Add a crushed garlic clove to the ½ cup melted butter and add 1 can small white potatoes. Serve with the remaining butter poured over the potatoes.
2. Substitute freshly chopped chives or frozen chopped chives for the garlic and serve as above.
3. Heat broilers with butter as above; just before serving brush with 3 tablespoons thin honey, heated, and sprinkle with toasted sesame seeds and salt.
4. Mix juice of 1 lemon with the melted butter, add 1 can pineapple chunks to the chicken and heat until bubbling. Baste frequently and add salt and paprika to taste. Serve with Minute Rice.
5. Brush broiler with butter as above, add 1 cup sherry, ½ cup currant jelly and ½ cup slivered almonds. Season to taste and baste frequently.
6. To above recipe, add the juice of 1 orange and 1 lemon. Reduce the sherry to ½ cup and add the slivered or grated rind of the orange and lemon. Serve garnished with orange slices and slices of cranberry jelly.
7. Disjoint broiler and keep hot in a low oven with 1 8-ounce can button mushrooms, 1 10-ounce can Italian tomatoes and 1 bay leaf. Season to taste and remove bay leaf just before serving. Sprinkle with parsley ground through a Mouli. Add 1 can white pearl corn or 1 can small white onions if desired.
8. Keep broiler hot or reheat broiler with ½ cup butter as in Method #1. Chop half a peeled cucumber fine, sauté for 1 minute in butter and mix the cucumber with 1 jar frozen

hollandaise sauce, heated over warm water. Sprinkle with a little chopped dill or parsley.

Any of the recipes suggested for ready-cooked broilers or chickens can be applied to frozen cooked chicken or canned chicken.

BROILED CHICKEN IMPROVEMENT

1 fresh-cooked broiler from delicatessen store. If frozen broiled broiler is used, thaw completely.	2 slices bacon 3 tablespoons warmed thin honey 2 tablespoons sesame seeds (toasted or plain)

salt and pepper

Secure bacon across breast of broiled broiler, season and heat in 450° F. oven until heated through. (In many cities it is possible to buy hot broilers fresh off the barbecue spit or fresh out of the infrared broiler; put it into a slow oven to maintain heat.) After broiler is hot, baste with honey, sprinkle with sesame seeds, reduce heat to 375° F. and bake, basting several times with honey and adding fresh seeds, for 10 minutes.

BARBECUED BROILER

1 ready-cooked broiler from delicatessen store. If frozen broiler is used, thaw completely.

Heat broiler in 400° F. oven until sizzling, basting every 2 minutes with a sauce made of the following ingredients. (If hot broilers can be purchased in your town, pick one up on your way home and finish it in the sauce in the few minutes it takes to reheat.)

½ cup melted butter	2 teaspoons tarragon
½ cup white wine	2 teaspoons rosemary
1 clove garlic, crushed	2 teaspoons ground ginger
1 tablespoon soy sauce	1 pinch curry powder

salt and pepper

8-MINUTE CHICKEN

1 pound raw chicken, cut into
medium dice
2 tablespoons butter or oil
1 4-ounce can sliced mushrooms
1 cup frozen chopped onion,
thawed
1 package frozen tiny peas,
thawed

½ 3-ounce envelope slivered
almonds
2 solid canned tomatoes, drained
1 10-ounce can concentrated cream
of mushroom or cream
of celery soup
2 tablespoons sherry
2 tablespoons sesame seeds
salt and pepper

Sauté chicken in butter or oil for 2 minutes, stirring constantly. Add mushrooms, onions, peas and almonds. Cover and simmer 4 minutes. Drain off butter or oil, add tomatoes, celery or mushroom soup, sherry, sesame seeds and seasonings. Serve as soon as peas are tender. Thin this with chicken broth or water and chicken bouillon cube, if thinner sauce is preferred. If preparing this recipe with thinner sauce, serve it with Minute Rice. Almonds may be toasted in butter and added to rice with the butter instead of adding them to chicken.

CHICKEN TETRAZZINI

1 2-pound can cooked chicken
½ pound fine noodles
1 quart water
3 chicken bouillon cubes
1 8-ounce can sliced mushrooms
salt, pepper and paprika

1 cup cream
1 can concentrated cream of
chicken soup
¼ cup sherry
½ cup grated Parmesan cheese

Turn oven to 450° F. On top of stove, bring water to a boil, add bouillon cubes, salt and noodles. Cook, covered, until noodles are almost tender, about 4 minutes. Drain and reserve broth, keep noodles hot in oven and continue boiling broth. In a second saucepan, heat cream with chicken soup and add just enough of the simmering broth to thin soup into a smooth sauce. Add mushrooms and chicken, cut into large pieces, and all jelly and liquid from chicken can. Cook, stirring, for 1 minute, add sherry, season well. Arrange noodles in shallow baking dish, pour chicken-mushroom mixture into the center and pour remaining sauce over noodles. Sprinkle with cheese and paprika and bake in oven until bubbling, 6–8 minutes.

CHICKEN IN RED WINE

If you live in a town where you can pick up a hot roasted or broiled chicken on your way home from work (or pleasure) then prepare it this way and keep it hot while you set the table.

1 3-pound ready-roasted chicken	1 8-ounce can button mushrooms
1 clove garlic, crushed	1 10-ounce can tomatoes
½ cup frozen chopped onion, thawed	½ cup red wine
	4 slices cooked tongue, cut julienne

salt, pepper and paprika

Disjoint chicken, lay it in a buttered casserole, add all other ingredients and heat in a 400° F. oven until chicken is hot through. Serve with ready-to-bake corn bread, hot out of the oven.

CHICKEN WITH ONION SAUCE

1 ready-cooked broiler, disjointed	1 teaspoon Kitchen Bouquet
1 can undiluted condensed onion soup	1 tablespoon flour, worked into 1 tablespoon butter
1 chicken bouillon cube	salt and pepper

Heat or reheat broiler in soup with bouillon cube, Kitchen Bouquet and seasonings. Take out broiler, arrange on a hot platter and stir the flour and butter combination into the soup. Cook over low heat, stirring constantly, until sauce thickens. Correct seasoning, pour over chicken and serve. If sauce is too thick, thin with a little bouillon or sherry to taste.

COLD CHICKEN IN CANTALOUPE

2 small cantaloupe melons, halved	1 teaspoon apricot jam
1 cold ready-cooked chicken or 2 1-pound cans chicken	½ teaspoon dried or fresh chopped tarragon
¾ cup mayonnaise	1 cup or 1 can seedless green grapes
1 slice onion, chopped	salt and pepper

Scrape seeds from melon halves and turn onto a platter to drain. In the meantime cut chicken meat into large chunks and bind with mayonnaise, beaten with onion, jam and tarragon. Add juice drained from melons and season well. Add grapes and fill the salad into melon halves. Set on individual plates and serve with bread fingers toasted with curry butter (curry powder to taste, mixed until smooth with soft butter).

CHICKEN LIVERS IN SOUR CREAM

1 1-pound package frozen chicken
   livers, thawed
¼ cup butter
1 8-ounce can button mushrooms

¼ cup warm brandy
1 cup sour cream
2 egg yolks
4 slices hot toast

salt and pepper

Sauté chicken livers in butter for 3 minutes, stirring frequently, add mushrooms and cook 3 minutes longer. Livers should be browned on the outside and pink on the inside. Add brandy and flame. Beat sour cream with egg yolks, reduce heat and stir into the livers. Season well and serve on toast.

CHICKEN LIVERS WITH APPLE RINGS

1 1-pound package frozen chicken
   livers, thawed
¼ cup butter
1 8-ounce can sliced mushrooms
½ cup frozen chopped onion,
   thawed

1 tablespoon brown sugar
¼ teaspoon cinnamon
1 jigger brandy
salt and pepper

Sauté chicken livers in butter with mushrooms and onion for 4 minutes, stirring. Add brown sugar and cinnamon and stir until dissolved. Continue to cook until livers are browned but still pink inside. Add brandy and flame. Serve with lightly browned apple rings.

APPLE RINGS: Cut 2 cored sweet apples into slices and brown lightly in butter, turning once. Do not peel the apple.

CHICKEN LIVERS DENISE

1 1-pound package frozen chicken
    livers, thawed
2 tablespoons butter
1 tablespoon flour
4 tablespoons white wine

1 tablespoon vinegar
¼ garlic clove, crushed
1 tablespoon chopped onion
1 tablespoon chopped parsley
salt and pepper

Brown livers in butter in a heavy pan, stirring with a wooden spoon until livers are just browned on all sides. Sprinkle with flour —be careful to sprinkle lightly—and stir flour until it is browned. Add wine and vinegar and cook, stirring until sauce is smooth. Crush garlic over the livers, add onion and parsley and season to taste. Serve at once on hot plates.

Although these livers are in the poultry chapter, they are good with cocktails. Cut them into individual pieces before cooking and stick a cocktail pick into each one after cooking and you have a good and hardy hors d'oeuvre for cocktail guests.

Another good place for these livers is Sunday morning with or without scrambled eggs, with or without a Saturday night before.

CHICKEN WING DINNER

1 pound chicken wings, fresh or
    frozen
1 egg, beaten
½ cup milk
¾ cup flour

1 cup bread crumbs
salt, pepper and ½ teaspoon curry
    powder
4 sprigs parsley, ground through
    Mouli, for garnish

If frozen chicken wings are used, thaw completely before cooking. Dip wings into seasoned batter made of milk and egg beaten into flour. Roll the coated wings in crumbs and fry in deep shortening at 375° F. for 6 minutes. Drain and serve at once.

Serve with 1 recipe Seafood Cocktail Sauce or Walnut Garlic Sauce.

You may be a confirmed Instant Epicure but we cannot imagine you without time on Christmas Day, Easter Sunday and, most important and traditional of all, on Thanksgiving Day. If you took the time to roast a turkey, and we hope you did, then you are in possession, for at least one day each year, of lots of cold roast turkey.

If you didn't roast your own turkey, then perhaps your mother had you over for Thanksgiving dinner and you shouldn't have gone home empty-handed. Any mother with leftover turkey to cope with should be delighted if you would take home enough for one or two of these dishes. In any case, we assume that somehow, somewhere, you obtained some cold roast turkey and that you can now use one of these Instant ways of making it better the second time around than the first.

TURKEY STEW

1 pound pressed turkey, cubed
1 package frozen peas, thawed
1 package frozen okra, thawed
½ cup bouillon
½ cup frozen chopped onion, thawed

1 No. 2 can creamed corn
1 10-ounce can tomatoes
4 English muffins, split with fork and toasted, or 4 pieces toast
¼ cup butter
salt and pepper

Prepare peas and okra according to package directions. Combine turkey, bouillon, onion, corn and tomatoes and heat to bubbling. Add peas and okra and season to taste. Serve on buttered muffins or toast.

TURKISH TURKEY

8 slices pressed turkey
½ cup frozen chopped onion, thawed
2 tablespoons butter
1 3-ounce package slivered almonds
½ cup small raisins

1 pinch ground cloves
1 pinch cinnamon
1 bay leaf
1 10-ounce can tomato soup
½ cup cream
salt and pepper

Sauté onion in butter until transparent, add soup and cream and stir until smooth and hot. Add almonds and raisins, ground cloves and cinnamon and the bay leaf. Heat turkey slices in this sauce and season well. Take out bay leaf and serve with cold apricot halves.

HOT TURKEY MUFFINS

4 thick slices pressed turkey
   (from delicatessen)
1 10-ounce can condensed cream of
   chicken soup
¼ cup cream
2 tablespoons sherry

4 English muffins, split with fork
   and toasted
¼ cup butter
4 slices ham, lightly broiled
4 parsley sprigs, ground through
   Mouli

salt and pepper

Heat turkey slices in soup and cream in a 375° F. oven for 4 minutes. Add sherry and seasonings and leave in oven until muffins are toasted and buttered. Lay half a slice of ham on each toasted muffin half and cover with half a slice of hot turkey on each slice of ham. Pour the hot sauce over it and sprinkle with parsley.

CHAPTER VI   *Vegetables*

$\mathbf{B}$ACK IN the happy carefree days when such things still existed I had a chauffeur-driven aunt who was taken out for an airing each afternoon. She always sat resplendently in the back of an enormous blue or maroon lined limousine which changed every few years from a Delage to a Daimler and, toward the end of her life, changed into a Lincoln (it was finally converted into a very roomy dog kennel). She always occupied herself with pleasant soothing tasks as she was driven about the country and she looked at the back of her chauffeur's head, which gave a sense of security we have never been able to emulate.

Her confreres enjoyed the passing scene, dozed, knitted, or gossiped with their chauffeurs through a braid-encrusted speaking tube provided for the purpose. They played with the ivory note pad on their left, or tinkered with their husband's humidor opposite or the make-up department on their right. There were flower vases and all was inlaid wood and discreet lighting. There were blinds and tasseled shades. But no matter what the interior of her limousine offered in the way of entertainment and no matter how beautiful the scenery without, my aunt shelled peas.

She would take along a great sack of them, an empty bag and a deep bowl, and as the car rolled along the peas were dropped into the bowl and the pods went into the empty sack and my aunt was deeply content. Cars were so designed that only her dignified white head and part of her impressive pearls were visible while she busily shelled away. Anyone would have supposed her hands to be idly folded in her lap.

When it was to be mushrooms for dinner, she peeled, when it was to be string beans, she strung and when it was carrots she julienned. Whatever dinner demanded she did it in the back of that car. When they arrived home she handed the cook, who always stood ready at the door, the fruits of her drive—ready and prepared for dinner. To my knowledge she never sliced onions or tried to wash spinach but she did everything else. She was always a placid, well-adjusted aunt who lived well into her nineties.

The only moral we can draw from all this is that we need not leave the kitchen tasks to be done in the kitchen. Most of them are as pleasant to watch as to perform and, while we cannot do them in our compacts and in our chic little motor bugs, we can do them in our living room. And if we are to be Instant Epicures we had better prepare ourselves to prepare food and cook it right where it is going to be eaten.

Vegetables and fruits lend themselves particularly well to living-room preparation and guest participation. Try coming into your living room with two pounds of beautiful large white mushrooms while your guests are at their cocktails. You will usually find that the unlikeliest man there knows it is as good for the psyche to slice mushrooms as to tear cellophane or toy with amber. It will turn out that he likes nothing better than something to do with his hands and he will interrupt his work only for a drag at his cigarette or a swallow of his drink. He will make a good job of the mushrooms and enjoy them the more when he eats them.

The Instant Epicure must learn to delegate work and to do in the living room what my aunt did in the back of her car.

A hostess hulling big red strawberries (in her white jersey dinner dress), especially if she does it neatly and efficiently, is much more attractive than the hostess who disappears into her kitchen and emerges hot and bothered, with no idea of where the conversation has gotten to or which jokes have been told. Stay with your guests;

as far as the vegetables are concerned you can either prepare them in the living room or boil frozen vegetables in no time flat. The only un-frozen vegetables we suggest in this book are the ones that cook in two to four minutes: zucchini, cucumbers, tomatoes and mushrooms.

If it is to be frozen vegetables for a first course, they can be cooking while the last cocktail is served; if they are to be served with the meat they can cook while the meat is broiling. There is no problem about their preparation but there is about their garnishment. Garnish them with something that will look attractive and add to the taste. Shaved almonds or bread crumbs can brown in butter while the vegetables boil. Grated coconut can be browned and set aside (it browns too suddenly to be left for an instant). A jar of frozen hollandaise can be heated in the top of the double boiler. Fresh herbs can go through a Mouli at the last moment. You can crumble canned chestnuts over your spinach or spike it with sherry. You can heat bottled garlic croutons for the frozen cauliflower or cover it with a julienne of delicatessen-store tongue. You can do almost anything. If you are going to serve vegetables you had better start inventing pleasantries or reading our suggestions—because the frozen vegetable boiled in water and served plain is a thing of the past.

The accepted French custom of making vegetables into a first course and serving potatoes (or pasta or rice) and salad with the meat is a good one, provided you make the vegetable worthy of being a course instead of a dull accompaniment. You don't have to go for a drive today—your vegetables come ready and prepared to be delicious, all you have to do is follow instructions and show a little imagination.

The Frozen Vegetables

The frozen vegetables are excellent and should be used constantly by Instant Epicures. The more constantly they are used, the more necessary it is to change and vary them slightly from time to time. You would not dream of duplicating your friends' meals when you invite them in return, and still you do not hesitate to give them the same lovely green peas they gave you. Even the manufacturers realize this and they have added combinations and variations, with the result that you now serve each other peas with onions in the French manner instead of plain green peas. The great monotony, on the whole, continues. The easiest way of adding variety is with toppings and garnishes. As far as combinations are concerned, you can combine almost all of them successfully. Cauliflower and broccoli or Brussels sprouts are all of a family and go well together. Corn and lima beans are an old combination which is better when you combine a package of each than when you buy two packages of succotash; that way you get more corn.

If you are going to follow our advice and buy a Mouli you can cover your vegetables with freshly minced herbs, freshly grated cheese or ground nuts. The shredder should make it possible for you to cover any vegetable with a julienne of ham or Bologna sausage. There is nothing new about the following garnishes except that they are too often forgotten.

ASPARAGUS

1. Cover 2 packages frozen asparagus, prepared according to package directions, with brown butter and a julienne of ham. Use 4 slices ham.
2. Fry 2/3 cup bread crumbs in ½ cup butter until brown, add more butter if preferred. Pour over asparagus, prepared as above, and cover with a grating of fresh Parmesan cheese. Push under the broiler to melt the cheese slightly, but not to brown it.
3. Prepare asparagus and buttered crumbs as above. Cover with a film of freshly grated orange rind. Grate the orange right over the asparagus and serve at once.
4. Heat a jar of frozen hollandaise sauce and serve it with asparagus, prepared as above. Grate the rind of a lemon over the asparagus and serve sprinkled with freshly ground parsley.

ARTICHOKES

1. Prepare 2 packages fresh frozen artichokes according to package directions and serve with a warm butter sauce made of 2/3 cup lightly browned butter in which ½ cup thawed frozen chopped onion has been heated with 2 tablespoons small capers. Sprinkle with freshly ground parsley and serve hot.
2. Add 2/3 cup lightly browned butter to artichokes prepared as above. Sprinkle with ½ cup grated Parmesan cheese and push under broiler until cheese is browned.

WAX BEANS

1. Prepare 2 packages fresh frozen wax beans according to package directions and pour over 2/3 cup butter, browned with ½ 3-ounce package shaved almonds.
2. Wax beans can also be prepared with ½ cup crumbs, browned in 2/3 cup butter and a julienne of 4 slices Bologna sausage.

CAULIFLOWER

1. Prepare 2 packages fresh frozen cauliflower according to package directions and pour over a sauce made of 1 package frozen peas, cooked until very soft and quickly mashed through a Vegetable Master or mincer. Thin peas into sauce consistency with cream and season well.
2. Fry bacon until crisp, drain, crumble and sprinkle over cauliflower, prepared as above. Add a little browned butter to which 1 pinch of sugar is added before browning.

GREEN BEANS

1. Prepare 2 packages French-cut string beans according to package directions and serve covered with chopped parsley and grated walnuts (use your Moulis), using about ¼ cup of each, lightly browned in ½ cup butter.
2. Cover French-cut string beans with a mixture of chopped onion and sliced mushrooms, lightly browned in ½ cup butter. Use 1 3-ounce can sliced mushrooms and 3 onion slices chopped with a Batirex or vegetable mincer.

EASTERN VEGETABLES

3 tablespoons vegetable oil
1½ cups frozen chopped onion, thawed
1 garlic clove, crushed
1 jar pimento, diced
1 green pepper, seeded and roughly chopped

3 tomatoes, sliced thin
1 cup water
1 bouillon cube
2 tablespoons cornstarch
2 teaspoons soy sauce
2 tablespoons dehydrated parsley

Heat oil in pan. Fry onion 1 minute, add garlic and remaining vegetables, ½ cup water and bouillon cube. Cover and cook about 8 minutes, stir well, make sure cube is dissolved. Stir cornstarch and soy sauce with remaining water until smooth, thickened and clear. Add to vegetables. Take from fire, add parsley and serve.

TARANTO ASPARAGUS

1 can white asparagus   ¼ cup butter, melted
prosciutto ham   grated Parmesan cheese

Drain asparagus, wrap each stalk in a slice of prosciutto, lay seam-side down in a buttered baking dish. Sprinkle with 2 tablespoons butter and the cheese. Bake 5 minutes in a 400° F. oven. Pour over remaining butter and serve at once.

STRING BEANS AMANDINE

2 packages frozen string beans,   1 tablespoon dehydrated parsley
    French cut   1 envelope shaved almonds
½ cup frozen chopped onion,   3 tablespoons butter
    thawed   salt and pepper

Prepare beans according to package directions. In the meantime, fry onions, parsley and almonds in butter until onions are just turning gold. Drain beans, pour over sauce and serve.

WHOLE HEARTS OF ARTICHOKE IN HOLLANDAISE SAUCE

2 7-ounce cans whole hearts of   1 6-ounce jar hollandaise sauce
    artichoke   ½ lemon, juice only
            salt, pepper and paprika

Heat hollandaise sauce in top of a double boiler over simmering water. Make sure the upper section of the double boiler is not submerged in the water in the lower section. The sauce should be heated only by the steam from the water. Heat artichoke hearts in their own liquid, do not boil. Drain and arrange in a hot serving dish. Beat lemon juice into sauce, season with salt and pepper and pour over the artichokes. Sprinkle with paprika and serve with meat, poultry or fish or serve as a separate course.

ARTICHOKE HEARTS

2 packages frozen artichoke hearts, thawed and drained	6 anchovy filets, chopped
	½ clove garlic, crushed
½ cup dry white wine	6 sprigs parsley
½ cup bouillon	2 tablespoons butter
salt and pepper	

Cook artichoke hearts in wine and bouillon for 6 minutes. Remove the artichoke hearts and drain well, but continue to boil the broth rapidly. Stir artichokes with anchovies, garlic and butter and chop the parsley over the artichokes through a Mouli. Season to taste and add reduced broth.

There are certain vegetables which lend themselves particularly well to being prepared by someone else, preferably a large company. Spinach is one of these because it is so difficult really to get the sand out of it. As hard as you try, and no matter how much water you use, there is still a grain of sand that lands in your husband's or your guest's back tooth. But large companies produce immaculate spinach, and beets that are red and beautiful without all the color bleeding out of them. If you do not like the way they are sliced, you can buy the whole ones and slice them paper thin on your slicer and make beet salads and relishes as well as all the good buttered and oranged beets.

SPINACH PARMIGIANA

2 packages frozen chopped spinach, thawed and drained	cinnamon or nutmeg
	4 eggs, beaten
2 tablespoons butter	grated Parmesan cheese
salt and pepper	

Cook spinach in salted water for 2 minutes, drain. Combine with butter, salt, pepper and a tiny dash of cinnamon or nutmeg. Cook over low flame, stirring, for 2 more minutes. Turn off heat, leave saucepan on burner, add eggs and cheese and stir until well mixed. Correct seasoning and serve.

FRENCH SPINACH

2 packages frozen spinach
2/3 cup garlic-flavored croutons

2 tablespoons butter
1/4 cup sherry

sugar, salt and pepper

Prepare spinach according to package directions. Heat croutons in butter, shaking to coat all sides. Drain spinach well, add sherry and croutons and season to taste with sugar, salt and pepper.

ITALIAN SPINACH

2 packages frozen spinach
3 tablespoons raisins
1/4 cup sherry

3 tablespoons pine nuts
1 pinch sugar
salt and pepper

Heat raisins in sherry while preparing spinach according to package directions. Drain well, add raisins, sherry and pine nuts and season to taste with sugar, salt and pepper.

BEETS

1 1-pound can sliced beets
2 tablespoons cornstarch
1/2 cup pineapple juice
1/4 cup vinegar

1/4 cup sugar
1 pinch ground cloves
1 pinch ground cinnamon
1/2 cup crushed pineapple

1 tablespoon butter

Stir cornstarch into 1/2 cup of the beet juice in the top of a double boiler over boiling water. Add pineapple juice, vinegar, sugar, ground cloves and cinnamon and continue to stir for a few minutes until thickened. Add pineapple, butter and beets and cook until beets are heated through.

GLAZED BEETS

1 1-pound can sliced beets, drained	½ cup orange juice
3 tablespoons brown sugar	1 clove
6 tablespoons butter	salt and pepper

In a saucepan, melt brown sugar in butter and orange juice. Add clove and beets and stir gently until beets are hot and well coated. Take out clove. Reduce heat and cook, stirring once or twice, until sauce is reduced and beets are glazed. Garnish with orange slices or dill and serve with duck, lamb, chicken or beef.

Instant Mashed Potatoes

The instant or frozen mashed potatoes are so quickly and easily prepared that they are the blessing of every Instant Cook. The only trouble is that no one (except my son) can eat mashed or whipped potatoes every day. The answer is to mix them or build them into something different each time, so that when you come around the circle and have plain mashed potatoes they will come as a relief after all the trimmed varieties.

Always prepare potatoes according to package directions.

1. In spring, when fresh chives are available, mow your chive plant down about 2 inches with your kitchen scissors and chop them through a Mouli. Add butter, salt and chives to the mashed potatoes and serve them with fish, meat or poultry.
2. In spring you can also cover a mound of whipped potatoes with a bunch of scallions or spring onions cut across into thin slices. Try it with your next broiled lamb chops.
3. In summer, mince the leaves of half a bunch of watercress through a Mouli and mix them with the mashed potatoes.
4. Follow the above recipe and sprinkle ¼ cup chopped walnuts over the cress and potato mixture. Good with anything, but particularly with broiled fish.
5. Prepare 1 package frozen peas and 1 package frozen mashed potatoes according to package directions. Whip potatoes with butter and salt to taste and add the peas. Don't let anyone make any stale jokes about this combination.
6. Don't forget the old standby, Potatoes Vesuvio. Prepare two or three packages instant potatoes according to directions,

mound them in a serving dish and dig a crater in the center of the mound. Put ¼ pound butter into the hot crater and serve sprinkled with parsley ground through a Mouli.

7. Mix an egg yolk into 1 package prepared mashed potatoes. Spread into a small baking dish. Sprinkle with grated cheese and brown under the broiler.

8. Beat cream cheese into hot mashed potatoes, using 1 3-ounce package for 2 packages frozen mashed potatoes. Brown lightly under the broiler and serve.

9. To above mixture add 1 1-pound can drained and flaked crab meat, season well and brown under broiler. Serve with cucumber salad.

10. Stir 1 package prepared mashed potatoes until light, add ¼ cup grated yellow cheese, season well and add a little prepared mustard to taste.

SWEET POTATOES

1 1-pound can sweet potatoes, sliced	¼ cup raisins
2 tablespoons butter	¼ cup brown sugar
2 pieces crystallized ginger, diced	¼ cup orange juice
2 tablespoons orange marmalade	

Arrange potatoes in a buttered baking dish. Dot with butter, sprinkle with ginger, raisins and sugar. Mix orange juice and marmalade, pour over potatoes and bake at 375° F. until potatoes are heated through.

BAKED SWEET POTATOES

2 cans sweet potatoes, sliced	2/3 cup maple syrup
1 can sliced apples	1 4-ounce jar marrons (in vanilla)
(apple pie filling)	salt and pepper

Arrange potato and apple slices alternately in a buttered baking dish. Pour over syrup and top with marrons. Heat in a 400° F. oven for about 8 minutes until bubbling, basting frequently.

CANDIED SWEET POTATOES

2 cans sweet potatoes, drained   ¼ cup maple syrup
¼ cup butter, melted   ¼ cup pecans
                        salt and pepper

Dip potatoes in hot butter, arrange in a flat baking dish, add remaining butter and syrup and sprinkle with pecans. Season and bake in 400° F. oven for about 6 minutes, turning on broiler for last minute.

RED POTATOES

1 1-pound can tiny whole white   2 tablespoons milk
   potatoes, drained   ½ cup sour cream
¼ cup frozen chopped onion,   1 teaspoon paprika
   thawed   salt and pepper
¼ cup butter

Fry onions in butter until they are puffed and transparent. Add potatoes and cook, shaking frequently until they are lightly browned. Add milk, cover and cook a few minutes longer until potatoes are heated through. Season, stir a little sour cream into paprika, then add rest of cream and stir into potatoes.

MUSTARD POTATOES I AND II

Variation I

2 cans small white potatoes   1 tablespoon tarragon vinegar
2 tablespoons lard   3 tablespoons butter
2 teaspoons brown mustard   salt and pepper

Heat drained potatoes in lard, shaking to coat evenly. Add mustard and vinegar and season to taste. Add butter and fry for 5 minutes, stirring or shaking constantly.

Variation II

1 1-pound can tiny whole white   ¼ cup heavy cream
   potatoes   2 parsley sprigs
2 tablespoons butter   salt and pepper
1 tablespoon brown mustard, mild   ¼ cup crushed pecans or walnuts

Heat potatoes in butter in a covered skillet, shaking to coat them on all sides. Stir mustard into a little cream and gradually beat in the rest of the cream. Put the parsley sprigs through a Mouli and grind over the cream, or use dehydrated parsley. Add salt and pepper and beat the sauce once more until the cream is slightly thickened. Pour cream over the potatoes, reduce heat and cook a minute longer. Pour into a hot serving dish and sprinkle with nuts.

Never serve vegetables or potatoes in a heavy sauce when the meat is also drenched in sauce. When potatoes or vegetables are in a sauce, that sauce should, at the same time, enhance the fish or meat. These potatoes are particularly good with boiled tongue or ham, boiled fish or a fish pudding. You can also serve them with broiled meats or fish.

FRIED POTATOES I AND II

Variation I

1 1-pound can white potatoes, sliced	4 tablespoons butter or fat
½ green pepper, seeded and diced	1 teaspoon curry powder
1 cup frozen chopped onion, thawed	1 teaspoon brown mustard
	salt and pepper

Fry potatoes, pepper and onion in butter for 2 minutes. Add curry mixed with mustard, stir well and season to taste. Serve as soon as potatoes are lightly browned.

Variation II

1 1-pound can white potatoes, sliced	2 teaspoons chopped dill
1 garlic clove, crushed	2 teaspoons chopped chives
2 teaspoons chopped parsley	4 tablespoons butter
	salt and pepper

Fry potatoes, with garlic and fresh or dried herbs, in butter until the potatoes are lightly browned.

SPICED BANANAS

Bananas prepared in this way can be served with meat or poultry in place of a vegetable.

4 bananas, peeled and cut in
    half lengthwise
1 lemon
1 egg
1 tablespoon water

½ cup flour
1 pinch ground ginger
1 pinch ground cloves
1 pinch ground cinnamon
1 pinch salt

deep fat for frying

Squeeze lemon over banana slices. Beat egg and water together and brush on bananas, dredge in flour mixed with remaining dry ingredients and fry in deep fat at 380° F. until golden.

GRILLED ONION SLICES

2 large onions
              ¼ cup melted butter
salt, pepper and paprika

Slice peeled onions about 1/5 inch thick. Lay on a baking sheet, sprinkle with warm butter and bake in a hot oven about 5 minutes. Turn slices with a spatula. Season well and sprinkle with paprika, brown quickly under broiler and serve at once with meats or fish.

GLAZED ONIONS

2 jars onions, drained
¼ cup butter
1 tablespoon sugar

¼ cup heavy cream
6 pecan halves, crushed
salt and pepper

In a heavy skillet, brown onions in butter and sugar, shaking the pan until the onions are evenly browned. Add cream, stir for 1 minute longer, season to taste and serve sprinkled with pecans crushed with a rolling pin.

CUCUMBER AND ZUCCHINI

6 cucumbers, peeled and sliced
2 young zucchini, sliced
2 teaspoons vinegar

2 tablespoons butter
4 sprigs parsley, ground
through Mouli

salt and pepper

Simmer cucumber and zucchini slices in salted and vinegared water for 3 minutes, drain well. Sauté in butter with chopped parsley for a minute longer. Season and serve. Vegetables should be transparent but still crisp. If cucumbers and zucchini are young they may require only 1½ minutes' boiling.

CUCUMBER AU GRATIN

2 cucumbers, peeled
butter for pan
¼ cup grated cheese

¼ cup bread crumbs
1 tablespoon butter
salt and pepper

Slice peeled cucumbers about ⅛ inch thick. Arrange in a shallow, buttered, fireproof baking dish and sprinkle with cheese and crumbs. Season to taste, dot with butter and bake in a 375° F. oven for about 8 minutes.

Tomatoes

At a time when importing rare garden plants was the style, a Berlin doctor set out a plant in the corner of his garden that bore him disappointing flowers. The plant had come from tropical America and was scheduled to be dug up in the fall. To the amazement of all, it produced a round green fruit after the blossoms fell. The green fruit turned red in fall and became the show plant of Berlin. Similar plants had borne similar fruits in an English greenhouse and, as the fruit was obviously poisonous, it was destroyed. The doctor in Berlin, however, ate his and so the love apple was discovered.

The Italians call it *pomodoro*—"golden apple"—other nations call it "apple of love" or "apple of Paradise" (some insist that it was a tomato plant that led Adam and Eve into temptation). The Germans and Austrians call it just *Paradies,* and if you order a

Boiled Beef with Paradies it will be Boiled Beef with Tomato Sauce.

You are bound to find a lot of recipes here for tomatoes and mushrooms, both of which are "quick cookers"—and none for root vegetables that need half-an-hour boiling before you can even *think* about their preparation. The tomato is one of the Instant Cook's best friends and a very good thing to have. Since I have become an Instant Cook with a small city apartment and guests who follow close on my heels as I come home from work, I always have tomatoes on hand.

You can decide in the last moment where to use them most advantageously. Be careful—sometimes when you aren't watching, you may use them several times, or even find yourself using them throughout dinner.

Hors d'oeuvre: Slice 2 tomatoes, put a spoon of sour cream and a spoon of caviar on each slice and produce with a Martini. If the budget does not run to caviar, sprinkle cream with basil, onion or horseradish—season with salt and pepper if caviar is not used. This does not imply that you should use salty caviar. There is a very good caviar on the market in a small glass jar which is not salty; since each slice gets less than half a teaspoon of caviar, the smallest jar goes a long way. You can also put the tomato slices on Melba toast or toast and top them with crisp bacon, but this takes 3 minutes longer.

Soup: Chop 2 ripe tomatoes roughly and fill into 4 soup cups. Grind 4 sprigs of parsley over the tomatoes through a Mouli. Add anything you have left over, like a little chopped avocado, celery or apple. Set cups in refrigerator while you finish cocktails. Bring cups to the table and pour a ladle of cold madrilène over each tomato-filled cup. If you have ever been in Madrid you will know that *vrai* madrilène is a cold liquid soup, served at that instant when it is so cold it has a little thickness, but not when it is so cold that it is a jelly which can be cut into cubes with a knife.

Main Course: Grilled or stewed tomatoes with meat, fish or poultry. If the meat is without sauce, tomatoes can be in a cream sauce. Hot meats are good with slices of cold tomato.

Salad: Try tomatoes around a rice salad—Minute Rice of course—prepared early in the morning so it will be cold for the salad. Or tomato and watercress salad or just tomato salad.

Short of a ghastly ersatz tomato dessert, there is nothing to end your tomato dinner with except a savory—and what could be better than a pause after dinner and then a small rarebit on tomato slices? Beer is good with this, and the more you think about it the better it would seem to increase the tomato rarebit and have that for dinner, followed with cold fruit and preceded with those bacon rolls which are called anything from Angels On Horseback or *Anges à Chevaux* to Banana Roll-ups or Olive and/or Shrimp In Blankets. You can wrap bacon around oysters, shrimp-stuffed olives or chicken livers, or around banana, pineapple or avocado chunks. Stick a cocktail pick through them, fry them until the bacon is crisp and serve.

ITALIAN BAKED TOMATOES

1 16-ounce can tomatoes, drained	¼ cup grated Parmesan cheese
2 tablespoons tomato paste	salt, pepper and brown sugar
1 envelope pistachio nuts	to taste
½ cup bread crumbs	1 tablespoon butter

Mix tomatoes, paste and nuts and fill into a shallow pie plate. Season. Cover with a mixture of crumbs and Parmesan and dot with butter. Bake in a 375° F. oven until bubbling and browned.

TROPICAL TOMATOES

2 large tomatoes, sliced	1 tablespoon oil or melted butter
2 bananas, peeled and sliced	¼ cup grated cheese
salt and pepper	

Arrange tomato slices on an oiled broiler rack, about 3 inches from source of heat. Arrange banana slices on tomatoes and brush with oil or melted butter. Season well. Sprinkle with cheese and broil until cheese is browned. Serve with broiled meat or as a luncheon main course. Crisp bacon can be served with these tomatoes at a late Sunday breakfast.

CHEESE-STUFFED TOMATOES

4 small tomatoes, peeled
1 cup cottage cheese
4–6 mushrooms, quartered

¼ bunch chives or 2 tablespoons
frozen chopped chives,
thawed

salt and pepper

Scoop out tomatoes with a spoon. Blend cottage cheese with mushrooms, chives and seasonings until mushrooms are roughly chopped. Fill tomatoes with the mixture, sprinkle top with additional chives and serve with any meat course in place of cooked tomatoes. This is especially good with pot roasts or any meat that is served with a heavy gravy.

If no blender is available, chop mushrooms before mixing with cottage cheese.

GRILLED TOMATO SLICES

1 large tomato
¼ cup melted butter

½ cup seasoned bread crumbs
salt and pepper

Cut tomato into ¼-inch slices. Pour melted butter into a flat dish, dip tomato slices in it and dredge with seasoned crumbs. Add salt and pepper to taste. Arrange slices on a baking sheet and brown under broiler, turning once. Broil about 6 minutes in all. Brown any remaining butter, sprinkle over hot tomato slices and serve.

FRIED TOMATOES

4 medium tomatoes
½ cup corn meal
¼ cup frozen chopped onion,
thawed

salt and pepper
butter for frying
4 sprigs parsley, ground
through Mouli

Cut tomatoes across in thick slices, season, dredge with corn meal and fry in hot butter until golden, turning once. Sprinkle with onion and parsley and serve with grilled minute steaks or broiled fish.

CURRIED TOMATOES

4 ripe tomatoes
1 cup bread crumbs
2 tablespoons brown sugar
1 teaspoon curry powder
butter for pan
½ cup frozen chopped onion,
    thawed

2 teaspoons frozen chopped chives,
    thawed
1 can concentrated cream of
    tomato soup
½ cup cream
salt and pepper

Slice tomatoes across in 2–3 thick slices. Arrange in shallow, buttered pan. Combine crumbs, sugar, curry powder and seasonings and sprinkle over tomatoes. Stir onions and chives into soup, add cream and pour over tomatoes. Bake in a 375° F. oven for 10 minutes or until tomatoes are tender.

AMERICAN TOMATOES

4 tomatoes
1 No. 2 can creamed corn
2 egg yolks

2 tablespoons chopped green pepper
    or ½ tablespoon dried green
    bell peppers
salt and pepper

Cut lid from tomatoes and scoop out pulp (add it to soup or stew or blend it into tomato juice in your blender). Beat corn with yolks, peppers and seasoning and fill into tomatoes. Bake in a 400° F. oven until sizzling hot. The tomatoes should remain firm.

BALKAN BAKED TOMATOES

4 tomatoes, halved
3 tablespoons oil
4 parsley sprigs ground
    through Mouli
3 tablespoons dried or fresh
    mint leaves

2 tablespoons basil
1 garlic clove, crushed
¼ cup crumbs
salt and pepper

Arrange tomato halves, cut side up, in a buttered ovenware dish and brush top surface with oil. Mix parsley, mint, basil, garlic and seasonings and spread on oil. Top with crumbs and sprinkle crumbs with remaining oil. Bake in a 400° F. oven or broil under medium heat until crumbs are browned and tomatoes are tender, about 8 minutes.

TOMATO RAREBIT

2 cups grated cheddar cheese, or
½ pound
1 10-ounce can condensed
tomato soup
1 teaspoon mild mustard

½ teaspoon Worcestershire sauce
1 egg, beaten
salt, pepper and paprika
4 pieces toast
1 tomato cut into 4 slices
4 onion slices, optional

Stir cheese and soup in top of double boiler over boiling water until cheese is melted. Add mustard and Worcestershire and stir ¼ cup of the cheese mixture into the egg. Add to remaining cheese mixture in double boiler and cook, stirring constantly, for 4 minutes. Pour over tomato slices arranged on toast slices. Sandwich onion between tomato and toast if preferred.

PROVINCIAL FRIED TOMATOES

1 tablespoon oil
1 tablespoon flour
½ cup bouillon
½ cup frozen chopped onion,
thawed

2 tablespoons dehydrated parsley
1 4-ounce can sliced mushrooms
4 tomatoes, sliced
3 tablespoons butter
salt and pepper

Heat oil in pan, stir in flour until it is smooth, add bouillon and cook over low heat, stirring constantly, for 1 minute. Add onion, parsley and mushrooms and simmer just long enough to puff onions. In the meantime fry the tomato slices in butter for just a moment on each side, turning with a pancake turner. Season well, pour over the onion and mushroom sauce and serve. Add bouillon if a thinner sauce is preferred.

TOMATOES AND HORSERADISH

4 tomatoes
¼ cup melted butter into which a
   sliver of garlic has been
   pressed

1 jar frozen hollandaise sauce,
   thawed
¼ cup fresh grated or bottled
   horseradish, drained

salt and pepper

Scald tomatoes and draw off skins. Cut a thin slice from top
and bottom of tomatoes so that they will stand straight. Brush
with melted butter, season and broil for 5 minutes. Cover with
hollandaise mixed with horseradish and serve.

TOMATOES GRATINÉE

3 tomatoes, cut across into 4
   slices each
1 4-ounce can chopped mushrooms
2 slices ham, slivered
½ cup herbed crumbs (or
   prepared poultry stuffing)

½ teaspoon each, dried oregano,
   chervil and basil
½–⅔ cup grated Parmesan cheese
1 tablespoon butter
salt and pepper

Arrange tomato slices in buttered baking dish. Cover with
mushrooms, ham and herbed crumbs. Add dried herbs and seasonings and sprinkle heavily with cheese. Dot with butter and bake in
a 375° F. oven until cheese is browned.

POLISH TOMATOES

4 tomatoes, sliced
1 cup bread crumbs
½ cup butter
½ garlic clove, crushed

1 slice ham, slivered
4 parsley sprigs, ground through
   Mouli
salt and pepper

Arrange tomato slices in a buttered baking dish and fry
seasoned bread crumbs in butter with the garlic until browned.
Spread crumbs on tomatoes, cover with ham slivers and parsley.
Season and bake in a 400° F. oven for 4 minutes.

TOMATES À LA MÉNAGÈRE

This sounds better in French than in English, which would be Tomatoes in the Manner of the Housewife.

4 tomatoes
½ cup sausage meat
½ cup frozen chopped onion, thawed

½ cup sauerkraut
¼ cup butter, melted
salt and pepper

Cut lid from tomatoes, scoop out pulp and fill with a mixture of onion, sausage meat and sauerkraut. Pour over melted butter and bake until sizzling hot in a 400° F. oven.

BAKED GREEN TOMATOES

4 green tomatoes, sliced
2 eggs, beaten

1 cup bread crumbs
salt and pepper

Dip tomato slices in egg and seasoned crumbs, repeat and bake in a hot oven, 400° F., or push under the broiler. Whether they are baked or broiled they should be served with beef or lamb, and they are ready when the crumbs are browned.

ALGERIAN TOMATOES

4 tomatoes, halved
½ cup frozen chopped onion, thawed
1 cup garlic-flavored croutons
¼ cup butter, melted

1 egg, well beaten
salt and pepper
½ envelope slivered almonds, optional

Scrape seeds from tomato halves and discard. Scoop out pulp with a spoon, add onion, croutons, butter and egg and season to taste. Stir the mixture and fill it into tomato halves. Sprinkle with almonds and set tomatoes into a shallow ovenware dish. Add ¼-inch water and bake in a 400° F. oven until tomatoes are tender and almonds are lightly browned, about 8 minutes.

TOMATO CREAM

1 pound tomatoes, peeled and
    quartered
4 slices onion
4 sprigs parsley

½ teaspoon each dried tarragon,
    dill and oregano
½ teaspoon celery salt
½ cup heavy cream, whipped

salt and pepper

Blend tomato, onion, parsley, herbs and seasonings until smooth. Fold into stiffly whipped salted cream and serve with hot fish, meat or potato dishes.

If no blender is available, chop the tomatoes and onion very well with a mincer; the parsley can be ground through a Mouli.

TOMATOES AND MUSHROOMS À L'ARLÉSIENNE

4 tomatoes, peeled
½ pound mushrooms, sliced
2 tablespoons butter
½ lemon

1 onion, chopped, or ¾ cup
    chopped, frozen onion,
    thawed
6 parsley sprigs put through Mouli

2 tablespoons oil

Arrange sliced tomatoes and mushrooms in a buttered, shallow pan. Season to taste and squeeze the juice of half a lemon over the dish. Sprinkle with onions, parsley and finally with the oil and bake in a 400° F. oven for 8 minutes.

Mushrooms

Mushrooms, otherwise known as the Fungi, are one of nature's pleasantest contributions to our table. They combine well with eggs, cheese, meat, fish, poultry and other vegetables. They cook quickly, taste good and contain practically no calories.

We speak, of course, of the harmless, neat, white mushroom that is available to all of us in this enlightened supermarket age. The poisonous varieties are practically unbuyable and any attempt to destroy your mortal enemy with a mushroom had best be abandoned.

In the mushroom family there are lots of skeletons in closets. The priceless and delectable truffle is first cousin to that incredible smokepot, the puffball, and the stinkhorn. The common field mushroom (Agaricus campestris) is sister under the skin to the Amanita phalloides (the most dangerous deadly death cup). The fake death cup, which the name would imply as edible, is actually as poisonous as the deadly death cup. That lovely coppery affair with white dots, that German Kobolds sat on in tales by the Brothers Grimm, is deadly, while the French cèpe and chanterelle are harmless.

The only mushrooms available to most of us are the ordinary cellar-grown white mushrooms, dried mushrooms from Italy and France, and canned mushrooms, which range from "button" through "sliced" to "chopped." Children are no longer taught to distinguish between the edible and the poisonous varieties and mycologists are almost as extinct as novels in which the heroine was destroyed with a mushroom.

The element of danger has been removed and we are left only with the delicacy and the pleasure.

The mushroom does not bloom, it has no flowers or leaves. It is in itself its own fruit—a sort of elemental thing that consists largely of water and, though we hate to mention it here, it is a parasite. It contains no chlorophyll, it is white, gray, yellow or reddish, but never green. Some varieties grow underground, others jump out of the ground like mushrooms after a rainstorm. It was thought, in the days before cosmetic specialists, that the rubbing on of a mushroom could bring about the rubbing off of freckles from a lady's face.

Mushrooms enhance other ingredients in recipes and they are good by themselves. They are not sufficiently appreciated or understood, and so we give you recipes for their quick preparation. For lack of time (your cooking time) we sadly omit such table delights as Steamed Parasols, Puffballs in Batter, Fungus Pie and Horse Button Stew.

MUSHROOM PURÉE

1 pound mushrooms	½ cup heavy cream
½ 10-ounce can onion soup, cream type	salt and pepper
	1 pinch allspice

Chop mushrooms—stems and caps—in blender or with a 6-bladed chopper. Heat in soup and cream, season and serve on toast or as a filling in heated tomatoes. The longer you can cook the mixture, over very reduced heat, the thicker it will get.

WASHINGTON MUSHROOMS

1 pound small mushrooms	1 tablespoon flour
3 tablespoons butter	1 dash mushroom essence
2/3 cup bouillon	½ envelope shaved almonds
2 tablespoons butter	1 tablespoon butter
salt and pepper	

Fry mushroom caps and sliced stems in butter until glossy, add half the bouillon and simmer. Stir butter and flour together in a small pan over low heat, add remaining bouillon and stir until smooth. Combine mushrooms and sauce over reduced heat and stir well. In the meantime fry almonds in butter until lightly browned. Add to mushrooms, season to taste and serve.

BERMUDA MUSHROOMS

1 pound large mushrooms	¾ cup seasoned and herbed crumbs
1 Bermuda onion, sliced	(poultry stuffing)
¼ cup bouillon	¼ cup melted butter
salt and pepper	

Arrange onion slices in a buttered pie dish. Add bouillon and sprinkle with seasoned and herbed crumbs. Sprinkle with butter, cover with mushroom caps (if there is time the chopped or sliced stems can be added). Pour over the remaining butter and broil about 3 inches from flame for about 6 minutes, or until mushrooms are tender. If you have time earlier in the day to slice the mushrooms, the broiling time can be cut down to 2 minutes.

The two schools of thought regarding the peeling of mushrooms should unite. They should agree to leave all good, fresh mushrooms unpeeled and peel only the ones that have turned brown. Also, peel mushrooms with blemishes or scars.

CAPRI MUSHROOMS

1 pound mushrooms
1–2 tablespoons butter or oil
1 clove garlic, crushed
2 tomatoes, sliced thin, seeds
    removed

salt and paprika
2 parsley stalks, ground through
    Mouli

Brown mushrooms in butter with garlic. Add tomatoes, season and cook a few minutes longer. Serve sprinkled with parsley.

COSMOPOLITAN MUSHROOMS

1 pound mushrooms, sliced
2 tablespoons frozen chopped onion,
    thawed
¼ cup butter

2 tablespoons flour
½ cup cream
½ cup chili sauce
1 dash mushroom essence
salt and pepper

Sauté mushrooms and onion in butter for 2 minutes. Remove with a slotted spoon and keep hot. Reduce heat, stir flour into butter remaining in pan. Gradually add cream and chili sauce, stirring constantly until smooth. Return mushrooms to sauce and cook just long enough to reheat. Serve with meats or pastas. Also a very good first course with toasted cheese bread.

FRENCH MUSHROOMS

1 pound large mushrooms
2 tablespoons oil
¼ cup white wine
¾ cup herbed crumbs
    (poultry stuffing)

½ clove garlic, crushed
2 tablespoons butter
salt and pepper

Remove stems from mushrooms and simmer caps, covered, in oil and wine over low heat. In the meantime chop or blend the stems until they are fine. Add them to the crumbs, garlic and seasonings and fry in butter until brown. Turn mushroom caps with stem side up. Fill crumb mixture into caps and push under the broiler until crumbs are brown.

HUNGARIAN MUSHROOMS

1 pound small mushrooms	4 tablespoons butter
½ cup frozen chopped onion, thawed	1 tablespoon paprika
	½ cup sour cream
salt and pepper	

Fry onion in butter until golden, add mushrooms and paprika and stir until smooth. Add sour cream and season well. Cook over very low heat for a minute longer but do not allow cream to boil. Serve with any chicken or meat recipe. Also very good with fish. Increase cream if served with a dry meat.

Canned button or sliced or chopped mushrooms can be substituted for most of these recipes. The flavor will not be quite as strong, so add bottled mushroom essence to taste.

HERBED MUSHROOMS

1 pound small mushrooms, stalks removed	½ teaspoon chives
3 tablespoons butter	½ teaspoon tarragon or oregano
6 parsley sprigs	1 tablespoon tomato paste
½ teaspoon chervil	¼ cup heavy cream
	1 egg yolk
salt and pepper	

Fry mushrooms in butter until glossy. Add parsley ground through a Mouli and the remaining dried or dehydrated herbs. If fresh herbs are available, grind them with the parsley. Stir mushrooms well, reduce heat and add tomato paste, cream and yolk beaten together. Cook, but do not boil, until sauce is hot. Season and serve. If there is time to chop or slice the mushroom stalks they can be added with the caps.

SATANIC MUSHROOMS

1 pound mushrooms
2 tablespoons butter
1 tablespoon lemon juice
4 shallots, finely chopped
4 sprigs parsley, ground
      through Mouli

½ cup heavy cream
4 slices buttered toast
1 4-ounce jar hollandaise sauce
paprika, salt and pepper

Sauté mushrooms in butter for 1 minute, add ½ cup water, lemon juice and seasonings and simmer for 2 minutes. Add shallots and parsley and cook 2 minutes longer. As soon as the shallots are transparent add cream and cook until bubbling. Arrange mushrooms and sauce on toast slices, spoon over hollandaise, sprinkle with paprika and brown under the broiler for just a moment.

SKEWERED MUSHROOMS

24 large mushrooms
2 limes

¼ cup melted butter
salt and pepper

Quarter one of the limes. Thread 6 mushrooms onto each skewer, thread 1 lime quarter on the end of each. Sprinkle mushrooms with juice squeezed from second lime. Brush with butter and season well. Broil about 3 inches from source of heat. Turn so that both sides are equally browned. Serve at once with hollandaise sauce.

MUSHROOMS BORDELAISE

2 large cans button mushrooms
2 tablespoons butter
1 tablespoon minced shallot or onion

1 tablespoon minced chives
1 tablespoon minced parsley
½ lemon, juice only

salt and pepper

Cook drained mushrooms in butter with shallot, chives and parsley until they are heated through. Shake or stir frequently. Add lemon juice and season to taste. Serve very hot with meats, as a first course, or as an appetizer with cocktail picks.

CHAPTER VII

Pastas,
Rice
and Breads

Pastas

T HE PASTA family is an enormous one with all sorts of cousins, aunts and minor relations. You can stick to the better known macaroni and spaghetti (and they will stick to you) or you can extend your interests to include fuselli, sea shells, egg bows and bow ties. There are rigati, fettucelli, mostaccioli, fidelini and margheritas. If you learn them all you can sing them to *Il Trovatore* or *Santa Lucia* and no one will ever know you aren't fluent in Italian.

If you have an Italian market in your town, you can find many more in lovely boxes with a little window in the front so you'll know what you are doing. They are all pastas and all spring from the ancient and distinguished macaroni family. Lasagna is part of this family, but it takes more time, unhappily, to cook than even an Italian Instant Epicure can find. It does come in frozen packages, as do pizzas and macaroni. Spaghetti dinners and spaghetti sauces come in cans. Ravioli comes in jars; there is nothing Italian and wonderful that does not come bottled (as Chianti), jarred or packaged. Nothing except the sunshine.

You do not need this book to tell you to open a can of this or that Italian specialty, but you can use our suggestions for combining part fresh and part canned products, and remember always to use nice fresh Parmesan cheese. Buy it in pieces and grate it with one of those little nut and cheese graters that we urged upon you at the beginning of this book. Do not just shake cheese out of a cardboard shaker, which you bought a year ago—remember that besides being Instant you are an Epicure and stale cheese is something no epicure should own, much less use. The container cheeses are excellent, but buy small fresh ones and use them up as soon after they are opened as possible.

Pastas make wonderful Sunday suppers, weekday luncheons, and they are an excellent buffet item. When you travel in Italy you learn that they are the answer to all meals and all courses except sweets. In Rome, where you naturally do as the Americans do, you go to one of the Alfredos. There was an original one and now there are several. You order Fettuccini Alfredo, which means noodles with butter and cheese, a little fresh-ground black pepper, a little of Alfredo's charm and the golden spoons which Mary Pickford and Douglas Fairbanks gave him in that bygone day when stars appreciated stars. Some of the Alfredos add a little cream, all of them make their own noodles, and when you think about eating buttered noodles in Rome you think it's pretty silly, but when you actually do eat Buttered Noodles Alfredo in Rome you discover that dreams can be made of pasta and rhapsodies can come from Parmesan cheese, grated at the right moment.

Pastas are paste, combinations of flour and water and, when we want to be as impossible as we can be, we compare our best friend's chef d'oeuvre to library paste. You may be able to put up wallpaper with combinations of flour and water, but if you buy it in different proportions called pasta you can base your entire cooking repertoire on them. They are invaluable to the Instant Epicure, they cook in minutes and are as varied and interesting as all else that stems from Italy (and the Italians got them from China, kindness of Marco Polo).

When cooking spaghetti, macaroni or noodles, follow package directions. If they do not specify exactly, allow 1 teaspoon salt for every quart of water and boil rapidly, stirring several times until the pasta is *al dente*. *Al dente* is the Italian way of saying it should be just tender with a little body, never soft or mushy. Drain immediately and let cold water run through the pasta for a moment, not long enough to cool it off. Only the thinnest spaghetti can boil in time to be included as part of the Instant Epicure's repertoire; noodles (we also call them fettuccini) boil faster and can be served with any of the sauces that are suggested for the other pastas.

The canned sauces are good, or combinations can be made with the canned sauces and other ingredients. The bases of the sauces, thick tomato sauce or bouillon, should be used out of a can, the additions of meat, chicken livers, clams or mushrooms can be made with fresh or frozen ingredients. If there is not enough time to make additions, just add basil and oregano and freshly grated Parmesan cheese to canned spaghetti sauce.

NOODLES (FETTUCCINI) WITH SHRIMP

½ pound noodles or fettuccini (medium thin)
1 pound raw peeled shrimp
½ cup frozen chopped onion, thawed
¼ cup butter

1 cup canned tomatoes
1 pimento, chopped
¼ cup chopped green pepper, optional
½ teaspoon dried oregano
salt and pepper

½ cup grated Parmesan cheese

Cook noodles according to package directions. In the meantime fry shrimp and onion in butter for 2 minutes, turn the shrimp and fry 2 minutes longer. Add tomatoes, pimento and green pepper and continue to cook until noodles are drained. Add oregano to sauce, correct seasoning and pour over noodles. Sprinkle with cheese and serve.

To make fettuccini with shrimp and vegetables, prepare recipe as above and add 1 package frozen peas, artichokes or okra to the sauce just before it is served. The vegetables have to be prepared separately according to package directions.

NOODLES (FETTUCCINI) WITH BEEF

½ pound noodles or fettuccini,
  medium thin
1 pound ground beef
1 8-ounce can sliced mushrooms
½ cup frozen chopped onion,
  thawed

¼ cup butter
3 beef bouillon cubes dissolved in 1
  cup boiling water
¼ cup red wine, optional
1 cup sour cream

Boil noodles according to package directions. Brown meat, mushrooms and onion in butter until the meat is no longer red. Add the bouillon and red wine and cook until the noodles are just al dente. Drain noodles, put them on a hot serving platter, stir sour cream into the sauce and pour over the noodles. Serve at once. As the bouillon cubes are very salty it will probably not be necessary to use more salt.

SPAGHETTI WITH MEAT SAUCE

½ pound thinnest spaghetti
½ pound ground beef
½ cup frozen chopped onion,
  thawed
1 garlic clove, crushed
¼ cup oil

1 10-ounce can tomato sauce
1 10-ounce can tomatoes
½ teaspoon each, dried oregano and
  basil
salt and pepper
grated Parmesan cheese

Prepare spaghetti according to package directions. In the meantime sauté beef, onion and garlic in oil until the beef is no longer red. Add tomato sauce, tomatoes, herbs and seasonings to taste and simmer until spaghetti is al dente. Drain at once, cover with the hot sauce and sprinkle generously with freshly grated Parmesan cheese.

To the above recipe you can add any leftover vegetables, canned sliced mushrooms or chopped green pepper. If green pepper is added, about ½ cup or to taste, sauté it with the onions and meat.

SPAGHETTI WITH CLAMS

½ pound thinnest spaghetti
1 1-pound can minced clams
½ cup frozen chopped onion,
  thawed

1 10-ounce can Italian tomatoes
1 10-ounce can tomato sauce
1 teaspoon dried basil
1 pinch dried dill

salt and pepper

Prepare spaghetti according to package directions. In the meantime simmer clams with remaining ingredients. When spaghetti is al dente, drain well, cover with the hot clam sauce and serve at once. Pass grated cheese separately, if desired.

SPAGHETTI WITH MUSHROOMS

Follow above recipe, substituting 1 1-pound can button mushrooms for the clams and omitting the dill. Sprinkle with grated Parmesan cheese and serve.

SPAGHETTI WITH BACON

½ pound thinnest spaghetti, broken into 1-inch lengths
8 slices bacon, cut into ½-inch squares
2 tablespoons brown sugar

1 1-pound can Italian tomatoes
1 10-ounce can tomato sauce
salt, pepper and Worcestershire sauce

Prepare spaghetti according to package directions. In the meantime fry bacon until brown, add sugar, tomatoes and seasonings to taste and simmer until spaghetti is al dente. Drain spaghetti well, season sauce to taste with salt, pepper and Worcestershire sauce and pour over the spaghetti. Pass grated Parmesan cheese separately.

MACARONI IN CASSEROLE

1 1-pound can macaroni and cheese sauce
butter for casserole
½ cup chopped ham, or any leftover meat

1 package frozen peas, prepared according to package directions
salt and pepper
½ cup grated Parmesan cheese

Spread half the macaroni in a 1-quart buttered casserole. Top with the ham and hot peas and cover with rest of macaroni. Season and sprinkle with grated cheese. Bake in a 400° F. oven for 10 minutes or until top is browned and macaroni is bubbling.

MACARONI AND TUNA CASSEROLE

1 1-pound can macaroni and
  cheese sauce
1 can tuna fish
1 can button mushrooms

1 10-ounce can Italian tomatoes
½ cup chopped stuffed olives
1 cup bread crumbs
salt and pepper

butter for casserole

Divide tuna fish into chunks, mix with macroni, mushrooms, olives and tomatoes and pour into a 2-quart buttered casserole. Top with seasoned bread crumbs and bake in a 400° F. oven until bread crumbs are lightly browned and macaroni is bubbling.

SPAGHETTI AND CHICKEN LIVERS

2 1-pound cans spaghetti with
  tomato sauce
1 1-pound package frozen chicken
  livers, thawed and cut into
  quarters
½ cup frozen chopped onion,
  thawed

3 tablespoons butter
½ teaspoon dried oregano
1 pinch cinnamon
salt and pepper
½ cup grated Parmesan cheese

Fry chicken livers and onion in butter until they are lightly browned, a minute or two. Add oregano and seasonings to taste and combine with spaghetti in a buttered casserole. Sprinkle with cheese and bake in a 400° F. oven until bubbling; serve at once with green salad and hot Italian bread.

Use canned macaroni and spaghetti in any of the combinations where freshly cooked noodles or spaghetti are suggested. Heat in the oven in a buttered casserole or heat on top of the stove in a double boiler over rapidly boiling water.

HUNGARIAN NOODLES I AND II

When a recipe calls for broken noodles, just break them in your hand or fill them into a measuring cup and break them by pressing them down until they are tightly packed.

Variation I

½ pound wide noodles, broken
1 1-pound can beef stew
½ cup frozen chopped onion,
    thawed
¼ garlic clove, crushed
1 tablespoon butter

1 teaspoon paprika
2 bouillon cubes
2 cups water
½ teaspoon caraway seeds
¼ green pepper, sliced across into
    rings

salt and pepper

Prepare noodles according to package directions. Fry onion and garlic in butter for 2 minutes, add paprika and stir well. Add bouillon cubes and water and cook until cubes are dissolved. Add beef stew and caraway seeds and continue to cook until meat is hot. Add drained noodles, season and serve hot, garnished with green pepper rings.

Variation II

To above noodles add:

1 1-pound can small white onions

1 10-ounce can tomatoes

Add onions and tomatoes to noodles at the same time as the beef and increase seasoning to taste.

S P Ä T Z L E

1 egg
2/3 cup water
2¼ cup flour

½ teaspoon salt
2 tablespoons butter

Beat egg and water into flour, season and press mixture through a collander into 2 quarts of rapidly boiling salted water. Cover and boil 3 minutes. Spätzle are done when they come to the surface. Drain very well and stir with butter. ½ cup brown bread crumbs may be added. Serve with beef stew, veal stew or Gulyas.

Rice

We have finally reached the point in this book when epicures must regret their Instant state. Up to now and after this all has been and all will again be well, but when it comes to rice, lovely slow-cooked rice, there will have to be a moment of silent regret. Nothing and nobody can make a Risotto Milanese or a Saffron Rice in minutes, but the manufacturers of canned and Minute Rice have done everything to soften the loss for us and to substitute an ersatz which is as nearly perfect as if we had had that extra half hour before dinner.

We give you here the best that can be done in the time (the Instant) you have to prepare dinner, and although it is not exactly a Riso Con le Code de Gamberi it is fast and uncomplicated and it tastes good.

Rice has been a staple in the East for centuries; it has simmered in Spain and Italy, in the Near East, Latin America and the South to give the endless enjoyment and nourishment that only rice can give. Whether we are Instant or slow epicures, an appreciation of rice belongs to the attributes of every epicure and if it is correctly used it should enhance any menu you can devise.

Most Americans think of it as Rice Pudding, which is one of those dishes that can be both the best or the worst thing you ever ate. They think of it as part of curry or part of a Chinese meal, but very few prepare it as an accompaniment for The Roast or The Bird.

Risi Bisi, rice with green peas, is served with little veal cutlets. The risottos are served as a meal in themselves or as an accompaniment for any of the meat dishes. The pilaf or pilau rices from the Near East should accompany the skewer recipes in the Outdoor Cooking chapter. When meat is juicy, or served with a sauce, the rice can be dry. When the meat is dry the rice should be prepared with a broth or tomato sauce so that it too will not be dry.

Rice has fed millions for centuries and some forms of it are ready for the future when there will still be rice lovers but fewer people who love rice and have time to prepare it besides.

RISI BISI

2 cups Minute Rice
1 package frozen peas

2 tablespoons butter
salt

Prepare rice and peas according to package directions. Drain peas well and combine them with the rice. Add butter and stir gently until melted. Season to taste and serve with broiled meats.

RISI E BISI I THROUGH III

Variation I

2 cups Minute Rice
1 package frozen peas
2 tablespoons butter

¼ cup grated Parmesan cheese
2 sprigs parsley, ground through
    Mouli

salt and pepper

Prepare rice and peas as above, stir in cheese and parsley after butter is melted. Season and serve with meat or as a meal in itself.

Variation II

2 2/3 cups Minute Rice
1 package frozen peas
½ cup frozen chopped onion,
    thawed

2 tablespoons butter
½ cup chopped ham, tongue or
    Bologna sausage
¼ cup grated Parmesan cheese

salt and pepper

Prepare rice and peas according to package directions. In the meantime, sauté onion in butter until transparent, add ham and stir well. Combine all ingredients, add cheese and season to taste. This can be served as a main dish.

Variation III

Prepare Risi e Bisi as in Variation II, substituting bacon, cut into squares with a kitchen scissors, for the ham and omitting the butter. Fry bacon until transparent, add the onions and continue to fry until bacon is crisp. Add rice, peas, cheese and season well. Serve as a main dish. A little of the bacon fat may be drained off if preferred.

LOBSTER AND LIME RICE

½ garlic clove, crushed
¼ cup butter
1 1/3 cups Minute Rice
1 1/3 cups water

1 teaspoon salt
1 6-ounce can lobster
2 tablespoons dehydrated parsley
1 teaspoon grated lime rind

2 teaspoons lime juice

Sauté garlic in 2 tablespoons butter ½ minute. Add Minute Rice, water and salt and mix only long enough to moisten the rice. Bring quickly to a boil over high heat, take from heat, cover and let stand 5 minutes. In the meantime, sauté lobster, parsley, lime rind and juice in remaining butter until heated through. Add to rice, mix lightly and serve.

GINGER RICE

1 egg, boiled just 5 minutes
1 1/3 cups Minute Rice
¼ teaspoon salt
1 1/3 cups boiling water
½ teaspoon ground ginger
¼ cup of oil or shortening

1 cup slivered meat, ham or
    any canned meat
1 tablespoon soy sauce
2 tablespoons frozen chopped onion,
    thawed
salt and pepper

Boil egg and set aside in warm water. Add rice and salt to boiling water and mix just long enough to moisten rice. Cover, remove from heat and let stand five minutes. Heat ginger in oil in a large pan, add meat and stir until lightly browned. Add the rice, soy sauce and onion and season to taste. Place egg on rice and mix the egg into the rice as it is served.

There are many good additions to Minute Rice prepared according to package directions. These additions will enhance the rice, and provide variety to your meal.

To every 1 1/3 cups Minute Rice (one package) add 1 table-spoon tomato paste and 1 teaspoon dehydrated parsley.

To every 1 1/3 cups Minute Rice add 1 tablespoon fresh or frozen chopped chives and 1 tablespoon fresh or dehydrated chopped parsley.

To every 1 1/3 cups Minute Rice add ½ cup canned mushrooms, sliced or chopped. Substitute the mushroom liquid for part of the water required for preparing the rice.

To every 1 1/3 cups Minute Rice add 1 teaspoon each, butter and orange marmalade, and ½ sliced banana. This is very good with duck.

To every 1 1/3 cups Minute Rice add 1 tablespoon browned butter and 2 tablespoons heavy cream, a pinch of ground cinnamon and sugar to taste. Serve as dessert or serve with stewed fruit as a light luncheon dish.

To every 1 1/3 cups Minute Rice add enough French dressing to moisten lightly. Cool and serve instead of a salad with any meat dish.

RICE WITH HAM

1½ cups sliced ham, cut julienne
¼ cup chopped frozen onion, thawed
1 4-ounce can sliced mushrooms
¼ cup butter

2 cups boiling water
1 teaspoon prepared mustard
1 dash Tabasco sauce
¼ cup chili sauce
2 cups Minute Rice

salt and pepper

Sauté ham, onion and mushrooms in butter for 3 minutes. Add water, liquid from the mushrooms, seasoning and sauces and bring back to a boil. Add rice, mix just long enough to moisten, cover and take from heat. Let stand 5 minutes. Fluff with a fork and serve at once.

RICE SUKIYAKI

½ cup frozen chopped onion, thawed
¼ cup butter
1 pound beef cut in thin strips, sirloin or any tender cut
1 4-ounce can sliced mushrooms
1 1-pound can bean sprouts, drained
¼ cup sliced water chestnuts, optional

2 tablespoons soy sauce
2 cups fresh spinach or watercress
1 bouillon cube dissolved in
1½ cups hot water
1⅓ cups Minute Rice
6 scallions, sliced across
salt and pepper

Sauté onion in butter for 1 minute, add beef and brown on all sides. Season and stir in mushrooms, bean sprouts, chestnuts and soy sauce. Cook 2 minutes, add spinach and cook 1 minute longer. Add bouillon cube dissolved in hot water, rice and scallions and simmer covered for 5 minutes. Do not overcook. Pass additional soy sauce separately.

SEAFOOD RICE

1 ¼-pound can sliced mushrooms	1 cup water
2 tablespoons butter	½ cup mayonnaise
1 pound shelled shrimp, sliced	2 teaspoons salt
lengthwise	1⅓ cups Minute Rice
1 pound scallops	2 tablespoons brandy

1 pinch each, pepper and paprika

Sauté mushrooms, shrimp and scallops in butter in a large skillet for 4 minutes. Mix water, mayonnaise and salt into the skillet mixture and bring to a boil. Stir in rice, cover and simmer 5 minutes, stir in brandy, correct seasoning and serve.

RICE WITH BEEF AND BLEU CHEESE

½ cup bread crumbs	1⅓ cups frozen chopped onion, thawed
¼ cup milk	
1 pound ground beef	1 clove garlic, crushed
1 egg	1 1-pound can tomatoes
¼ cup crumbled Bleu cheese	1⅓ cups Minute Rice
¼ cup butter	1 cup water

salt and pepper

Soak bread crumbs in milk until milk is absorbed, add beef, egg and cheese and mix lightly. Shape into small balls and sauté in butter in a large skillet with the onion and garlic until onion is transparent. Add remaining ingredients, mixing only until the rice is moistened. Bring to a boil over high heat, cover, remove from heat and let stand five minutes.

CONTINENTAL RICE

1 can condensed cream of chicken
    soup
¼ cup frozen chopped onion,
    thawed
1 teaspoon salt
½ teaspoon each, dried thyme,
    parsley and celery flakes
½ cup dry white wine

1 cup water
1-1/3 cups Minute Rice
1½ cups canned or cooked diced
    chicken
½ teaspoon paprika
1 4-ounce can sliced mushrooms,
    drained

Heat soup, onion, salt, herbs and wine to a boil in a sauce-pan. Pour half the mixture into a 1½-quart casserole, add rice (straight from the box) and chicken, making two layers of each. Add remaining soup mixture, spread with mushrooms and bake in a 400° F. oven 10 minutes. Stir well, sprinkle with paprika and serve. This dish can be prepared ahead of time and reheated or it can be left in a low-heat oven until needed.

CRAB MEAT AND RICE CASSEROLE

1 package frozen peas
1 can condensed cream of mushroom
    soup
1¼ cups milk
¼ cup frozen chopped onion,
    thawed

1 teaspoon lemon juice
1-1/3 cups Minute Rice
1 6-ounce package frozen crab meat,
    thawed
½ cup grated Parmesan cheese
salt, pepper and paprika

This recipe can be prepared in two different ways, depending on time.

Method I: Prepare peas and rice according to package directions. Drain peas, combine with rice, onion, lemon juice and crab meat. Season well, spread with cheese, sprinkle with paprika and bake in a 400° F. oven until cheese is browned. Omit milk in this method.

Method II: Prepare peas according to package directions. Heat soup, milk, onion and lemon juice to a boil in a sauce pan. Pour half the mixture into a 1½-quart casserole, add rice right from the box, crab meat and peas and cover with remaining soup mixture. Sprinkle with cheese and paprika and bake covered in a

400° F. oven for 10 minutes or until cheese is browned and casserole is bubbling.

The second method is ideal for a casserole that has to be quickly prepared but is not needed immediately. It can be left in a slow oven until needed.

RICE AND LOBSTER CASSEROLE

1 package frozen artichoke hearts
1 1/3 cups Minute Rice
1 8-ounce can lobster, or ½ pound frozen lobster, thawed
1 can condensed cream of mushroom soup

¾ soup can water
½ cup sherry
salt, garlic salt and pepper
2 slices processed American Cheese, cut into triangles

Prepare artichoke hearts and rice according to package directions, reducing the cooking time for the artichoke hearts by about 2 minutes. Cook them only until they are just tender, not soft. Heat lobster meat with the soup and water in a 1½-quart casserole. Add the well-drained artichokes and rice and season to taste. Add sherry and top with cheese. Push under the broiler or into a 450° F. oven until cheese softens and browns a little.

CHICKEN AND RICE WITH HERBS

1 1/3 cups Minute Rice
½ teaspoon salt
1 1/3 cups boiling water
1 can cream of chicken soup
1 cup cream
¼ cup sherry
¼ teaspoon Worcestershire sauce

1 cup cooked or canned diced chicken meat
1 4-ounce can sliced mushrooms
1 canned pimento, cut fine
2 parsley sprigs, ground through Mouli

Add Minute Rice and salt to boiling water and mix just long enough to moisten rice. Cover and remove from heat and let stand 5 minutes. In the meantime heat soup and cream and stir until smooth. Add sherry and Worcestershire sauce and season to taste. Add rice, chicken, mushrooms, pimento and parsley. Place in a 400° F. oven just long enough to heat through. Serve at once, or place in a slow oven to stay hot until needed.

Breads

Besides all sorts of geographical and political differences between Americans and Europeans, there is the marked difference in our attitude toward hot yeast breads. Until recently the European considered any hot breads almost as dangerous to the national well-being as that most hazardous of all mad American undertakings—sleeping with an open window. He willingly ate baker's bread fresh out of the oven, but he could not agree to heated or toasted breads. When they were eaten with an iced beverage he could only mourn the inevitable passing of the Western Hemisphere.

Fortunately, love and understanding have finally come to the Europeans. Love of hot breads, iced drinks, cold bedrooms and electric blankets. They have, at long last, come to understand that all is either hot or cold in America, nothing is lukewarm. With the discovery of ice cream bars, fried chicken-in-a-basket, chilled fountain drinks and hot breads, the mortality rate in Europe has not gone up appreciably. Americans did not, in fact, die because they ate hot breads but because they were old, or struck by lightning. We can, apparently, eat this deadly, dangerous, heated bread and still live to a ripe old age.

In Instant Epicureanism (and Instant Epicures have reason to want to live longer, if anything, than other people) the use of quick hot breads goes far to unite a meal. It is a sort of liaison between food and haste, it toasts or bakes quickly and bridges the gap between the courses. It is an accompaniment that leads from cocktails or soup to meat. It weaves a spell around the salad and it makes a choppy meal into a feast. Give them a hot loaf of bread, full of garlic and butter, give them a good red wine, and after that you can relax. If your main course is sketchy they'll never know the difference, and when they go home they'll remember the crunching loaf and forget the indifferent casserole you produced.

BROILED ITALIAN BREAD

8 1-inch-thick slices Italian bread
2 garlic cloves, crushed
¼ cup soft butter

2 teaspoons dried marjoram,
    oregano or parsley
salt

Stir garlic into soft butter, add dried, or fresh minced, herbs and spread on bread slices. Sprinkle with salt and push under the broiler. Serve hot.

CINNAMON TOAST WITH APPLE SAUCE

4 slices bread
½ teaspoon cinnamon

½ cup sugar
1 egg, beaten

1 15-ounce jar apple sauce

Mix cinnamon, sugar and half the egg. Spread mixture thickly on bread slices and bake about 8 minutes in a 425° F. oven. Serve with apple sauce for dessert.

This is also good served with hot maple sauce or hot cherry sauce. The fruit can be served with the cinnamon toast or you can cut the toast into fingers, before baking, and pass it separately. If you ever serve tea in the afternoon, hot cinnamon toast is the perfect accompaniment.

ITALIAN BREAD

1 loaf Italian bread
½ cup soft butter
½ cup frozen chopped onion,
    thawed

½ garlic clove, crushed
1 cup grated Parmesan cheese
salt

Cut loaf across diagonally in 1-inch slices, not cutting through bottom crust. Mix butter, onion, garlic and cheese and season to taste. Spread a little of the mixture into each slice. Bake on a baking sheet in a 400° F. oven for 10 minutes.

SEEDED BREADS

1 loaf Italian or French bread, or
   1 Hero sandwich loaf per
   person

½ cup butter
2 tablespoons poppy seeds
salt

Cut bread into thick slices, not cutting through bottom crust. Spread soft butter thickly over top of loaf, letting some go down a little way between the slices. Spread poppy seeds and salt thickly on top of butter and bake in a 400° F. oven for 10 minutes.

You can substitute caraway seeds and rough salt for poppy seeds, or substitute sesame seeds for poppy seeds.

HERBED MUFFINS

4 English muffins
½ cup butter
2 tablespoons dried herbs, chives,
   parsley, oregano and basil

¼ cup salted nuts, roughly
   crushed
salt

Split muffins with a fork, spread with butter mixed with herbs, nuts and salt. Push under broiler until edges are browned.

HOT RYE BREAD

1 loaf sour rye bread
½ cup butter, softened

1 onion, put through mincer
½ teaspoon salt

¼ teaspoon ground caraway seeds

Cut loaf down length in 2 or 3 strips, not cutting through bottom crust. Cut across in thick slices so that bread is divided into chunks but not cut through. Mix butter with onion, salt and caraway and spread between and over cubes of bread. Set on a baking sheet and bake in a 400° F. oven for 10 minutes or until heated but not browned. Serve with soups or salad, frankfurters, cheeses or baked beans.

CURRIED BREAD

8 slices white bread   ½ cup butter
1 tablespoon curry powder

Melt butter in a flat baking pan, mix with curry powder and lay bread slices into pan. Turn so that they are buttered on both sides. Bake in a 400° F. oven for 8–10 minutes or until bread is lightly browned.

CARAWAY SALT STICKS

1 loaf unsliced bread   2 tablespoons caraway seeds
¾ cup butter, melted   1 tablespoon rough salt

Cut loaf into ¾- to 1-inch-thick slices and cut slices into ¾- to 1-inch fingers or sticks. Brush with melted butter and sprinkle caraway seeds and rough salt over the butter. Bake on a buttered baking sheet in a 400° F. oven for 10 minutes or until lightly browned. Serve hot with beer and frankfurters or with any salad or soup. Very good with potato salad.

PAIN RETROUVÉ

8 thin slices French bread   1 teaspoon sugar
4 eggs   butter for frying
1 cup milk   powdered sugar for sprinkling
¼ cup cream   orange rind
1 tablespoon orange juice

Beat eggs into milk, cream, orange juice and sugar. Dip bread slices into mixture, and fry in hot butter until brown on both sides. Sprinkle slices with powdered sugar as soon as they come out of the frying pan. Grate orange rind over each slice and serve.

The buttered and garnished breads are a great addition to a meal that might otherwise be skimpy. Combined with a strong soup or a crisp salad they are a meal in themselves. They can be served with any egg or cheese dish to turn luncheon into a proper meal when unexpected guests arrive.

All the breads are available at the bread counters of your markets. Frozen fresh chives and chopped onions are at the frozen-food counters and they cut down the time needed to prepare the loaves. Melted butter can be dribbled between the slices if there is no time for softening butter.

If you have an herb garden you can produce lovely toasted loaves all summer that will add enormously to your popularity.

BAKED FRENCH LOAF

1 longest loaf French bread
½ cup soft butter
¼ cup minced chives, frozen or fresh

2 tablespoons soft butter
2 tablespoons crumbled Roquefort cheese
salt and pepper

Cut loaf into 1-inch-thick diagonal slices, cutting almost to bottom crust. Stir chives into soft butter and spread between slices. Stir Roquefort cheese with remaining butter and spread on top of bread. Wrap in aluminum foil, leaving top open. Bake in a 400° F. oven for 10 minutes, or until lightly browned.

HOLIDAY BREAD

1 loaf unsliced raisin bread
½ cup melted butter

1/3 cup sugar
½ teaspoon cinnamon
½ 3-ounce envelope broken pecans

Cut loaf lengthwise into 3 parts by cutting twice down length of loaf. Do not cut through bottom crust; cut across into 1½-inch-thick slices but do not cut through bottom crust. Spread melted butter over top of loaf and brush down between the bread slices. Sprinkle with mixture of cinnamon and sugar, sprinkling most of it on top. Sprinkle top with broken pecans and let a few go down between the slices. Bake as above.

ONION BREAD

1 loaf unsliced Italian bread   salt
2–3 onions, thinly sliced   ½ cup soft butter

Cut loaf almost down to bottom crust into 1-inch-thick slices. If it is a wide loaf cut once down center. Spread soft butter between slices and over top of loaf. Insert an onion slice between each bread slice and season with salt. Bake in a 425° F. oven for 10 minutes.

BREAD SLICES

12 thin slices white bread   ½ cup soft butter
     salt

Butter thin bread, sprinkle with salt and bake in a 425° F. oven with any of the following spreads or toppings. The bread should be toasted and the topping melted in 4 to 8 minutes.

1. Sprinkle with minced parsley, chives, dill or any preferred herb.
2. Spread with anchovy paste, marmalade, cinnamon and sugar or Roquefort cheese.
3. Sprinkle with grated Parmesan cheese, caraway seeds, poppy seeds or sesame seeds.
4. Spread with mustard or minced onion.
5. Combine any of the above and eat with salads, eggs, cold meats or afternoon or breakfast tea.

SLICED WHITE LOAVES

1 loaf thin-sliced white bread   ¾ cup melted butter
     salt

Brush each slice of bread with melted butter, sprinkle with salt and reshape loaf. Put into a bread pan or wrap in foil, leaving top open. Bake in a 450° F. oven for 10 minutes.

Add any of the following ingredients to the butter: ¼ cup cut chives, ¼ cup chopped parsley, ½ cup grated cheese, 1 teaspoon curry powder, ¼ cup minced scallions or onions, or any preferred herb.

SLICED RYE LOAVES

1 round loaf sliced rye bread   ½ cup melted butter
                     salt

Brush slices with butter as for sliced white loaves. Season and bake as described above.

Add any of the following ingredients to the butter: 1 teaspoon caraway seeds or 1 teaspoon poppy seeds, or ¼ cup minced scallions or onions.

TOASTED BRIOCHE

4 brioches from the bakery   ½ cup soft butter
                     salt

Slice each brioche into 4 slices and spread with soft butter. Sprinkle with salt and lay on a baking sheet. Bake in a 450° F. oven until edges are brown and butter is melted. Watch carefully, this goes very fast. If there is more time follow same procedure but leave in a 200° F. oven while you prepare dinner. Let brioches dry out and increase heat to brown brioches only during last 4 minutes of baking. Serve with anything. It is a lovely way of having bread.

The Brown-and-Serve Rolls

The half-baked Brown-and-Serve Rolls and Bread are so good that we can do no more than recommend them. However, like everything else, they can take a little change or improvement at times and we follow with some suggestions that do not prolong their baking time.

The small round rolls can be slashed across the top and any of the following ingredients can be inserted in the slash:
1 orange section, white membrane and pits removed
1 wedge American or cheddar cheese
1 sliver butter and 1 teaspoon grated Parmesan cheese

1 teaspoon honey, 1 teaspoon broken walnuts and 1 pinch cinnamon

1 teaspoon apricot jam, 1 teaspoon sugar sprinkled over

1 teaspoon apricot jam and 1 teaspoon brown sugar sprinkled over

2 teaspoons softened cream cheese, either chive cheese or pimento

2 teaspoons garlic butter (combine 1 crushed garlic clove with ½ cup soft butter and ½ teaspoon salt)

Bake the rolls according to package directions. The time required is approximately 10 minutes in a 400° F. oven.

The loaves of bread can be spread with melted butter, garlic butter and any of the seeds and herbs. Or they too can be slashed and prepared as the regular baked loaves. After the Bake-and-Serve loaf is prepared with the spread, bake it according to the directions on the package.

Biscuits

Use the type of biscuits that are cut and ready for the oven —most of them will bake in a 450° F. oven in 10 minutes. Follow directions on the package.

Arrange biscuits in a buttered baking pan. Use a layer cake pan or any pan that will press the biscuits close together. Brush top with melted butter and sprinkle with poppy, sesame, caraway or celery seeds.

You can also paint top with egg beaten with water (1 tablespoon water per egg) and sprinkle with rough salt and shaved almonds. Or sprinkle with cinnamon and sugar and shaved almonds.

CHAPTER VIII

Salads, Dressings and Relishes

Salads

WHEN WE look back on the stories that were read to us when we were children, they all seem to have been tales of diminishment. "Hans In Luck" started with a sack of gold and ended with a mill-stone. The ten little nigger boys dwindled until there were none, Casper wouldn't eat his soup and faded (in our edition) to a picture of a thread. Even Mother Hubbard's cupboard became bare.

I do not know what those stories were supposed to teach us, unless it was to prepare us, as we grew older, for constantly diminishing time. Once it took a day, or even more, to prepare a proper dinner; later it came down to starting dinner some time in the early afternoon. Then it became "After Five Cooking," then "20-Minute Cooking" and now we stand on the verge of "Instant Cooking" (we'll call it "From-One-to-Ten-Minute Cooking") and after that—pills. Variously flavored and colored pills and beverages to swallow them with, or maybe we'll give ourselves shots in the arm. No one will have a kitchen; kitchens will be preserved in museums and we'll go to look at them as we look at Pompeii or the Catacombs today.

So—while it lasts—while we still have an instant in which to cook food—let's enjoy it. Let's eat those things that would be ruined if they were cooked for longer than 3 minutes. Let's not try to cook those things, which really require 30 minutes, by pressurizing them or forcing them into a fraction of their proper cooking time. And *let's make lots of salads.*

The time-consuming, elaborately molded salad is pretty much a thing of the past, and so is the salad that has to be arranged like a still life. We need not waste time with hollowing out orange baskets or with piping green cream cheese into pear halves. And we certainly don't have to create fruit pictures out of angelica and maraschino cherries.

We've boiled the whole thing down to the "Tossed Green Salad" and the combined salad and a combination of the two. You simply prepare one or more salad greens and dump them into a salad bowl with dressing. When it comes time to serve the salad you toss it around and that's all. The combined salad only means that you put lettuce or other salad greens in a bowl with tomatoes or cucumbers or any other ingredients and toss or stir it with dressing. When you serve it forth it does not look pretty but it tastes wonderfully well. Even if it is now a rather wilted and unrecognizable mixture you can always recall the fact that you saw it before it was tossed and that odd-looking lump is a combination of Roquefort cheese, bread crumbs and pimento.

Another thing that has come into the fore with the fast tossed salad is the deep salad bowl. I am reminded of a famous Philadelphia plastic surgeon who did the most painstakingly delicate jobs imaginable. If any of his patients had seen him toss a salad (which he did over the table and clear through the dining room into the living room) they would never have entrusted their faces to him. The deep salad bowl is the answer. They come now in wonderful deep tulip shapes, a little wider at the top but deep enough to prevent oily lettuce leaves from flying around the table.

The salad can, of course, come at any time during the meal. In some parts of the country it is a first course, in other parts it has to follow the meat. Many restaurants just put it next to you so that you can eat it before, with or after the main course. All they ask you to do is to choose between French, Russian and Roquefort dressing. A salad can be served in place of a vegetable and fruit salads can end the meal in place of a dessert. Chef's salads, Caesar salads and many others are a meal in themselves, while such delicacies as shrimp or lobster salads are a gala meal.

The salad is flexible and it's fun. It can absorb leftovers and it is the perfect accompaniment to the broiled meats that every Instant Epicure lives on. It is also a boon to the people who get on their scales each day and a help to the people who have to watch their budgets.

There are so many lovely salad combinations that it is quite impossible to give recipes for more than a scratch on the surface. We list a few combinations here without detailed recipes because it is only necessary to combine the ingredients in proportions that please your own taste and pour on the dressing in a rough ratio of about two tablespoons for four people. Use the commercially bottled dressings or prepare one that comes in an envelope and needs only vinegar, oil and water added. Or, of course, prepare your own or make your own addition to the prepared dressings. See salad dressings farther along in this chapter.

Ten Simple Salad Combinations

1. Lettuce, chopped raw mushrooms, chives and herb dressing.
2. Lettuce, green onions, chopped celery, chopped stuffed olives and chili dressing.
3. Endive, avocado, crumbled Roquefort cheese and French dressing.
4. Romaine, apple slices, ham slivers and Italian dressing.
5. Romaine, canned grapefruit sections and French dressing.
6. Watercress, avocado slices, garlic croutons and French dressing.
7. Spinach leaves, Boston lettuce, iceberg lettuce and Russian dressing.
8. Spinach leaves, shoestring beets, French dressing and a little sour cream.
9. Iceberg lettuce, sliced radishes, mustard mayonnaise and parsley.
10. Boston lettuce, sliced tomatoes, grated Parmesan cheese and Italian dressing.

GOURMET'S SALAD

2 tomatoes, peeled and halved
1 No. 2 can pineapple chunks,
    drained
½ green pepper, chopped through
    mincer

1 can French string beans, drained
½ cup heavy cream
celery salt, salt and pepper
1 small head Boston lettuce

Arrange lettuce leaves around salad bowl. Place 4 tomato halves in center. Combine pineapple, green pepper and string beans and dress with cream flavored with salts and pepper. Mound mixture over tomatoes and serve. If preferred, a little French dressing can be mixed with the cream.

ATECA SALAD

1 can French string beans, drained
4 lettuce leaves
½ cup bottled Italian dressing
1 onion, sliced thin and divided into
    rings

½ clove garlic, crushed
¼ teaspoon each dried chervil,
    oregano, rosemary and
    tarragon

Arrange beans on lettuce leaves in a salad bowl. Shake dressing with garlic and herbs, pour over beans. Cover with onion rings and serve.

BEET SALAD

1 16-ounce can sliced beets, drained
1 small white onion, sliced thin
1 small head Boston or Bibb lettuce

2 tablespoons Italian dressing
2 tablespoons orange mayonnaise
salt and pepper

Arrange beets and onions on lettuce leaves in salad bowl. Mix dressing and mayonnaise, season to taste and pour over salad. Mix just before serving.

SALAMANCA SALAD I AND II

Variation I

1 Spanish onion, sliced very thin
1 tomato, peeled and sliced thin
1 cucumber, sliced thin

4 lettuce leaves
¼ cup French dressing, or to taste
½ cup bread crumbs

salt and pepper

Arrange overlapping slices of onion, tomato and cucumber on lettuce leaves. Pour over dressing and sprinkle salad with seasoned crumbs.

Variation II

Prepare onion, tomato and cucumber on lettuce leaves, as above. Pour over a dressing made of 2 tablespoons French dressing, 2 tablespoons mayonnaise and 2 tablespoons tiny white pearl cocktail onions. Omit bread crumbs and serve.

EGG SALAD

4 poached eggs, or 4 5-minute eggs, shelled
½ bunch radishes, sliced

mayonnaise
1 small head Boston lettuce
salt, pepper and paprika

Line salad bowl with lettuce leaves. Arrange eggs in center and surround with a ring of radish salad (sliced radishes bound with mayonnaise). Sprinkle with seasonings and serve.

HUMBERTO SALAD

2 tomatoes, peeled and sliced
1 small head Boston or Bibb lettuce
¼ cup Italian dressing
1 pimento, minced

1 tablespoon frozen minced chives, thawed, or fresh chopped chives

Arrange tomato slices and crisp lettuce in salad bowl. Just before serving add dressing mixed with minced pimento. Sprinkle with chives and toss just before serving.

ROMAINE SALAD

1 head romaine lettuce
1 cucumber, sliced on slicer
4–6 spinach leaves, torn into pieces
1 tablespoon mayonnaise

2 tablespoons French dressing
1 teaspoon capers
1 teaspoon pickle relish, drained
salt and pepper

Break romaine lettuce leaves into quarters, mix with cucumber and spinach leaves. Combine mayonnaise, dressing, capers and relish and shake or stir well, pour over salad. Correct seasoning and serve.

BURGOS SALAD

4 tomatoes, peeled and sliced	1 teaspoon finely minced basil
1 onion, sliced thin	¼ cup French dressing
6 sprigs parsley, ground through Mouli	¼ cup crumbled Roquefort cheese
	salt and pepper

Arrange tomatoes and onion in a salad bowl. Season and sprinkle with parsley and basil. Pour over dressing and sprinkle with cheese. Mix and serve.

MIKADO SALAD

4 tomatoes, peeled and sliced	1 garlic clove, crushed
½ cup frozen chopped onion, thawed	1 teaspoon dried chervil
	½ teaspoon dried tarragon
2 tablespoons chopped chives, frozen or fresh	¼ cup French dressing

Combine sliced tomatoes, chopped onion and chives. Mix garlic and dried herbs with dressing and pour over the tomatoes. This salad is nicer with fresh cut chives when obtainable.

Cabbage comes ready-shredded. In some cases it is even combined with shredded carrots and other ingredients that enhance the coleslaw. Here are two recipes for using the prepared packages as the Danes and Germans do.

DANISH COLESLAW

2 packages prepared coleslaw or 2 cups finely shredded cabbage	1 tablespoon vinegar
	2 tablespoons frozen chopped chives, thawed
¾ cup sour cream, whipped	1 4-ounce wedge Danish Blue cheese, crumbled
1 tart apple, peeled, cored and sliced	
salt and pepper	

Combine all ingredients except the cheese. Chill until needed, sprinkle with the cheese and serve. If this slaw is prepared long before it is needed, omit the apple until just before serving.

GERMAN COLESLAW

2 packages shredded cabbage
¼ cup sour cream
¼ cup French dressing
1 teaspoon dry mustard

1 teaspoon caraway seeds
1 tablespoon frozen chopped onion, thawed
3 tablespoons grated cheese

salt and pepper

Beat sour cream with remaining ingredients, season to taste and pour over well-drained shredded cabbage.

Since very good white potatoes now come in jars and cans we include five potato salads here. Drain the potatoes well before using them and dry them with a kitchen towel.

GERMAN SUPPER SALAD

1 1-pound can potatoes, sliced
1 large dill pickle, sliced
1 apple, cored and sliced
1 jar herring in white wine

1 onion, sliced thin
4 sprigs parsley, chopped through Mouli

Sauce

½ cup mayonnaise
1 tablespoon tarragon vinegar

1 tablespoon bottled French dressing
1 tablespoon sour cream

1 tablespoon brown mustard

Arrange all ingredients in a serving platter or tray. Mix the sauce and pour it into a separate sauce bowl. Let guests serve themselves or pour the sauce over the salad and mix salad at the table just before serving it. Pass buttered black bread separately.

SOUR CREAM AND DILL POTATO SALAD

1 1-pound can tiny whole white potatoes	½ sweet apple, cored
	¼ cup tarragon vinegar
3 stalks celery	½ cup sour cream
1 slice onion	2 teaspoons minced or dry dill
salt, pepper and paprika	

Drain potatoes. Dice celery, onion and unpeeled apple and combine with potatoes in a salad bowl. Pour over vinegar and season with salt and pepper. Just before serving beat sour cream with half the dill and pour over salad. Stir with a wooden spoon to coat potatoes well. Correct seasoning and sprinkle with paprika and remaining dill.

SALADE ANDRÉA

1 can small white potatoes, drained	6 tablespoons mayonnaise
1 can French string beans, drained	salt and pepper
3 tender celery stalks, sliced	Boston lettuce leaves
2 tomatoes, sliced	

Combine potatoes and beans with celery and carefully fold in mayonnaise. Season and arrange salad in a lettuce-lined bowl. Garnish with a ring of tomato slices.

SALADE ALSACIENNE

1 1-pound can potatoes, sliced	1 teaspoon minced onion
1 1-pound can sliced beets	salt and pepper
¼ cup mayonnaise	4 lettuce leaves
1 tablespoon grated horseradish	4 parsley sprigs
1 teaspoon each, dried chervil and tarragon	Boston lettuce leaves

Drain potatoes and beets well. Mix mayonnaise, horseradish, herbs and onion and season to taste. Just before serving arrange lettuce leaves in a salad bowl. Pour the sauce over potatoes and beets and mound the salad in the center of the bowl. Chop parsley over the salad through a Mouli and serve at once. Mix in the last moment, otherwise the beets will stain the potatoes red.

POTATO SALAD UNDER GREEN SAUCE
(In Blender)

2 1-pound cans small white potatoes,
    sliced
¾ cup mayonnaise
2 tablespoons tarragon vinegar
2 tablespoons white wine
1 teaspoon lemon juice
½ clove garlic, crushed

12 parsley sprigs, stems removed
6 sprigs watercress, stems removed
2 spinach leaves
½ bunch scallions or spring onions,
    with 1 inch of green tops
2 anchovy filets
pepper to taste

Combine mayonnaise with all remaining ingredients in blender and blend just long enough to chop greens and scallions roughly. Pour over potatoes and serve. If anchovies are omitted, substitute salt to taste.

In many well regulated households there are certain tasks left to the man of the house. In this field the salad, or at least some of the salads, should run neck and neck with mixing drinks and broiling meat.

Any man who lets his wife usurp these duties isn't a man, he's a parasite or one of those types who doesn't know or care what he is eating, in which case his wife has long since given up cooking anyway.

But for the man who mixes all decent, manly salads and leaves the cottage cheese and coleslaw type of luncheon salad, including fruit salads, to his wife, here are a few hints. They are usually not necessary; men seem to come into the world with an instinct for mixing salads.

To wash Boston lettuce, remove the outside leaves. Cut out the stem by cutting a hollow in the bottom of the head which will permit the leaves to fall apart without breaking or unnecessary handling. Wash the leaves lightly. The innermost leaves and heart are usually so protected that they don't require washing. Spread on a towel or wrap in a towel or shake in a French lettuce basket so that the leaves are dried. The wrapped leaves can be placed in the refrigerator or they can be spread out on a towel in a cool place until needed. The filled lettuce basket can be whirled and then hung in a cool place until needed.

Iceberg lettuce can be used as it comes after the outside leaves and stem have been removed. Romaine lettuce should be treated like Boston lettuce. Being less delicate, it can be a little more vigorously handled and shaken. Endive stalks should be trimmed, the root end should be cut off about ¼ inch up and the outside leaves removed.

Bibb lettuce and escarole are handled like Boston lettuce.

Watercress has to have rough stems removed. All wilted or crushed sprigs have to be discarded. Wash remaining leaves, shake in a towel and wrap in aluminum foil. Store in refrigerator until needed.

TOSSED GREEN SALAD

2 heads Boston lettuce	1 small head romaine lettuce
½ bunch watercress	1 bunch scallions, roughly sliced
1 small head chicory,	½ cucumber, sliced thin on a
inside leaves only	metal cutter
6 tablespoons French dressing	

Prepare lettuces and cress and combine with scallions and cucumber in a large deep salad bowl. Pour over the dressing. Toss lightly but well enough so that all leaves are coated. Serve at once.

Spinach leaves and any other salad greens can be added or subtracted. Just see that they are dry and crisp.

RICARDO'S SALAD

1 garlic clove	¼ teaspoon dry mustard
1 tablespoon coarse salt	3 tablespoons oil
¼ teaspoon anise seed	1 tablespoon tarragon vinegar
10 black peppercorns	6 dashes Maggi seasoning
2 heads Boston lettuce	

Substitute any other lettuce or combinations of salad greens for the Boston lettuce according to your taste.

Separate the lettuce leaves. Wash them separately and shake them well. Refrigerate the leaves, wrapped in a kitchen towel, while mixing the dressing. Lettuce can be prepared at any time and can stay in the refrigerator until needed. Mix the dressing in your (unwashed) wooden salad bowl. Add the crisp dry lettuce, toss and serve.

Mix the dressing as follows:

Crush garlic into salad bowl through a garlic press. Add salt and anise seed and crush together with a wooden spoon, bearing down heavily. Add peppercorns and continue to crush with spoon until they are coarsely broken. Mix in mustard and stir in oil. Add vinegar, stir again and add Maggi seasoning. Dunk a lettuce leaf into the dressing and taste.

At this point I asked Ricardo whether the usual cookbook phrase should follow, "Taste and correct seasoning." But he said it was just to taste, period. He tells me that he doesn't taste for anything, any more than the average man tastes the first swallow of wine for anything. If the first test leaf tastes good he serves the salad; if it doesn't taste good he serves the salad. Perhaps with regret but never with any attempt to change it.

BACON SALAD

1 small head Boston lettuce	salt, pepper and sugar
½ head iceberg lettuce	2 slices bacon
1 tablespoon tarragon vinegar	

Arrange crisp lettuce in salad bowl, sprinkle with seasonings: use salt to taste, grind black pepper over the lettuce, and add a good pinch of sugar. Cut bacon into ½-inch squares with a kitchen scissors and fry until brown. Add vinegar to bacon and stir well in the pan. Pour over the lettuce, mix and serve at once.

Tender canned artichoke hearts lend themselves to many combinations. Drain them well and add them to Boston lettuce, add a few capers to Italian dressing and pour it over the salad. Do not toss or stir too hard, as the artichoke hearts break very easily (like any heart) and have to be handled thoughtfully.

SALAD OF ARTICHOKE HEARTS

1 7-ounce can whole hearts of
    artichoke, drained
½ teaspoon dry mustard
½ cup mayonnaise
2 tablespoons chopped scallions
    or onion
¼ clove garlic, crushed

½ teaspoon dried or
    fresh tarragon
½ lemon, juice only
salt, pepper and paprika
½ head lettuce
2 tablespoons capers
3 parsley sprigs

Stir mustard into a little mayonnaise until smooth, add remaining mayonnaise, scallions, garlic, tarragon and lemon juice. Season to taste with salt, pepper and paprika. Arrange lettuce leaves in a salad bowl. Combine artichoke hearts and mayonnaise sauce and mound in the center of the bowl. Sprinkle with capers and grind the parsley sprigs over the artichokes through a Mouli.

STROMBOLI

1 8½-ounce can hearts of artichoke,
    drained
1 7-ounce can or fresh cooked
    crab meat
1 small jar black caviar

¼ cup mayonnaise
¼ cup Italian dressing
½ teaspoon each dried oregano,
    tarragon, chervil and parsley
6 Boston lettuce leaves

Combine artichokes, crab meat and caviar and arrange on lettuce leaves in a salad bowl. Beat mayonnaise, Italian dressing and herbs and pour over the salad. Mix before serving.

The gourds make good salads. Don't let the cooking of the zucchini frighten you. If it is young and tender and thinly sliced it cooks for only a minute. Cucumbers are sliced raw. If you have a metal slicer it takes only a minute and the top of your middle finger. Watch it.

ZUCCHINI SALAD

4 small zucchini
1 lemon, slivered rind, and
    1 tablespoon juice
salt

¼ cup Italian dressing
½ teaspoon each, dried oregano,
    chervil and tarragon

Peel thin yellow rind from lemon with a potato peeler and cut into thin slices with a kitchen scissors or knife. Slice zucchini thin and plunge into boiling, salted water for 1½ minutes. Take out with a slotted spoon, drain well. Pour commercial Italian dressing, to which dried herbs and lemon juice have been added, over the zucchini while they are hot. Sprinkle with lemon rind and serve. If there is time, place salad in refrigerator until needed.

GRAPE AND ZUCCHINI SALAD

4 small zucchini
¾ cup seedless grapes, chilled

¼ cup bottled French dressing
½ teaspoon oregano

salt and pepper

Slice zucchini thin on a metal slicer and drop into boiling salted water. Boil about 3 minutes, or until slices are slightly transparent. Drain, season and cool. Combine with grapes and dressing and sprinkle with oregano.

TURKISH CUCUMBER SALAD

4 cucumbers, peeled and sliced thin
on metal slicer
1 clove garlic, crushed

1/3 cup cottage cheese
1/3 cup sour cream
salt and pepper

½ bunch fresh chives in season

Arrange sliced and drained cucumbers in a bowl. Season well. Mix garlic, cottage cheese and sour cream into a thick sauce in the blender. Add chives to the sauce while it is blending. Pour sauce over the cucumbers and add 4 cold (deep-freeze type) ice cubes and serve at once.

If no blender is available, chop the chives well with a vegetable mincer and crush the garlic in a press.

ONION AND CUCUMBER SALAD WITH SOUR CREAM DRESSING

1 small head Boston lettuce
4 small white onions, sliced thin and separated into rings
1 cucumber, sliced thin on a metal slicer

½ cup sour cream
1 small lemon, juice only
1 teaspoon each of dried or fresh chopped dill, chervil, tarragon and parsley

salt and freshly ground black pepper

Prepare lettuce, onion rings and cucumber slices in a salad bowl. Beat or whip sour cream with remaining ingredients and pour the dressing over the salad. Mix just before serving.

PARIS SALAD

2 heads lettuce
1 cucumber, sliced thin on metal slicer
2 tomatoes, peeled, seeded and sliced

½ cup or 1 4-ounce can sliced mushrooms, drained
¼ cup mayonnaise
1 tablespoon tart herb dressing

Arrange lettuce in bowl, cover with cucumber slices. Cover cucumber with tomato slices and end with mushrooms. Pour over mayonnaise mixed with herb dressing and toss just before serving.

The next four salads are the hearty Sunday-night-supper type. With an omelet or a rarebit, or all by themselves with toasted bread, they make wonderful meals. Don't forget the red wine or Sangría.

HAM SALAD

¼ pound boiled sliced ham, cut into long slivers with kitchen scissors
2 Boston lettuces
¼ cup frozen chopped onion, thawed
2 tablespoons grated Parmesan cheese

½ small iceberg lettuce
10 crisp, washed spinach leaves
¼ cup French dressing
1 teaspoon brown mustard
1 teaspoon small capers
4 sprigs parsley, ground through Mouli

Combine first 6 ingredients in a large salad bowl. Mix dressing with mustard and capers and pour it over the salad. Grind parsley over the top and toss just before serving.

PASTORAL SALAD

1 jar or can small white onions, drained
2 tablespoons sweet pickle relish, drained
6 anchovy filets, chopped
1 can tuna fish

1 tablespoon capers
10 stuffed olives, sliced
1 tablespoon each, chopped or dry parsley, chives and chervil
salt and pepper
lettuce leaves

½ cup French dressing

Combine all ingredients and arrange on lettuce leaves. Pour over dressing. Stir the salad just before serving.

Make a meal of this with toasted English muffins and red wine.

SALADE CATALAN

1 head romaine lettuce
20 ripe pitted olives, sliced
1/3 cup French dressing

¾ cup cold cooked meat—ham, tongue, veal or chicken, cut julienne

Break inside leaves of the romaine into pieces and arrange in a salad bowl. Cover with olives and top with julienne of meat. Pour dressing over salad and mix just before serving.

SWISS CHEESE SALAD I AND II

Variation I

½ pound Swiss cheese, slivered or diced
½ cup French dressing

1 teaspoon prepared mustard
½ cup frozen chopped onion, thawed

salt and pepper

Mix dressing, mustard, onion and seasonings in bowl, add cheese and mix. Surround with lettuce leaves and serve.

Variation II

½ cup mayonnaise
1 diced celery stalk
3 sliced radishes

4 parsley stalks, ground through
Mouli
½ cup chopped nuts

Follow Swiss Cheese Salad I, substitute mayonnaise for French dressing. Add celery, radishes and parsley to recipe and garnish with nuts.

P E A S A N T   S A L A D

Whenever a recipe calls for crushed nuts, place the nuts between 2 pieces of waxed paper and crush them with a rolling pin. This method works with pecans, pistachios, walnuts and cashews, but Brazil nuts, almonds, filberts and macadamia nuts have to be chopped.

1 head Boston lettuce
½ garlic clove
1 stale bread crust
1 teaspoon dried chervil
1 tablespoon crushed pecans or
walnuts

2 tablespoons chopped chives, fresh
or frozen
2 tablespoons mayonnaise
1 tablespoon French dressing
1 teaspoon prepared mustard

Rub salad bowl and bread crust with garlic. Arrange clean, crisp lettuce leaves in bowl with bread crust, sprinkle with nuts, chives and chervil. Mix mayonnaise, French dressing and mustard and pour the sauce over the salad. Mix the salad just before serving it, and remove the crust.

E N D I V E   S A L A D

8 stalks endive
¼ garlic clove, crushed
½ cup herb dressing

1 wedge Blue or Roquefort cheese
1 tablespoon fresh chopped or
dry chervil

Trim endive, cut in quarters lengthwise and divide over 4 salad plates. Crush garlic into dressing and shake well. Pour over endive. Divide cheese over the salad and sprinkle with chervil.

ENDIVE AND APPLE SALAD

4 stalks endive, cut into strips
4 slices Swiss cheese, cut into strips
1 apple, peeled, cored and cut into
  long slivers

4 lettuce leaves
2 tablespoons Italian dressing
1 tablespoon chopped pimento

Cut endive stalks into 4–6 long strips. Cut cheese into long thin slivers across the width of the cheese slices and mix with the endive strips. Arranging all in the same direction, add apple strips and arrange salad on lettuce leaves on 4 plates. Pour over dressing and garnish with pimento.

DUTCH APPLE SALAD

2 apples, peeled, cored and sliced
2 onions, sliced thin
1 head Boston lettuce
1 teaspoon lemon juice

1 teaspoon grated or slivered lemon
  rind
¼ cup French dressing
paprika

Combine apple and onion slices and arrange on lettuce in a salad bowl. Add lemon juice and rind to dressing and pour over the salad. Sprinkle with paprika and serve.

CHERRY SALAD

1 large can pitted sweet cherries
½ envelope slivered almonds
1 head Boston lettuce
½ bunch watercress

¼ cup French dressing or more
  to taste
1 pinch cinnamon
1 teaspoon paprika

½ 4-ounce package cream cheese

Arrange lettuce and watercress in bowl, add cherries and almonds. Mix dressing with cinnamon and paprika and pour it over the salad. Just before serving rice the cheese through a medium-fine strainer over the surface of the salad.

FRUIT SALAD

1 8-ounce can grapefruit sections, drained	½ envelope pistachio nuts
1 head Boston lettuce	1 tablespoon apricot jam
½ bunch watercress	2 tablespoons French dressing
	salt and pepper

Arrange grapefruit, lettuce, watercress and nuts in bowl. Stir jam into dressing. Season to taste and pour over salad in bowl. Toss and serve.

SALAD BELLE HÉLÈNE

1 can pineapple chunks	¾ cup whipped cream topping
4 lettuce leaves	½ cup ketchup

Arrange drained pineapple chunks on lettuce leaves and pour over a sauce of whipped cream folded into ketchup. Serve cold.

Salad Dressings

There are now such good salad dressings on the market that we suggest keeping a few of them on hand in your refrigerator. Mix your own when there is time, or decant the bottled variety and mix with such additions as you prefer. If you need the dressing suddenly, hold the bottle under the warm-water tap until the oil is liquified.

There is a second method of obtaining excellent dressings, which is to mix an envelope of dressing base with vinegar and oil. The envelope gives proper proportions, although I find that the water can be omitted and the amount of water substituted by half oil and half vinegar. This may sound like heresy, but the fact remains that our lettuces and other ingredients may not be quite as dry as the manufacturer hopes and so a little water goes into the dressing in any case.

Of the bottled varieties, you must lay them in according to your taste. For the average household and for the following recipes we would suggest a bottle each of: French dressing, Italian dressing, herb dressing, and Roquefort dressing.

The Italian dressing can have half a teaspoon of oregano added to the bottle. Chopped onion, pimento and capers can be added when the dressing is used, but should not be added to the bottle. A split garlic clove can be put into the bottle if you want the real Italian taste.

The herb dressing can be shaken up with any additional herbs, fresh or dried, that you fancy: chervil, chives, tarragon and oregano.

French dressing can stay as it is and have minced onion added for some salads.

The Roquefort dressing is good thinned half and half with French dressing.

If you are going to stock oil and tarragon vinegar and the little envelopes of dressing base, then be sure to have a supply of French and Italian envelopes as well as any others that tempt you. They are all good.

If you mix your own, prepare them and store them or mix them in the bowl, as in Ricardo's Salad.

We bring you 2 blender mayonnaises and a few blender dressings, that can be made in less than a minute and stored.

ROQUEFORT DRESSING I THROUGH III

Variation I

1 4-ounce wedge Roquefort cheese, at room temperature	2 tablespoons tarragon vinegar
6 tablespoons oil	2 tablespoons lemon juice
	salt and pepper

Crush cheese with a fork, stir in oil, vinegar and lemon juice until smooth. Season to taste. Thin with oil if dressing is too thick.

Variation II

Add ¼ cup mayonnaise, ¼ cup sour cream and 2 teaspoons anchovy paste to the above. Ducks take to water as this dressing takes to sliced tomatoes and onions.

Variation III

To one recipe Roquefort Dressing, Variation I, add 2 tablespoons sherry. Thin with sour cream if dressing is too thick.

COMBINATION DRESSING I AND II

Variation I

1/3 cup bottled French dressing (use one of the sharp dressings)

1/3 cup bottled Roquefort dressing

1/3 cup mayonnaise

Stir well and serve over tomato, tossed green, egg or orange salad.

Variation II

¼ cup bottled herb dressing
¼ cup mayonnaise
¼ cup heavy cream
2 tablespoons minced onion

1 teaspoon each, dried tarragon, chervil and oregano
1 tablespoon prepared mustard

Beat all ingredients. Rub salad bowl with garlic and discard (garlic). Half fill salad bowl with crisp greens, pour over as much dressing as desired, about 1 tablespoon per person, toss salad and serve.

CELERY SEED DRESSING

1 teaspoon salt
1 teaspoon dry mustard
1 tablespoon sugar
1 tablespoon minced onion

1 pinch anise seed
½ cup vinegar
½ cup oil, cold
1 ice cube
¼ cup heavy cream, chilled

1 teaspoon celery seed

In a salad bowl stir salt, mustard and sugar with a wooden spoon. Add anise seed and bear down hard enough with the spoon to grind the seeds. Add onion and grind it into the dry ingredients with the back of the wooden spoon. Stir in vinegar, add oil and beat with ice cube until dressing is thickened. Remove what is left of ice cube, beat in cream and celery seed and serve with mixed or green salads or vegetable salads.

ITALIAN DRESSING

1/3 cup tarragon vinegar
1 teaspoon salt
1 teaspoon dry mustard
2 teaspoons sugar
1 teaspoon paprika
¼ teaspoon black pepper

2/3 cup oil
1 garlic clove, split
1 pimento, minced
1 teaspoon smallest capers
½ teaspoon each dried oregano and
  chervil

Stir a little of the vinegar into the dry ingredients until salt and sugar are dissolved and mustard is smooth. Add remaining vinegar and stir well. Add oil and stir or shake until the dressing is smooth.

Add the garlic clove, pimento, capers and herbs and set dressing aside until needed. Remove garlic, shake well and use dressing at the rate of 2 tablespoons of dressing for a mixed salad for 2 people.

FRENCH DRESSING

1 teaspoon salt
2 teaspoons sugar
3 teaspoons prepared mustard

freshly ground black pepper
1 garlic clove, split
3 tablespoons tarragon vinegar

6 tablespoons oil, cold

Shake all ingredients in a bottle until thick and smooth. If oil is too warm add an ice cube. Remove cube and keep dressing cold until needed. Do not keep it so cold that the oil will coagulate, but cold enough to be lightly thickened. Just before using, take out garlic clove.

SPICED FRENCH DRESSING

1 cup oil
1/3 cup lemon juice
3 tablespoons sugar
3 tablespoons ketchup
1 tablespoon Worcestershire sauce

1½ teaspoons salt
1 teaspoon dry mustard
½ teaspoon paprika
1 slice onion
½ clove garlic, peeled

2 drops Tabasco sauce

Blend all ingredients until smooth. Serve with mixed green salads, seafood and vegetable salads.

BLENDER FRENCH DRESSING

1½ teaspoons salt
1 teaspoon paprika
¼ teaspoon pepper
1 teaspoon dry mustard
2 teaspoons sugar

½ cup tarragon vinegar
3/4 cup oil
¼ cup tomato ketchup
1 thin slice onion
2 sprigs parsley, stems removed

Put all ingredients in blender and blend until parsley and onion are finely minced.

BLENDER MAYONNAISE
WITH VARIATIONS I THROUGH IV

1 egg
½ teaspoon salt
2 tablespoons tarragon vinegar

¼ teaspoon dry mustard
1 pinch each, sugar and white pepper
1 cup oil

Blend egg with dry ingredients, vinegar and 2 tablespoons of the oil for a few seconds, until smooth. Open top of blender and add remaining oil in a thin stream. When the oil is all added the mayonnaise will be thick. Stir with spatula, blend for 1 second longer and chill until needed.

Variation I

ONION MAYONNAISE

To 1 recipe Mayonnaise add 2 onion slices and 4 parsley sprigs (stems removed) and blend until onion is finely chopped.

Variation II

TARTAR MAYONNAISE

To 1 recipe Mayonnaise add 2 onion slices, 2 parsley sprigs and ½ tablespoon capers and blend until onion is chopped (do not blend until it is minced). Mix with ¼ cup drained pickle relish and serve with deep-fried oysters, scallops, clams, fish foods and shell fish. Increase relish or add chopped dill pickle to taste.

Variation III

LEMON MAYONNAISE

To 1 recipe Mayonnaise add 2 teaspoons lemon juice (reduce vinegar accordingly) and 2 curls of lemon rind cut from lemon with a potato peeler. Blend until rind is minced.

Variation IV

CURRY MAYONNAISE

To 1 recipe Mayonnaise add 1 teaspoon curry powder and 2 tablespoons chutney. Blend until chutney is chopped medium fine. Increase curry powder to taste.

OLIVE DRESSING

1 8-fluid-ounce bottle Italian dressing	6 large stuffed olives, sliced
1 3-ounce section Roquefort cheese	½ teaspoon dried oregano
	1 dash Worcestershire sauce

Pour ¼ of the Italian dressing into salad bowl. Stir in crumbled Roquefort with a wooden spoon and add Worcestershire sauce and oregano after cheese is soft and smooth. Stir in remaining dressing and olives and add crisp mixed greens. Use Boston lettuce, iceberg and/or romaine, tomatoes, cucumbers; in fact use this dressing with any mixed or plain salad.

SPANISH DRESSING

1 cup oil	1½ teaspoons sugar
2 teaspoons salt	2 slices onion
1 teaspoon pepper	2 slices green pepper
½ cup tarragon vinegar	1 pimento, canned
4 sprigs parsley, stems removed	

Blend until pepper and onion are finely chopped. Serve with vegetable, green, fish, avocado and meat salads.

GARLIC DRESSING

1 garlic clove, crushed	1 pinch anise seed
1 teaspoon salt	1 teaspoon minced parsley
½ teaspoon freshly ground pepper	3 tablespoons tarragon vinegar
6 tablespoons olive oil	

Crush garlic into a wooden salad bowl, add salt, pepper, anise seed and parsley and crush together into a paste with a wooden salad spoon. Stir in vinegar and add oil very slowly, stirring constantly. Put mixed salad greens into the bowl and set aside until ready to serve. Fatigue (or mix) greens and dressing for a minute, then serve.

MINT DRESSING

1 cup oil	¼ teaspoon black pepper
1/3 cup tarragon vinegar	2 teaspoons minced onion
1½ teaspoons salt	2 teaspoons chopped mint

Combine all ingredients in a bottle and shake well. Pour over grape, melon ball or avocado salad.

COOKED SOUR CREAM DRESSING

¼ cup orange juice

¼ cup sugar

1 scant teaspoon dry mustard

¼ teaspoon salt

1 egg

1 cup sour cream

onion salt, or 1 dash onion juice

In the top of a double boiler stir orange juice into sugar, mustard and salt. Add egg and beat until smooth. Place over simmering water and stir or whisk until thick. Place in refrigerator to cool. Stir in sour cream, correct seasoning and serve over green, avocado or fruit salads. Grate the orange rind, if you didn't discard it, over the salad.

CUCUMBER SALAD SAUCE

¼ pound cottage cheese

1 cup yogurt

2 tablespoons cut chives

½ teaspoon Worcestershire sauce

salt, pepper and paprika

Stir or blend cheese and yogurt until smooth, add remaining ingredients and pour over sliced cucumber salad. Dust with a little paprika.

SOUR CREAM DRESSING

½ pint heavy sour cream

2 tablespoons tarragon vinegar

1 tablespoon brown sugar

1 teaspoon dry mustard

1 teaspoon lemon juice

¼ teaspoon paprika

salt and pepper

½ bunch chives, or 2 tablespoons frozen chives, thawed

Whip sour cream until smooth and thick. Beat in vinegar, sugar, mustard, lemon juice and paprika. Season dressing well and pour over thinly sliced cucumbers, radishes or any crisp vegetable salad. Sprinkle with chives. This is also a good dressing for coleslaw, which can be purchased ready cut at most markets.

Relishes

The relish is supposed to do all that the name implies for the dish that it accompanies. It is supposed to enhance meats and fish, lend them spice and interest and generally pep up the whole situation.

The relish tray that looks so attractive is usually a combination of appetizers and savory additions to the main course. Often it includes cottage cheese and jellies, in which case it is supposed to enhance the bread or rolls and butter. Celery and olives, carrot sticks and radishes are assembled with bottled sweet pickles, mustard pickles and sliced dill pickles. Here are a few quickly made relishes that can be added. Chutney, salted nuts, fried coconut, pistachios and pickled watermelon rind are good additions, depending on the menu. All you need is one of those pretty divided dishes and you are off. After that you can compose from cranberry sauce to a can of button mushrooms mixed with sharp mustard and French dressing.

TOMATO RELISH

1 jar tomato paste	2 tablespoons heavy rum
¼ cup brown sugar	1 teaspoon grated lemon rind
salt and pepper to taste	

Stir all ingredients together and serve with meats.

COTTAGE CHEESE RELISH

1 1-pound container cottage cheese	½ cup frozen chopped onion, thawed
½ teaspoon salt	
½ teaspoon celery salt	½ cucumber, put through vegetable chopper
½ cup sour cream	paprika and black pepper

Add salts, cream, chopped onion and cucumber to cottage cheese and beat until well mixed. Arrange on relish tray and sprinkle with crossed lines of paprika and black pepper.

RAW CRANBERRY RELISH

1 package fresh cranberries, stems
    picked off
       1 3-ounce envelope walnuts, broken

2 oranges, quartered
1 cup sugar, or to taste

Put berries and oranges through food chopper and drain well. Add nuts to sugar and stir into pulp. Moisten with as much of the drained-off juice as desired. This relish will keep in refrigerator. Serve with poultry or meat.

GARDEN RELISH

4 tomatoes, peeled and quartered
1 green pepper, seeded
1 cucumber, roughly sliced
½ cup frozen chopped onion,
    thawed

½ teaspoon salt
½ teaspoon celery salt
black pepper

Put tomatoes, green pepper and cucumber through food chopper and drain well. Add onion, salts and freshly ground black pepper. Chill and serve.

RED RELISH

2 16-ounce cans chopped beets,
    drained
½ small head of cabbage
¾ cup sugar, or to taste
1 teaspoon salt

1 teaspoon dried dill
2 tablespoons grated horseradish,
    drained
1 cup tarragon vinegar
1 teaspoon caraway seeds

Put cabbage through food chopper and add to well-drained beets. Add sugar, salt, dill and horseradish to vinegar and shake or stir until sugar is dissolved. Pour over mixed beets and cabbage. Correct seasoning and serve sprinkled with caraway seeds.

PICKLED BINGS

1 1-pound can Bing cherries,
    drained
¼ cup brown sugar

½ cup vinegar
salt to taste

Bring ½ cup cherry juice to boil with sugar and vinegar.
Pour over cherries. Season to taste and chill. Increase sugar or salt,
depending on sweetness of cherries.

FRIED PINEAPPLE

6 slices canned pineapple
flour for dredging
paprika
butter for frying

3 tablespoons chopped nuts—pecans,
walnuts or cashews
6 sprigs parsley

Sprinkle well-dredged pineapple slices with paprika and fry
in butter until brown on both sides, about 2 minutes per side.
Sprinkle with nuts and garnish center with parsley. Use to garnish
meat or poultry. Arrange around pork chops, ham steak, duck or
lamp chops.

PINEAPPLE RELISH I AND II

Variation I

1 10-ounce can pineapple chunks,
drained
1 cup vinegar

½ teaspoon cinnamon
½ teaspoon ground cloves
½ teaspoon broken ginger root
1 lemon

Drain pineapple. Heat vinegar with ground cinnamon and
cloves and ginger root and stir until spices are dissolved. Grate
lemon rind over the pineapple chunks and pour over the spiced
vinegar. Add a little of the pineapple juice to taste and chill until
needed.

Variation II

1 can pineapple chunks
½ cup vinegar
¼ teaspoon ground cinnamon

½ teaspoon ground cloves
¼ teaspoon ground ginger
1 tablespoon curry powder
¼–½ cup brown sugar

Drain pineapple and add juice to vinegar. Add next four
ingredients and heat to boiling. Add sugar and pineapple chunks
and cook 4 minutes. Serve hot or cold with meats, curries or turkey.

RED PEPPER SAUCE

1 jar pimento	red wine
1 red pepper, seeded and sliced	salt and paprika

Blend pimento and red pepper in blender, adding enough red wine to make a thick relish. Season with salt and paprika and serve with meat or fish.

MINT RELISH

2 large bunches mint, leaves only	1 small onion, sliced
2 tablespoons candied ginger	½ teaspoon paprika
½ lemon, juice and 1 large curl of rind	salt and pepper to taste

Blend all ingredients in blender until ginger, lemon rind and onion are coarsely chopped. Serve with meat, fish or poultry.

HOT MUSTARD

3 tablespoons dry mustard	6 drops sesame oil or olive oil
1 tablespoon vinegar	

Stir mustard to remove lumps, gradually stir in oil and then the vinegar. Stir in more vinegar, if necessary, to make a smooth, medium-thin mustard relish. Serve with shrimp, beef or fish dishes.

PICKLED MUSHROOMS

2 10-ounce cans button mushrooms	2 tablespoons mixed pickling spices
tarragon vinegar	2 tablespoons oil
salt and pepper	

Empty mushrooms and half their liquid into a small saucepan, add vingear to cover. Add spices and oil and season to taste. Simmer until flavors are well absorbed, about 8 minutes. Cool and store. Drain off liquid when serving.

CHAPTER IX

Sauces

Pᴇᴏᴘʟᴇ ᴀʀᴇ always saying the most dreadful things. They speak of food as "yummy" and "scrumptious" and they speak of adult women (themselves and their friends) as the "girls." As long as they have an inexpensive car they call it a car; when it finally turns into a good one they speak only of its make, even though it is still just a car. By the time they say, "The Ferrari is in the parking lot," the answer, as everyone knows, is, "Which Ferrari?" And anyway it should be garaged. When they speak of cooking and food they hit bottom.

From Dunks and Dips to Drops and Dainties, from Crisps and Crunches to Frizzles and Wiggles. They go from Upside-Down to Roly-Poly and Tangy and Zippy. There is, in fact, a series of words and phrases that can be recited slowly until all appetite is gone and a slight feeling of illness is induced, and that is called the Ugly Word Diet Method.

But all this is as nothing compared to the attitude they take and the words they use when it comes to sauces. They can win an Oscar or a Nobel prize with becoming modesty, but when it comes to a sauce that they have just produced successfully it is always in the first person possessive. It is never just that simple, unassuming little sauce, it is *my* sauce and the better it tastes the louder the stress on the *my*.

If sauces still took a full day to prepare and were still based on stocks that took the two days before that to prepare, if they still had to be reduced for hours and forced through the finest hair-mesh sieve and oiled and buttered, then there might be some justification for all this possessiveness. As it is, we no longer wear ourselves or our elbows out over them, we usually open some jars and bottles and we concoct a little mixture that may be a passably good sauce but it certainly need not be *my* sauce.

This element of personal pride may be irritating but when it comes to a light and smooth hollandaise, it becomes completely insufferable. The creator of this masterpiece cackles away as loudly as the hen which laid the eggs that went into it. Makers of good hollandaise act as though they thought ticker tape should rain down upon them while they serve up *their* hollandaise.

After sauces the next items of uncontrolled pride in the kitchen are omelets and soufflés, but even at worst it usually only goes to: "There are six eggs in this omelet," not, "*I* always use six eggs in *my* béarnaise." All this from men and women who can produce plays, sing arias, race horses, paint paintings or make millions. They still count their real accomplishments as a bagatelle compared to the fact that they got *their* hollandaise to the table and into their guests before it curdled.

Sauce making has (in a lot of words) ceased to be an art or a talent that only a few are endowed with. It's fun to make sauces and the quicker they go the greater the pleasure. It is a way of adding interest and flavor to a dish, it is a way of moistening dry foods or of enlivening dull ones. Sauces can add piquancy and they can add comfort—smooth, creamy comfort—to a food that would otherwise be harsh or brittle. Sauce making is no longer the thing on which your epicurean reputation depends. You can take all the pleasure you want in making sauces, just so long as you don't take pride in them. There are far too many people today who know how to buy a good sauce and how to open the jar. The most that you can do is produce original sauces and quick ones.

Escoffier's sauces were masterpieces. The highest schools of cookery in France and Italy evolved sauces that were dreams of lightness or diabolically hot and tantalizing. There were the great mother sauces and their daughters, there were even little second-cousin-from-the-country sauces. There were also, in that sauce-creative period, some eternal sauces. Those were the ones that were poured over everything you ate, whether fish or fowl, boiled or broiled; they completely drowned out everything from steak to scallops. They were the sauces that succeeded in making everything taste exactly alike and drove traveling Americans and Englishmen back to their native shores where they could find their broiled meats in their natural juices and not drowned in mushroom or tomato sauce or the plain brown paste known as *tunke* that blanketed so many Central European dishes.

But those days are over. Today we dream up a sauce out of a jar of jam or we concoct one out of an avocado. We call it *the* sauce without any mother complexes and while we are watching our language we don't speak of sauce making as "sorcery"—ever. And to the next person who says, "I'll whip up *my Beauharnaise* for you," the answer is, as everyone knows, "Which Beauharnaise?"

MEDIUM CREAM SAUCE

2 tablespoons butter	1 cup milk, warmed
2 tablespoons flour	¼ teaspoon salt
	1 dash pepper

Melt butter in top of double boiler over boiling water. Stir in flour with a wooden spoon until the roux* is smooth and the flour is cooked, about 2 to 3 minutes. Add milk gradually and continue to stir until sauce is thick, about 4 to 5 minutes. Stir vigorously with a whisk to make sauce smooth, season and use as recipes require for sauces and soups. Increase butter and flour for a thicker sauce, increase milk for a thinner sauce.

BROWN SAUCE

2 tablespoons butter	1 cup bouillon
2 tablespoons flour	¼ teaspoon salt

* French word for combined butter and flour. There is no English word.

Brown butter in a saucepan, stir in flour and continue to stir over low heat until smooth and brown, about 2 to 3 minutes. Add bouillon gradually and stir until sauce is thick, about 4 to 5 minutes. Stir with a whisk until smooth, season and use as required.

Increase butter and flour for a thicker sauce. Thin with bouillon. Sauté 1 tablespoon minced onion with the butter and strain the sauce before serving. Any of the brown sauces can be made out of this simple base. Add tomato purée and garlic, Madeira or slivered ham. M. Escoffier may be turning in his grave, but you can still produce a sound brown sauce in less than ten minutes.

The next eight sauces appear here instead of among the salad dressings, as they are sauces which can also be served with meats, vegetables, fish or fruit. Some are good poured over poached eggs, and others are good with smoked fishes. They can be used interchangeably and all of them are good for salads.

SAUCE ANTIBOISE

1 cup mayonnaise	¼ cup tomato purée
2 teaspoons anchovy paste	2 tablespoons chopped or dried
or more to taste	tarragon

salt and pepper to taste

Stir all ingredients into mayonnaise and serve cold with fish. Very good also with fish puddings, Swedish fish balls or five-minute eggs.

GREENWICH MAYONNAISE

1 cup mayonnaise	2 tablespoons grated horseradish
¼ cup thick apple sauce	salt and pepper to taste

Mix all ingredients and serve with ham, pork roast, tongue or duck. This is also good with herring.

SAUCE GÉNOISE

1 cup mayonnaise

6 sprigs parsley

6 leaves washed spinach

1 envelope shelled pistachio nuts

salt and pepper to taste

Blend mayonnaise with spinach and parsley for one minute. Add nuts and season well. Serve cold with hot fish, meats or vegetables.

If blender is not available, chop spinach and parsley fine and blend well with the mayonnaise.

SAUCE VALENTINE

¾ cup mayonnaise

3 tablespoons grated horseradish, drained

3 tablespoons brown mustard

1 tablespoon dried tarragon

Mix all ingredients and serve with cold meat.

ORANGE MAYONNAISE

1 cup mayonnaise

1 orange, slivered rind and juice

salt and black pepper

Stir the slivered rind and orange juice into mayonnaise. Season to taste and serve with asparagus, avocado or endive salad.

HORATIO MAYONNAISE

1 cup mayonnaise

5 minced anchovy filets

1 tablespoon minced chives

juice of ½ lemon

Mix all ingredients and serve with hot or cold fish, hard-cooked eggs or meat.

FLORIDA MAYONNAISE

1 small banana, peeled and cut
 into slices

½ cup mayonnaise
¼ cup chopped pecans
cream to thin

Blend all ingredients, thin to taste with cream and serve with grapefruit salad or mixed fruit salad. Very good with grape salad.

If no blender is available, the banana can be mashed by hand and the pecans chopped finely with a chopper.

AVOCADO DRESSING

1 large, ripe avocado
2 slices onion
2 tablespoons mayonnaise
2 tablespoons sour cream

2 teaspoons lemon juice
1 clove garlic, crushed
3 dashes Tabasco sauce
salt and cayenne to taste

Peel and stone avocado and blend into a smooth paste. Add all other ingredients and blend until onion is finely minced. Serve over sliced oranges, fruit salad or green salad.

If no blender is available, chop the onion well, or use 2 tablespoons frozen chopped onion, thawed, of course.

HOT BREAD CRUMB SAUCE
I THROUGH III
For Potatoes, Vegetables, Meat or Fish

Variation I

6 tablespoons dry bread crumbs
salt and pepper

1 tablespoon chopped chives
¼ cup butter

Fry everything together until crumbs are golden brown. Pour over hot canned whole white potatoes, heated cauliflower or asparagus, or broiled fish steaks. Very good on wax beans.

Prepare any frozen vegetable according to package directions while the crumb sauce is cooking. Take sauce from heat the moment crumbs are the right color and pour over the well-drained vegetable.

Variation II

6 tablespoons dry bread crumbs   salt and pepper
1 tablespoon grated or slivered   ¼ cup butter
    orange rind

Prepare sauce as Hot Bread Crumb Sauce I, substituting the orange rind for the chives. This is a specialty for hot green asparagus. Garnish the platter with orange slices for a main course. Pour the crumb-orange sauce over the hot drained spears.

Variation III

6 tablespoons dry bread crumbs   salt and pepper
½ envelope shaved almonds   1/3 cup butter

Prepare sauce as Hot Bread Crumb Sauce I and serve over French-cut beans and broiled fish.

The next twelve sauces are all Instant Sauces, although they are suggested as accompaniments for tongue, ham, duck and main dishes which are not included in this book. You may have simmered a ham on Sunday or you may want to serve a heated canned ham. We give you the sauces anyway, since you may have only a moment to prepare the sauce for a meat that you put away in the freezer last summer. Cold sliced meats can be bought at any delicatessen, they can be served cold with some of these sauces or they can be heated in the sauce.

COLD MOSCOW SAUCE

2 tablespoons prepared mustard   1 teaspoon sugar
2 tablespoons oil   1 thin slice onion
2 tablespoons vinegar   salt to taste

Put all ingredients in the blender and blend into a smooth sauce. Serve with any meat dish. Especially good with boiled beef, ham, tongue or steaks.

If no blender is available, chop the onion well before adding.

APPLE HORSERADISH SAUCE

1 jar apple sauce

½ cup fresh grated horseradish or drained bottled horseradish

Mix and serve with hot ham or tongue.

RAISIN SAUCE

2 tablespoons brown sugar
½ teaspoon dry mustard
¼ teaspoon salt
pepper to taste
2 tablespoons tarragon vinegar

¾ cup apricot nectar or orange juice
¼ cup molasses
½ cup raisins
¼ cup orange marmalade

1 tablespoon butter

Stir dry ingredients together, gradually add vinegar and nectar. Add molasses, raisins and marmalade and boil 2 minutes. Take from heat, stir in butter and serve with ham, tongue or game.

HANOVER SAUCE

3 tablespoons sugar
1 orange, slivered outer rind
1 tablespoon lemon juice

2 tablespoons prepared mustard
2 tablespoons oil
2 tablespoons port wine

Crush orange rind and sugar together with a wooden spoon. Stir in remaining ingredients and serve with game or duck.

HORSERADISH SAUCE

1 cup sour cream
¼ cup grated horseradish, drained

1 pinch sugar
salt to taste

Combine all ingredients and serve with boiled beef or ham. It is also good with fish or game.

MINT SAUCE FOR ROASTED LAMB

1 cup red currant jelly   ½ teaspoon sweet basil
¼ cup tarragon vinegar   3 tablespoons chopped fresh mint

Melt jelly over hot water. Add vinegar, basil and mint and serve hot or cold with roasted lamb.

MUTTON SAUCE

¼ cup currant jelly   ¼ cup chopped parsley
½ cup port   ¼ cup chopped mint

Chop parsley and mint through a Mouli or in blender. Melt currant jelly over hot water, add port and chopped herbs. Salt to taste and serve with thick broiled mutton chops and mustard potatoes.

MINT SAUCE

⅓ cup mint leaves, ground   1 tablespoon brown sugar
    through Mouli   2/3 cup white wine vinegar
                    salt and pepper to taste

Heat sugar in vinegar until it is dissolved, stir in mint leaves and serve with roast lamb.

WALNUT GARLIC SAUCE

2 slices bread   3 cloves garlic, crushed
½ cup cream   2 tablespoons vinegar
½ cup walnuts   1 teaspoon oil
                    salt and pepper to taste

Soak bread in cream and press out well. Crush walnuts with rolling pin, add garlic and bread and pound to a paste. Slowly stir in vinegar and oil and add a little cream if necessary to make a thick sauce. Season and serve with meat, fish or poultry.

CRANBERRY APRICOT SAUCE

1 16-ounce can apricot halves,
    drained
1/3 cup brown sugar
1½ teaspoons dry mustard
1 can whole cranberry sauce

Blend all ingredients until finely chopped or press apricots and cranberry sauce through a sieve. Heat and serve with meat or poultry.

HOT CHERRY SAUCE

2 cups pitted Bing cherries
1 glass red currant jelly
½ cup port
½ cup sherry
½ cup orange juice
1 tablespoon slivered orange rind
2 tablespoons lemon juice
1 teaspoon slivered lemon rind
¼ teaspoon brown mustard
2 dashes Maggi seasoning
salt to taste

Drain cherries and simmer them with all remaining ingredients, over low heat, until currant jelly is dissolved. Serve with tongue, venison, ham or any smoked pork.

CUCUMBER SAUCE FOR CHICKEN

1 3-ounce package cream cheese,
    at room temperature
1 cup yogurt, beaten
2 tablespoons chopped frozen
    chives, thawed
½ cucumber, roughly sliced
1 dash Worcestershire sauce
salt and pepper
¼ teaspoon paprika

Blend cheese and yogurt until smooth, add remaining ingredients and blend until cucumber is finely chopped. Serve with hot broiled chicken.

If no blender is available, chop cucumber finely with a vegetable mincer.

SAUCE MIGNONETTE

If you can possibly get Tellicherry pepper (Tellicherry is in India) you will find that the flavor is better than any other black pepper. White Flower Farm at Litchfield, Connecticut, went far to make Tellicherry famous by importing the pepper for everyone who came for white flowers and left with white flowers and black pepper.

1 cup tarragon vinegar	2 tablespoons coarsely ground
2/3 cup chopped shallots	or crushed black pepper

Heat vinegar, add shallots and simmer until they are transparent. Add pepper to taste and serve with steak or filet.

PARSLEY SAUCE

8 spinach leaves	½ bunch chives
½ bunch parsley, stems removed	2/3 cup oil
2 sprigs chervil	1/3 cup vinegar
6 sprigs tarragon	salt and pepper to taste

Blend spinach leaves to a paste, gradually add vinegar and remaining herbs, blend 1 minute longer. Season to taste and serve with cold meats and fish. This sauce can be made with parsley only, if other herbs are not available. Serve also with eggs, poultry or vegetables. Very good with tomatoes or cauliflower. Wonderful with rice.

If no blender is available, use a vegetable mincer and a Mouli to chop or grind the vegetables.

Fish need sauces too, and here are eight that may be good with meat or poultry, but their primary reason for being is to go with the fish course. They are welcome in Lent, or for anyone who wants to change a bland white fish into something more interesting. The frozen trout, which are available in all markets now, boil in a few minutes and, served under one of the following sauces, they make a gala hot or cold dish. Salmon steaks are wonderful with the cucumber or anchovy sauces and when you don't know what to do with fish, start with the sauce and just push the fish under it.

WATERCRESS SAUCE

1 bottle Italian dressing   1 bunch watercress, stems removed

Mince watercress in blender or chop it through a Mouli. Use ¼ bottle of dressing to ¼ bunch watercress. Combine minced watercress and dressing and serve with hot or cold fish or with cold chicken. This is an excellent sauce with boiled salmon or trout. Also good with broiled swordfish.

SWEDISH CUCUMBER SAUCE

Although the Swedes eat this with boiled and broiled fish, it is good with a fat and tender broiled broiler.

½ bunch chives, cut in half across   1 tablespoon tarragon vinegar
1 cucumber, cut into thick slices   1 slice onion
½ cup heavy cream, whipped   ½ teaspoon salt
1 tablespoon sugar   salt and pepper to taste

Blend dry ingredients and vinegar, add chives, onion and cucumber and blend long enough to chop cucumber. Fold mixture into whipped cream, add salt if necessary.

If no blender is available, use a vegetable mincer for the chives, cucumber and onion.

SEAFOOD COCKTAIL SAUCE

¾ cup bottled cocktail sauce   2 teaspoons Worcestershire sauce
1 tablespoon lemon juice   2 teaspoons grated onion
1 tablespoon prepared horseradish,   1 dash Tabasco sauce
    drained   salt and pepper

Combine all ingredients and chill. Serve with crab meat, lobster, clams or shrimp. Garnish with lemon wedges.

AVOCADO SAUCE

1 medium avocado
1 teaspoon mustard
2 tablespoons lemon juice
2 tablespoons sour cream

2 tablespoons grated onion
1 dash Worcestershire sauce
salt and pepper
cream for thinning

Mash peeled avocado with remaining ingredients, season to taste and thin to desired consistency with cream. Serve with cold fish or shell fish, orange salad or sliced tomatoes.

ANCHOVY SAUCE FOR HOT SALMON

½ cup butter
1 tablespoon anchovy paste
2 tablespoons chili vinegar

1 tablespoon water or consommé
1 grating of nutmeg
salt and pepper

1 egg yolk

In a double boiler over boiling water whisk butter with anchovy paste, vinegar and consommé until mixture is light and creamy. Season to taste and whisk in egg yolk just before serving.

BULGARIAN SAUCE FOR FISH I AND II

Variation I

¼ cup butter
2 tablespoons parsley, ground
    through Mouli

1 cup ground nuts—walnuts or
    pecans
2 tablespoons lemon juice

salt

Melt butter, add nuts and cook long enough to brown very lightly. Add parsley, lemon juice and salt, and serve with fish. Boiled or broiled fish is especially good with this sauce.

Variation II

Substitute ½ envelope shaved almonds for the ground nuts and pour the sauce over sautéed, boiled or broiled fish. The dish then becomes Trout or Sole Amandine.

SAUCE LIVOURNAISE

1 tablespoon vinegar
salt and freshly ground black pepper
2 egg yolks

½ cup oil
4 sprigs parsley chopped through
     Mouli

1 pinch nutmeg

Stir vinegar with salt and pepper, add egg yolks and stir until light. Gradually stir in oil, adding drop by drop for just a few minutes, then add more quickly. Correct seasoning, add parsley and serve with a dusting of nutmeg. Good with cold meats, fish or salads.

HOLLANDAISE SAUCE

4 egg yolks
1 tablespoon lemon juice

⅔ cup butter
salt and white pepper

Whisk the yolks with the lemon juice in the upper section of a double boiler, over simmering water, until they are creamy. Add the butter, tablespoon by tablespoon, whisking after each addition, until it is completely incorporated before adding the next piece. Season and serve.

To avoid curdling of the sauce, be sure the simmering water in the lower section of the double boiler does not touch the upper section. If the sauce should curdle, add a tablespoon of boiling water, take from heat and whisk until sauce is smooth again.

Set Hollandaise Sauce over warm water if it is not served at once.

Blender Method

Rinse blender in hot water, dry and whirl yolks with lemon juice until smooth. Add hot melted butter in a thin stream, as for mayonnaise, season and serve. Be sure the blender is still warm when the yolks and lemon juice are whirled.

Dessert Sauces

For years now we've been eating brown Betties and puddings for the sake of the hard sauce. And why not? I've always wanted to serve large rosettes of cold hard sauce for each guest and pass a sauceboat of apple-raisin-crumb sauce separately. Some of the paler, blonder desserts are literally only an excuse for the sauce and if there is no sauce there is really no point in eating calories just for fun. Ice creams, plain cakes, fruits and canned puddings are not only improved by sauces, they cry for them.

If you are caught suddenly dessertless, just cut a slice of pound cake into fingers and serve it under any one of the dessert sauces. Pour raspberry sauce over fresh raspberries or strawberries. Serve sherry sauce over sliced oranges or over bought gingerbread. Serve hard sauce with any hot dessert that will melt the sauce and enhance the dessert.

HARD SAUCES I THROUGH IV

Variation I

½ cup soft butter
1½ cups brown sugar
¼ cup strong black coffee

1 dash coffee essence or 1 teaspoon
  instant coffee
1 pinch nutmeg or cinnamon

Cream butter and sugar. Stir in coffee, in which instant coffee should be dissolved, and flavor with nutmeg or cinnamon to taste. Chill until needed.

Variation II

½ cup soft butter
1½ cups confectioners' sugar
12 blanched almonds put through
  Mouli nut grinder

1 tablespoon brandy
1 dash almond essence

Prepare as above and chill until needed.

Variation III

½ cup soft butter
2 tablespoons rum or brandy

1½ cups confectioners' sugar

Beat butter and sugar together and gradually add rum or brandy to taste. Chill until needed.

Variation IV

½ cup butter
1 tablespoon hot cream, or milk
1½ cups confectioners' sugar

1 egg yolk
1 teaspoon cinnamon
1 drop vanilla

Combine sugar and cinnamon. Beat butter, cream, sugar and yolk together until smooth. Add vanilla and chill until needed.

SHERRY SAUCE

3 egg yolks
½ cup sherry

1 tablespoon sugar
2 tablespoons heavy cream

Beat yolks, sherry and sugar in the top of a double boiler, over simmering water, until the sauce thickens. Take from heat, beat in cream and serve over fingers of sliced pound cake, sliced oranges, gingerbread or ice cream.

HOT APRICOT SAUCE

¾ cup apricot jam
½ cup apricot nectar

1 3½-ounce envelope slivered
    almonds
½ cup apricot brandy

Heat jam with nectar, add almonds and brandy. Serve hot or cold with cold puddings, ice cream or babas. Serve with poached fruits, hot puddings, baked ham. Serve the sauce alone with plain cake or fill dessert glasses with the sauce and top with sour cream and dust with cinnamon.

COFFEE SAUCE

½ cup strong instant coffee
½ cup sugar
2 squares semisweet chocolate,
    melted

2 tablespoons butter
½ teaspoon vanilla
1 pinch cinnamon

Boil coffee and sugar 5 minutes. Stir in melted chocolate, butter, vanilla and cinnamon. Beat until smooth and serve with ice cream, puddings, cake or stewed pears.

VANILLA ICE CREAM SAUCE I AND II

Variation I

1 pint vanilla ice cream

1 egg, beaten until light with
2 tablespoons rum

Let vanilla ice cream soften slightly. This happens very quickly; do not let it get too soft. If you store ice cream in freezing compartment, move it to refrigerator and leave it for about an hour. Beat ice cream with electric beater or rotary beater. Beat in egg and rum. Serve sauce with fritters, puddings, brown Betty or poached fruits. Very good with babas, which can be bought at bakeries or in cans.

Variation II

1 pint vanilla ice cream,
    slightly softened

1 cup heavy cream
1 tablespoon rum

Whip cream and scrape out of bowl. Set in refrigerator. Beat ice cream and rum until it is light and smooth, fold in whipped cream and serve as Variation I.

COFFEE WHIP SAUCE

1 tablespoon instant coffee
¼ cup boiling water
¾ cup cream

¼ cup sugar, or to taste
3 egg yolks
½ teaspoon vanilla

In top of double boiler over simmering water, combine instant coffee and water. Stir until dissolved, add cream and sugar and beat until well mixed. Add egg yolks and cook, whisking constantly with a wire whisk, until sauce is light and creamy. Add vanilla and serve large portions of this sauce over small portions of vanilla ice cream, or over lady fingers.

RASPBERRY SAUCE

1 cup raspberry jam
1 cup white wine

1 cup whipped cream
sugar to taste

Blend or stir raspberry jam in white wine until smooth. Fold into whipped cream. Sugar to taste and serve with ice creams, puddings or poured over canned pears, peaches or apricots.

ORANGE SAUCE FOR PANCAKES

¼ cup sugar
¼ cup butter

¼ cup orange juice
¼ cup Grand Marnier or Curaçao
2 teaspoons grated orange rind

Heat sugar, butter and orange juice until it bubbles. Stir in liqueur and orange rind and heat small pancakes in the sauce.

CHAPTER X   *Desserts*

D<small>ESSERTS TAKE</small> to Instant Epicureanism as flowers take to sunshine; they burst into a bloom of new and delightful inventions. Tragic, isn't it, that all this should have happened when no one eats desserts any more?

Regarding the nonconsumption of sweets, especially by the man of today, the big strong executive type who has no weaknesses, who can reject dessert without regret—well, it isn't true. It's a fable he has cooked up to keep his wife thin and jittery. What he does during his day at the office or when he is on a business trip would shock you deeply. You might even divorce him if you could see him eating that chocolate fudge cake and putting all that sugar in his coffee.

It is high time that wives should know what goes on. The program is roughly as follows:

A cup of black coffee, one bite out of a piece of toast and an irritable rush from the house or apartment. There may or may not have been one hasty kiss, on the cheek.

Arriving at the office, he is greeted by his secretary. If he hasn't a secretary he is greeted by someone else's secretary and her immediate concern is whether she can now bring him his steaming-hot coffee full of sugar and cream with a piece of Danish. At the point the sugar has entered his blood stream, your husband is full of warmth, energy and good will.

In the middle of the morning there is a coffee break. If he is really an executive, not just the executive type, he has his coffee brought him in a cup and saucer, again with plenty of sugar and cream and a doughnut or possibly even a sugary jelly doughnut with the sweetest, most disgusting center of artificially colored goo you ever saw. Remember, this is the man who refused your mother's homemade birthday cake.

At lunch he finally is able to get the sugar his system requires. Whether he lunches in the executive suite dining room where the pastries and desserts are baked each morning, or whether they are catered—the chef or caterer knows the way to have his contract renewed. He gives his gentlemen desserts—cakes, pies, ice creams and combinations of cakes, pies and ice creams à la mode. If your husband eats at the nearest lunch counter his especially favorite waitress always serves him a piece of double chocolate fudge cake, something you haven't had since you were twelve. After coffee with lots of sugar and cream the glucose in his system is way over normal.

During the afternoon there are other coffee breaks and there are drinks. He loves whisky sours, and no wonder—they are made of three parts whisky, two parts lemon juice and one part sugar. If he has enough whisky sours he will have at least four to five parts sugar.

On the train going home he has a chocolate bar. This man is your husband, the man you love, the man who wonders why you are so tired after taking care of house, children, job, oil burner repair and both your mothers on one saccharin pill all day. This perfidious creature has a sugar count that would give his doctor a shock, but he won't eat dessert at home. He turns it down with virtue and fortitude and sets an example for you and everyone around him.

So . . . having deprived yourself of those Strawberries Romanoff and that Peach Nougat and having limited yourself to a little Scotch on the rocks . . . go out and eat a hot fudge sundae with whipped cream, nuts and a cherry and come home full of energy and pep and make a big fat Instant Dessert. Make it for yourself and your growing children and your guests and have a little fun out of food. There are no heavy cakes here; the desserts that can be made in minutes are light and cheerful. It would take all day to make those jelly doughnuts your husband sugars his waistcoat with each morning.

Desserts round out a meal; who wants to spend the rest of the night, after a dinner party, with the taste of oil, vinegar, garlic and black coffee? We don't say you should have a Baked Alsaka or a Mont Blanc every evening, but you should have a dessert, whether it be Cherries Jubilee or fresh cherries with Brie. Don't ever stop anything in the middle, least of all your dinner. Taper it off gently and kindly, go from a broiled meat with a salad to a fruit dessert. We've gone out of our way to bring you Instant Desserts and we don't want to feel that they are wasted.

If you go to the trouble of cooking for that ingrate you are married to and he has the temerity to refuse your Instant Pineapple Everest, you know what you can do with it. It kept Mack Sennett in business for years.

ORANGE ALASKA

2 large oranges, halved
1 pint ice cream—vanilla, peach
    or coffee
4 egg whites

2 tablespoons confectioners' sugar
1 tablespoon orange liqueur—
    Curaçao, or Grand Marnier
2 tablespoons granulated sugar

Cut oranges in half, scoop out with spoon. Fill shells with ice cream. Beat egg whites stiff with confectioners' sugar and flavor with liqueur. Mound or pipe on orange halves. Dust with sugar and brown under broiler or in a 400° F. oven. Put orange pulp through juicer and chill for breakfast.

PINEAPPLE EVEREST

4 pineapple slices, drained
½ cup cream, whipped
2 tablespoons confectioners' sugar

2 tablespoons finely chopped
    fresh mint

Top each pineapple slice with a mound of cream whipped with sugar. Dust with mint or fold mint into cream after whipping.

PEACH ALASKA

1 round commercial sponge cake
6 to 8 large canned peach halves
2 tablespoons brandy
1½ pints peach or strawberry
    ice cream

4 egg whites
1¼ cups confectioners' sugar
3 tablespoons granulated sugar

Arrange peach halves on sponge cake on an ovenproof platter. Sprinkle with brandy and cover with ice cream. Beat egg whites stiff with confectioners' sugar. Cover entire cake, sides and top, evenly with stiff egg whites, dust with granulated sugar. Push into a 400° F. oven until lightly browned, about 4 to 6 minutes. Serve at once. Alaska can also be browned under broiler.

FLAMED APRICOTS

1 No. 303 can whole peeled
    apricots, drained
1 cup port

¼ cup apricot brandy or
    brandy, warmed

Heat apricots in port but do not boil. Arrange in a dessert bowl, pour over brandy and ignite at the table. Serve after the flame dies down.

APRICOTS FINES BOUCHES

1 No. 2 can apricots, drained and
    chilled
6 tablespoons butter, or ¾ bar

2 egg yolks
2 tablespoons kirsch
1 tablespoon sugar
½ envelope shaved almonds

Melt butter in the top of a double boiler over simmering water. Add yolks, kirsch and sugar and whip or stir until the sauce becomes thick and creamy. Pour over the apricots and sprinkle with almonds. This can be served immediately or chilled until needed. The apricots have to be drained well.

BABAS

4 large babas from bakery or
   1 can small babas
¼ cup sugar

¾ cup orange marmalade
¼ cup Curaçao
1 teaspoon lemon juice
¼ cup chopped pistachio nuts

Cook sugar, marmalade, Curaçao and lemon juice in top of double boiler over boiling water until marmalade is melted. Stir sauce until smooth, heat the babas in the sauce until they are puffed and saturated. Serve sprinkled with pistachio nuts. Vanilla Ice Cream Sauce I or II is very good poured over the babas. The nuts should be sprinkled over the sauce.

BABAS AU RHUM

2 cans babas au rhum
½ cup heavy rum
½ cup apricot jam

1 pint vanilla ice cream,
   slightly softened

Place ice cream in refrigerator, not in freezer. In top of double boiler, over boiling water, heat babas in their own syrup, rum and apricot jam. In the meantime, beat the ice cream with a whisk or rotary beater until smooth. Serve hot babas with melted jelly-rum sauce in dessert dishes. Pass cold ice cream sauce separately.

PUFFED PANCAKES

¼ cup flour
1 tablespoon sugar
¼ tablespoon cinnamon sugar
3 eggs, separated

½ cup sour cream
¼ teaspoon salt
½ lemon, sliced paper thin
1 tablespoon lemon juice

Stir flour, sugar and salt together. Beat egg yolks until pale and creamy. Stir in dry ingredients. Beat egg whites stiff with a pinch of salt and fold into yolks. Cook by spoonfuls on a buttered griddle, turning once. Serve sprinkled with cinnamon sugar. Cut lemon in half, squeeze ½ on pancakes and slice other half paper thin for garnish.

Cinnamon sugar is a mixture of 1 part cinnamon to 10 parts sugar.

WINE CHAUDEAU

Chaudeau is the perfect dessert, provided you have a hand electric beater. Chaudeau must be beaten while it is in a double boiler on top of the stove.

You also need a partner—whether a life partner or a friend makes no difference—someone who will help you to cope with the Chaudeau, which rises suddenly.

Set out the glasses from which the Chaudeau will be eaten. They should be large compotes, champagne or punch glasses, anything which will hold about 2 ladlefuls of Chaudeau.

With beater in hand and partner at your side with ladle in hand, you can start.

1 cup light Chablis   3 egg yolks
2 tablespoons granulated sugar

Beat sugar and yolks in the upper part of a double boiler and place it over gently simmering water in the lower section. Immediately start beating the yolks and sugar and in a moment add the Chablis. Keep beating the mixture. It will become creamy yellow and very light. It will rise and as it comes to the top your partner can scoop out ladlefuls for the first 2 glasses.

Beat for a few more seconds, until it does not seem to be rising any further. Divide the rest in the remaining glasses and serve at once. You can pass small petit fours with this.

All this will take less than five minutes. You'll both be back at the table before you are missed.

The entire family of desserts that spring from the expansion of egg yolks when beaten over warm water are boons for the Instant Epicure. There is no doubt that they go quickly and non-epicures don't understand them at all.

ORANGE ZABAIONE

4 egg yolks
¼ cup sugar
½ cup Marsala

2 tablespoons orange Curaçao
2 tablespoons orange juice
1 tablespoon grated orange rind

Beat yolks and sugar in top of a double boiler until thick and light in color. Add Marsala, Curaçao and orange juice. Place over boiling water in lower section of double boiler. Beat until mixture rises and doubles in bulk. Serve in stemmed glasses and sprinkle with orange rind.

ZABAIONE MICHEL

5 egg yolks
¾ cup sugar

¼ teaspoon vanilla
1 lemon, grated rind
¾ cup port, sherry or Madeira

Beat yolks, sugar, vanilla and lemon until light and thick. Stir in the wine, and place the mixture in the top of a double boiler over gently boiling water. Whisk or beat until the mixture thickens and rises. Pour into stemmed glasses and serve warm or cold with souvaroffs.

ZABAIONE

3 egg yolks
3 tablespoons sugar
½ cup Marsala or Madeira

Beat yolks and sugar in the top of a double boiler until they are creamy and almost white in color. Add the Marsala and set over gently boiling water in the lower section of the double boiler. Continue to beat until the Zabaione rises and doubles in volume. Take from heat and serve at once in stemmed glasses.

CRÈME BACHIQUE

6 eggs, separated
1¼ cups sugar
5 tablespoons heavy rum

Beat yolks and sugar until almost white and creamy. Flavor with rum and just before serving fold in the stiffly beaten egg whites.

LEMON MOUSSE

4 lemons, grated rind only   ½ cup sugar
6 eggs   3 tablespoons water

Beat sugar and yolks until creamy and light, gradually add the grated rind of 3 lemons. Whisk over boiling water until light. Cool and fold in the stiffly beaten egg whites and remaining grated lemon rind.

LEMON FOAM

2 egg yolks   2 tablespoons lemon juice
2 tablespoons sugar   grated rind of the lemon

Beat ingredients over hot water and serve over sponge cake.

ORANGE DESSERT

In an attractive English cookbook there is a recipe for a "Quick" dessert. The author writes: "As the name implies, this recipe comes to us from America. . . ."

So that is our reputation abroad, and here is another Instant. You could drag it out by chilling it.

1 basket raspberries or strawberries   sugar to taste
2 large oranges   1 jigger Curaçao or kirsch

Cut the oranges in half. With a sharp spoon take out the sections, as though you were going to eat them. Place sections in a bowl. When the halves are empty, scrape out the white pulp.

Crush any small soft berries and keep the good ones. Mix the orange sections with sugar and the crushed berries, return them to the shells, pile the good berries on top, flavor with the liqueur and refrigerate until needed.

Pour over a little more liqueur just before serving.

ORANGE MOUSSE

½ cup sugar   4 oranges, juice and grated rind
                        6 eggs, separated

Beat sugar and yolks until creamy and light, gradually add orange juice with the grated rind of 3 oranges. Whisk over boiling water until light. Cool and fold in the stiffly beaten egg whites and remaining rind.

DRYBUS
(for 2 people)

1 cup red wine   ¼ teaspoon ground cloves
¼ teaspoon cinnamon   vanilla
1 tablespoon sugar or to taste   1 egg yolk

Heat ¾ cup red wine, add cinnamon, sugar and cloves and stir until dissolved. Add 1 dash vanilla and place over boiling water. Beat yolk with remaining ¼ cup wine. Add to hot wine and beat over low heat until it rises and doubles in volume. Serve at once in stemmed glasses.

NEROS

4 squares semisweet chocolate   1 pinch of salt
4 eggs, separated   ½ teaspoon vanilla

Melt chocolate in the top of a double boiler over boiling water. Take from heat as soon as softened. Beat in yolks, salt and vanilla and set aside. Beat egg whites stiff, fold into chocolate and pour into crystal bowl. Eat at once with lady fingers or chill as long as possible and serve with whipped cream.

MAYONNAISE AU CHOCOLAT

4 eggs, separated   1 tablespoon butter
6 tablespoons sugar   3 tablespoons rum
                  4 squares semisweet chocolate

Melt butter and chocolate over hot water. Take from heat. Beat well, add yolks to the mixture, beating after each addition until smooth. Beat in sugar and rum and cool. Fold in the stiffly beaten egg whites.

BALANCE

6 eggs, separated   ½ teaspoon vanilla
6 squares semisweet chocolate   ¼ cup sugar

Beat melted chocolate, yolks and sugar until light and thick, fold in vanilla and stiffly beaten whites.

UNBALANCE

6 eggs, separated   6 tablespoons very strong coffee
6 squares semisweet chocolate   ¼ cup sugar

Beat chocolate, yolks and sugar until light and thick, fold in coffee with stiffly beaten whites. Fill into pots and chill until needed.

TROPICAL AMERICANA

1 package chocolate rum wafers   1 quart vanilla or coffee
1 tablespoon instant coffee   ice cream
1 cup water

Melt wafers mixed with instant coffee and water in top of double boiler over boiling water. Stir until smooth. Pour over vanilla ice cream in individual dessert cups and serve.

Here are fruit desserts for every occasion. When minutes matter, fruit has to take the place of the slow-cooking puddings and slow-baking cakes. If you cannot always end with cheese, fruit, nuts and continental closings, then try some of these; they are light, refreshing and easily prepared. With the proper trimmings they can look as attractive as any time-consuming construction of confectionery.

FRUIT WITH SOUR CREAM

As each fruit or berry comes in season there is a good way of serving it with sour cream. In each case there is a third ingredient added to change it from an ordinary dessert into one you can serve guests. The third ingredient also adds a little change in flavor or an accentuation of flavor.

Always whip or stir the sour cream to make it light and smooth, pour it over the fruit and sprinkle with the third ingredient. Serve very cold. In one or two cases, the fruit can be canned stewed fruit and when it is, it can be served either warm or cold. Stewed pears, cherries or apples are good when they are heated, especially if you add a jigger of warm rum or brandy. Figs can be used fresh or canned, but they should always be served cold, as should the various berries and melon balls. If the fruit is sour, beat or whip the sugar into the cream.

figs, fresh or canned	sour cream	grated or slivered orange rind
(if a liqueur is used, add Curaçao, Cointreau or Grand Marnier)		
black cherries	sour cream	powdered cinnamon mixed with sugar (kirsch liqueur)
seedless green grapes	sour cream	brown sugar
stewed or fresh pears	sour cream	grated chocolate
canned or fresh pineapple	sour cream	grated coconut and mint leaves
melon balls	sour cream	minced chutney and walnuts
strawberries	sour cream	grated orange rind (Curaçao)
raspberries	sour cream	shaved almonds and 1 dash almond extract
sliced peaches	sour cream	slivered almonds and 1 dash maraschino
sliced stewed apples	sour cream	brown sugar and cinnamon
apricot halves	sour cream	shaved almonds (apricot brandy)
blue plums, halved	sour cream	grated orange rind, toasted crumbs and 1 pinch ground cloves (rum)

JAMAICA FIGS

1 No. 303 jar figs, drained   2 tablespoons rum
½ cup cream, whipped   ½ cup chopped toasted almonds
                    powdered sugar to taste
        Flavor whipped cream with rum, add sugar to taste, pour over
figs and dust with chopped almonds.

BANANAS FLAMBÉE

4 bananas   ¼ cup powdered sugar
3 tablespoons butter   ¼ cup kirsch

        Gently brown skinned bananas on all sides in butter in a
heavy skillet and sprinkle with sugar. Arrange on a silver or metal
serving dish. Pour over the kirsch and flame. Serve when the flame
dies down.

BAKED BANANAS

6 ripe bananas, peeled and cut in   juice of 1 lemon
        half lengthwise   1 can whole cranberry sauce
butter for pan   sugar to taste
                    1 orange, sliced

        Arrange bananas in a buttered baking dish, stir lemon juice
into cranberry sauce, add sugar to taste and pour over the bananas.
Bake in a 400° F. oven for about 8 minutes, or until bananas are
soft and sauce is bubbling. Garnish with orange slices.

STRAWBERRIES MICKEY

2 baskets strawberries, hulled   ½ cup heavy cream, whipped, or
½ lemon, juice and grated rind   ½ cup whipped cream
1 ounce kirsch   topping
3 ounces Curaçao   ½ pint vanilla ice cream

Sprinkle strawberries with lemon juice, rind and liqueurs and set in refrigerator. Whip cream until stiff, beat vanilla ice cream until soft and smooth, fold in cream. Pour over strawberries, stir at table and serve. Raspberries may be substituted for strawberries, or use half raspberries and half strawberries. The liqueurs may be increased or decreased to taste.

ANTILLES MELON

1 large cantaloupe	1/3 cup powdered sugar
1 can pineapple chunks	½ cup water
½ cup kirsch	1 lemon, quartered

Cut lid from top of melon, remove seeds and scoop out the meat with a spoon, leaving the shell intact. Boil syrup from pineapple can, kirsch, sugar and water rapidly for 6 minutes, cool. Dice the melon meat, add the pineapple and melon to syrup and refill the melon shell. Put on lid, chill until served. Serve surrounded by lemon leaves and lemon wedges.

OPORTO MELONS

2 medium cantaloupes or	port
4 very small individual ones	

Cut ends of melon across so the halves will stand evenly. Cut melons in half, scoop out seeds, fill with port and serve. If small ones are obtainable, cut lid from top, scoop out seeds, fill with port and return lid.

THE PORT OF PORTO

2 small melons	sugar to taste
1 basket strawberries	port

Cut melons in half, scrape out seeds and drain. Hull strawberries, sugar them lightly and arrange them in the 4 melon halves. Add as much port as each melon half will hold, and serve.

Strawberries in port are good without the melon and a melon filled with port is good without the strawberries. Omit either fruit but don't omit the port.

BAKED PINEAPPLE

1 can sliced pineapple
melted butter

grated coconut
2 tablespoons Curaçao

Drain pineapple, boil syrup rapidly to reduce to half. Dry pineapple slices, dip in melted butter and dredge with coconut. Place on a baking sheet and bake in a 350° F. oven for 4 minutes. Add Curaçao to syrup and pass separately with baked pineapple slices.

MIXED FEELINGS

1 No. 10 can sliced apples
1 No. 2 can pineapple chunks

1 can grated coconut
3 tablespoons butter

Arrange apples and pineapple chunks in serving dish, chill as long as possible. Fry coconut in butter, stirring constantly until golden. Spread over fruit and serve.

Fry coconut in a heavy pan over low flame. It turns brown suddenly, so watch carefully and as soon as it starts to go deep brown take from heat and stir until evenly browned. Drain on brown paper for a moment.

AMBROSIA IN HASTE

1 cup grated coconut
1 can pineapple chunks

1 basket fresh strawberries
1 lime, quartered

Moisten strawberries with pineapple juice from can. Roll strawberries and pineapple chunks in coconut and serve cold with lime wedges.

MIXED AMBROSIA

1 8-ounce can grapefruit sections
1 4-ounce can orange sections
1 cup grated coconut
½ cup confectioners' sugar
2 jiggers Grand Marnier

Arrange drained grapefruit and orange sections in a serving dish. Sprinkle with sugar and Grand Marnier and chill for as long as possible. Before serving spread coconut over fruit.

CANDIED FRUIT AND APPLE

1 can sliced apples
1 jar mixed candied fruit
½ cup rum
1 cinnamon stick
2 slices commercial pound cake cut into 4 rounds with cookie cutter (optional)
Heavy cream, also optional

Heat apples in their own juice. Heat candied fruit in rum with the cinnamon. Take out the cinnamon. Serve together on pound cake rounds. Pass cream separately, if desired.

SPICED PRUNES WITH WALNUTS

2 16-ounce jars prunes, drained
2 oranges, thinly sliced
¼ cup brown sugar
¼ cup rum
1 tablespoon vinegar
¼ teaspoon cinnamon, or to taste
1 pinch salt
1 cup chopped walnuts

Place prunes in serving dish and cover with orange slices. Combine remaining ingredients, heat to boiling, stir well and pour over fruit.

PRUNEAUX AU VIN

1 1-pound jar prunes, drained
½ teaspoon cinnamon
2 cups red wine
1½ tablespoons sugar

Boil wine, cinnamon and sugar uncovered for 8 minutes. Add prunes, and cool. Pour into a jar and chill until served. These will keep for 2 or 3 days in refrigerator. Serve with thin lemon slices, sour cream beaten with a little rum, a sprinkling of shaved almonds or a sprinkling of grated coconut.

GINGER PEARS

1 1-pound can pear halves, drained   1 jar raspberry jam
6 gingersnaps, crushed   1 lemon, juice only
                                  port (optional)

Crush gingersnaps with a rolling pin; roll pears in crumbs. Heat raspberry jam; thin to taste with lemon juice. Add port and pass separately with the pears. Arrange pear halves in compote dishes. Add enough sauce to half cover pears and sprinkle generously with gingersnap crumbs.

BRANDY PEARS

1 1-pound can pears   ½ cup brandy
1 jar mixed candied fruits   1 envelope broken walnut meats

Heat candied fruits and walnuts in brandy and add pear juice to taste. Pour over canned pear halves and serve.

ICED GRAPES
(Bowling Balls)

1 pound large sweet grapes   1 egg white, lightly beaten
                              confectioners' sugar

Dip stemmed grapes in egg white and roll in sugar. Arrange them in a pyramid on a dessert platter as you would stack bowling balls, chill until served.

CRÈME DE COGNAC À LA MINUTE
(per person)

1 egg   1 teaspoon sugar or to taste
            2 tablespoons brandy

Blend or beat ingredients until smooth and creamy. Fill into stemmed glasses and serve as dessert with small petit fours or serve as a liqueur after dinner.

CRÈME DE KIRSCH WITH BLACK CHERRIES
(per person)

1 egg   1 1-pound can pitted black cherries,
1 teaspoon sugar   well drained
2 tablespoons kirsch

Follow recipe for Crème de Cognac à la Minute, pour the Crème over black cherries and serve as dessert.

For more elaborate purposes, arrange cherries around large scoops of vanilla ice cream, cover with Crème de Kirsch and if you don't care how richly you gild the lily, sprinkle with shaved almonds. When used as a sauce, count 2 eggs for 3 people.

CHERRIES JUBILÉE

1 No. 2 can pitted black cherries   ¼ cup brandy, warmed
1 tablespoon cornstarch   1 envelope shaved almonds
2 tablespoons cold water   (optional)
¼ cup kirsch, warmed   1 quart vanilla ice cream

Drain cherries, heat syrup to a boil, stir cornstarch with water and stir into syrup. Add cherries and simmer until heated through. Take from fire, add kirsch and brandy and flame. Spoon over ice cream and sprinkle with almonds.

BUTTERED RUM PEACHES

1 can or 2 packages frozen sliced
    peaches

2 tablespoons butter
2 tablespoons dark brown sugar

½ cup rum

Heat butter, sugar and rum with syrup from peaches. Add peaches and reheat, but do not allow to boil. Serve hot sprinkled with cinnamon, nutmeg or cocoa.

BURNT BRANDY PEACHES
(per person)

¼ cup brandy
1–2 tablespoons sugar

1 peach, peeled and sliced thin
nutmeg to taste

Heat brandy and sugar in a heavy pan. Add peach slices and ignite. When flame dies down, fill into dessert glasses, dust with nutmeg and serve.

PEACH CRÈME

3 peaches
1 cup cream, whipped

2 slices pound cake
½–2/3 cup sugar

Press peeled peaches through a sieve, stir in sugar to taste, gently fold in whipped cream and serve surrounded by fingers cut from trimmed pound cake. You may substitute 3 bananas or 1½ cups drained canned apricot halves for the peaches.

HONEYED PEACHES

6 large ripe peaches, peeled,
    stoned and sliced

1/3 cup honey
¼ cup rum

Heat honey and rum, pour over peaches and serve. If you have the time, crack the peach pits with a nutcracker and draw the skin from the little peach almond in the pit. Split the little almonds in half and sprinkle over the peaches.

HOT AND COLD PEACHES

8 canned peach halves
8 teaspoons butter
½ cup orange marmalade
½ teaspoon cocoa powder or
  nutmeg

¼ cup shaved almonds
½ pint vanilla ice cream
1 dash almond extract, optional

Place peach halves, cut side up, on a baking sheet. Place marmalade and butter on each. Dust with cocoa powder and sprinkle with almonds. Broil for 5 minutes, or until almonds are golden. Keep ice cream in refrigerator, not in freezer, beat until light and smooth, add almond extract and pass with peaches.

PEACH NOUGAT

2 packages frozen peaches,
  thawed and drained
½ cup cream, whipped
1 tablespoon confectioners' sugar

1 Italian nougat candy bar, crushed
4 tablespoons peach brandy or
  brandy

Arrange peaches in serving dish, sprinkle with brandy. Fold sugar into whipped cream, mound on peaches and sprinkle with crushed Italian nougat bar.

You can substitute any "crunch" type chocolate bar for the nougat. Crush with a rolling pin (chocolate must be cold when crushed), or melt bar over hot water, beat with 2 tablespoons cream and pass separately.

PEACHES AND PRESERVES

4 peaches
½ teaspoon vanilla
½ cup raspberry jam
¼ cup currant jelly

2 tablespoons orange marmalade
½ cup warm brandy, optional
¼ cup warm kirsch, optional
2 pints vanilla ice cream

Poach peaches in water to cover for a minute. Draw off the skins and return to the warm water. Add the vanilla and keep warm until ready to serve. Melt the jam, jelly and marmalade together in a chafing dish or top of a double boiler, add the peaches and stir to coat them with the preserves. Divide the ice cream over 4 dessert dishes, pour warmed brandy and kirsch over the peaches and flame. Add a peach to each serving of ice cream and pour the sauce over the peaches.

PEACH NUT

1 cup cream, whipped	2 teaspoons almond flavoring
½ cup grated coconut	½ teaspoon vanilla
4 peaches, peeled and sliced	powdered sugar to taste

Fold coconut, peaches and flavorings into whipped cream. Sweeten to taste and serve.

ORANGE MARMALADE ROLLS

These rolls can be served as an emergency dessert or they can be prepared for tea in the afternoon. They are also a very good addition to a late Sunday breakfast.

8 slices thin white bread, crusts removed	½ cup bitter orange marmalade
½ cup soft butter	cocktail picks

Butter bread, spread with marmalade and roll each slice up tightly. Secure with picks and lay seam side down on a buttered baking sheet. Butter the top of the roll lightly and toast under the broiler until the bread is golden. Draw out picks and serve at once.

RICH KNIGHTS

8 slices day-old white bread	1 tablespoon maple sugar
1 egg	½ teaspoon cinnamon
½ cup cream	1 pinch ground cloves
½ cup white wine	¼ cup butter for frying

Beat egg, cream, wine, sugar and spices well. Dip bread slices into mixture and fry on both sides in butter until golden. Serve hot with maple sugar or maple syrup.

RUM OMELET

Follow recipe for plain omelet made with 6 eggs, salt very lightly. Slide onto a platter, sprinkle with 2½ tablespoons sugar. Pour 5 tablespoons warmed rum over omelet and ignite. Serve after the flame dies down.

OMELETTE AUX CONFITURES

Follow recipe for plain omelet. Before folding lay a strip of jam (½ cup) along center of omelet, fold and slide onto a serving plate. Sprinkle with sugar. If you have a red-hot salamander, scorch crisscross pattern over top of omelet.

FRENCH CHOCOLATE ICING

5 tablespoons butter
2 squares semisweet chocolate

2 eggs, separated
icing sugar

Soften butter and chocolate over hot water. Sugar to taste and beat in egg yolks until thick and light. Fold in the stiffly beaten egg whites and spread on commercial angel or sponge cake. The icing hardens as it cools.

BUTTER CRÈME FÜLLE

Cream ½ cup sweet butter until it is very light and foamy. Stir in 1 well-beaten egg yolk and gradually add 2½ cups powdered sugar sifted with 2 tablespoons dry cocoa. Beat until light and add enough strong cold coffee to make the icing the right consistency for spreading. Use as above.

GREEN MINT AND LEMON ICE

1 quart lemon sherbet

¼ cup green mint

Fill 4 dessert cups with sherbet. Make a deep hole in the center with a knife handle, fill with green mint and serve at once. This is also good using orange sherbet and Curaçao.

There are many very quick, very attractive and delicious desserts that can be prepared in seconds if you have a blender. As a matter of fact, most of these are so good that they are reason enough to go out and buy yourself one (which can also be used for less fattening and more filling foods).

BLACK BEAUTY

2 cups chocolate ice cream
¼ cup crème de cacao, or to taste

¼ cup broken walnut meats
½ cup heavy cream, whipped

Whirl ice cream and liqueur in blender until smooth. Pour into chilled glasses or cups, top with whipped cream, sprinkle with nuts and serve.

BELGIAN FRUIT PUDDING
(for 6)

½ cup raisins
½ cup currants
1 5-ounce envelope walnut meats
1 4-ounce jar candied cherries
1 4-ounce jar mixed candied fruit

½ cup brandy
1 cup broken macaroons
2 15-ounce jars apple sauce
3 egg whites
3 tablespoons sugar

Combine fruits, nuts, brandy, macaroons and apple sauce in blender. Blend only long enough to chop roughly. Beat egg whites stiff, adding sugar gradually. Mound egg whites on fruit and push under broiler for 2 minutes, or until meringue is golden.

APRICOT PURÉE

1 No. 303 can apricot halves, drained
confectioners' sugar to taste

apricot brandy to taste
1 envelope shaved almonds

Whisk apricots in blender, sweeten to taste. Fill into 4 cocktail glasses, make a depression in the center of each and pour in a thimble of apricot brandy. Sprinkle with shaved almonds and serve.

STRAWBERRY CREAM

1 3-ounce package cream cheese
½ cup powdered sugar
½ cup heavy cream

2 tablespoons rum
2 packages frozen strawberries, thawed

Blend sugar, cream and rum with cream cheese until it is smooth, adding cheese gradually to mixture. Stir into strawberries and serve in dessert glasses.

ORANGE PRUNE WHIP

1 16-ounce jar prunes, pitted
½ cup orange marmalade
1 tablespoon lemon juice

3 egg whites
2 tablespoons sugar
½ cup broken walnut meats

Blend prunes, marmalade and lemon juice until smooth. Fold into egg whites which have been beaten until stiff with sugar. Serve dusted with nuts.

RASPBERRY CREAM

1 basket fresh raspberries
1 cup cream, whipped stiff
¼ cup sugar, or to taste

1 package frozen raspberries blended until smooth

Fold whipped cream into blended raspberries and sugar to taste. Divide into dessert glasses and cover cream with fresh raspberries. Serve with dessert wafers or small petit fours.

APPLE SAUCE

4 apples, peeled and quartered
¼ cup orange or any preferred
    fruit juice

¼ cup sugar
1 pinch cinnamon, or to taste

Blend fruit juice and 3 apple slices until smooth, gradually add remaining apple, sugar and cinnamon. Serve as dessert or with pork or duck.

EDEN APPLE SAUCE

2 15-ounce jars apple sauce
¼ cup pitted dates

thin rind of ½ lemon
sugar to taste

Blend apple sauce, dates and lemon rind until smooth. Sweeten and serve in chilled glasses.

Variations:

1. Substitute sieved prunes for dates and add 2 tablespoons raisins.
2. Substitute ¼ cup candied orange peel and ¼ cup broken walnut meats for dates.
3. Substitute 2 tablespoons candied lemon peel and 2 tablespoons candied orange peel for dates.

CHAPTER XI

Outdoor or Plug-in-anywhere Cooking

L ONG BEFORE the words "status" and "symbol" had been coined into a phrase, there were certain recognized proofs of one's standing in the social world. The place where you ate was second only to the place where you bathed.

Some time ago (we do not go back to Nero's marble days) indoor plumbing was the first rung up the ladder. Next it had to have water laid on. After you'd gotten it indoors *with* running water, it had to be concealed and soon after that it had to be tiled and then sunken. Now, for goodness' sake, it has to be a better second living room with leopard skins, open fireplace, real oil paintings and a Louis XVI bergère. There has to be a picture window even if you can only see into your neighbor's social stratification symbolized through the picture window of his bath-sitting room.

In the eating department, where your status has always shown, you started in the kitchen, graduated to the dinette and on to the dining room. When it should have ended right there everyone suddenly got up from the dining table and went out of doors. They had to eat in the patio (this was a matter of life and death).

If there was no patio the breezeway had to do. From there eating went to the side of your swimming pool. From the poolside it moved up to the penthouse terrace and now that there is no higher place to go, the status symbol of all times is not to use, or even recognize, those two words and to eat *anywhere*.

When we say *anywhere* we mean *anywhere* except in the dining room. It can be a tray across the bathtub; it can be flaming swords while you loll in the pit in your living room. It can be a meal spread out on the model stand in the studio, or in front of your new bath-living room fireplace. It can be an habachi or a roll-away broiler-bar-cum-stereophone. It can be any place that you can wheel your heating unit and plug it in—and that's living.

You can still have mesquite logs shipped in from Arizona for your streamlined cookout but it's really much easier and smarter to be a thermostatically controlled cook. There is no reason why the outdoor cook should have more time than the indoor cook and outdoor Instant Epicures need a group of quickly preparable menus. You don't have to cook in the kitchen just because you are in a hurry. Just plug in your oven or your skillet or your broiler and when it goes *bing!* throw on the meat and when it goes *bing!* again, eat it.

Don't let anyone catch you, even for an instant, in a chef's cap, asbestos gloves or with a silver steer-headed briquette tong. Lighter fluid is passé; if you have to display an emblem of your condition, just have the longest, most elegant roll-up extension cord in the world (it can be on a wheel like your garden hose) and all the in-and-outdoor electric outlets that you and your electrical engineer can think of. Plug yourself in wherever the fancy for food and drink strikes you.

This does not say that charcoal-broiled meats aren't wonderful, or that barbecue pits aren't worth the effort; it only means that they aren't absolutely necessary for those people who do not have half a day in which to build up the proper ashes and glowing coals. It is now possible for everyone, those who have time and those who don't, to eat where they are most comfortable, coolest, happiest and hungriest.

If a party is going well in the garden, don't break it up. Bring the food to the guests, not the guests (in pairs, as for Noah's Ark) to the food at a table set in the dining room. Eating out of doors at the end of an extension cord is a special thing that has more to do with freedom than with status. It is an escape from formality (remember the popular *fête champêtre*), from tradition and from service plates.

Formal dining-room eating meant a constant stirring up of guests and atmosphere. If they were just getting interested in each other over cocktails, they were seated at opposite ends of the table during dinner. After dinner hostesses took the ladies away for coffee while the host plied the gentlemen with liqueurs and politics. By the time they reassembled they rarely found each other again and certainly they never re-established the pleasant atmosphere of the cocktail hour. Seated at a table they couldn't wander around between courses and sit next to the person they were most interested in.

Informal eating is just as important when you are alone at home as when you have guests. You and your husband can relax and drift gradually from cocktail to dinner without the interruption of moving out of your comfortable chairs. You can listen to your favorite music, talk about everything you have to talk about and not subject your system to the strain of moving about. Just stay where you are and let the food come to you.

BROILED SHRIMP I AND II
ON ELECTRIC BROILER OR
ON OUTDOOR GRILL

Here again the actual cooking time is about 8 minutes, but you will have to give the preparation of the shrimp another 8 minutes within a day of broiling or grilling them. Prepare them in the morning before you go to work and grill them in the evening in just as long as it takes the broiler or the coals to get hot plus 8 minutes.

If you are planning to shell fresh shrimp, then remove shells but leave on tails so they can be held while eating. Split down back and rinse out vein. We suggest this for people who have time early in the day for preparations, but no cooking time later.

Variation I

2 pounds frozen peeled shrimp,
    thawed (large or jumbo)
½ bunch parsley, stems removed,
    ground through Mouli (½
    cup ground)
4 garlic cloves, crushed

1 cup frozen chopped onion, thawed
1 teaspoon dried rosemary
2 lemons, grated rind and juice
¾ cup oil
1 teaspoon salt
2 teaspoons Colman's mustard

Spread the split shrimp out flat. Arrange flattened shrimp in a shallow pan or on 2 pie plates and spread all other ingredients over them. Marinate in refrigerator for 4 hours. If there is not enough time, marinate for at least 2 hours. Spread shrimp on foil-lined broiler rack and push into top position, or as near heating unit as possible on an electric broiler, or place shrimp in a hinged wire rack and grill over coals in the outdoor barbecue grill.

Whichever method is used, spread the shrimp, after they are on the rack, with the marinade and all the chopped ingredients and grill until the shrimp are no longer transparent and the edges are browned (the backs will be pink).

Variation II

Prepare shrimp as for Method I.

¾ cup oil
1 bunch green onions, chopped
1 bay leaf
¼ teaspoon black pepper
½ teaspoon paprika

1 teaspoon salt
½ teaspoon marjoram
½ teaspoon rosemary
1 pinch nutmeg
2 lemons, grated rind and juice

Mix oil with all other ingredients, marinate shrimp from 2 to 4 hours, take out bay leaf and use marinade on shrimp as in Variation I.

OUTDOOR BROILED OYSTERS

4 dozen oysters in shell
½ cup butter
½ cup cocktail sauce

2 tablespoons grated horseradish
2 tablespoons lemon juice
salt and pepper

Roast oysters on metal grid over hot coals until shells open, about 8 minutes. Spear hot oysters and dip first in melted butter, then in cocktail sauce combined with horseradish and lemon juice.

If preferred, increase amount of butter, add lemon juice to butter and add a crushed garlic clove. Dip hot oysters into butter only and eat immediately.

BROILED FROGS' LEGS

24–28 pairs frogs' legs	1 teaspoon each chopped chervil,
1 pound butter, melted	chives, dill, oregano and
2 garlic cloves, crushed	tarragon
2 lemons, juice and grated rind	4 sprigs parsley ground through
½ teaspoon salt	Mouli
¼ teaspoon pepper	

Marinate frogs' legs in sauce made of butter, garlic, lemon, seasonings and herbs during the time that you are preparing the fire. When coals are right, spread frogs' legs on greased, hinged wire rack and broil 3 inches from coals for about 4 minutes on each side, or until they are white and tender. Brush constantly with marinade. Serve with remaining marinade and grilled bread.

Grilled Frankfurters

Allow from 1 to 2 pairs frankfurters per person. Grill whole or split, wrapped in bacon or in foil as follows:

WHOLE GRILLED FRANKFURTERS

4 pairs frankfurters	mustard
8 frankfurter buns, split	ketchup
½ cup soft butter	relish
	horseradish

Broil frankfurters on grill 3 inches from source of heat, turning frequently to brown all sides. In the meantime open buns and butter them lightly. Lay butter side down at side of grill to toast slowly. Turn frankfurters to grill evenly. They are done when they are sizzling hot and lightly browned (8 to 10 minutes). Place frankfurters on rolls, close rolls and allow guests to use any of the relishes and condiments, or they may want to make a combination. Grilled frankfurters can be cut down 1 inch with 2 cuts making a cross at each end. As they grill, the ends spread and make them look attractive. Do not toast rolls. Serve the frankfurters with heated canned baked beans, sauerkraut, coleslaw or potato salad. Add hot grilled bread, heated potato chips, cold radishes and add the mustards.

SPLIT GRILLED FRANKFURTERS

Split frankfurters lengthwise but do not cut all the way through. Spread out and grill. This goes faster than the whole frankfurter. Split frankfurters can be brushed with mustard or filled with relishes or slivers of cheese and folded back. Secure with wooden cocktail picks and grill as whole frankfurters.

BACON-WRAPPED FRANKFURTERS

Wrap plain or split and filled frankfurters in bacon. Secure with cocktail picks and grill, turning frequently until bacon is crisp, about 10 minutes. Serve with potato salad or coleslaw.

FOIL-WRAPPED FRANKFURTERS

Split frankfurters, fill with long strips of cheese and a little relish and mustard. Wrap loosely in foil, lay on rack and grill about 6 minutes, turning the package 2 or 3 times.

Quick Skewers

Stringing meat, vegetables, fruit and fish on skewers is a pleasant undertaking. Some of them take too much time on the grill to be included here, but others are done in 10 minutes or less.

Grill over hot coals, turning frequently, or adjust the skewers in an automatic rotisserie. Grill them over hot coals in an hibachi or under your kitchen broiler.

The following are all quick-broiling foods; string them up in any combination and broil until browned. Broil shrimp until opaque and pink. Take hamburger from coals when it is browned but before it shows any inclination to break.

Marinate filled skewers while coals or broiler is heating. If there is more time marinate longer. Baste or brush with marinade and use marinade as sauce unless a different sauce is suggested. The following combinations contain all the fast-broiling foods:

1. Alternate peeled and deveined shrimp with green pepper strips, tomato quarters and canned white onions. Marinate, baste and serve with a sauce of butter melted with lemon juice, grated lemon rind, crushed garlic and dried rosemary to taste.

2. Alternate cooked and shelled shrimp with large stuffed olives. Marinate with garlic butter. Add chopped almonds to remaining garlic butter and pass as a sauce.

3. Alternate apple wedges with cooked ham cubes, brush with oil while broiling. Brush with warmed honey for last 2 minutes. Serve with Cumberland Sauce.

4. Alternate canned pineapple chunks with ham cubes and treat as above.

5. Alternate oysters, wrapped in bacon, with mushrooms. Serve with tartar sauce. The bacon supplies enough fat for broiling.

6. Alternate small hamburgers, wrapped around small pieces of Bleu cheese, with tomato quarters and mushrooms. Brush with oil, dust heavily with paprika and serve with spiced ketchup, mustard and ground horseradish.

7. String chicken livers, wrapped in bacon, on skewers. Allow a second skewer for each guest and string it with mushrooms alternating with canned white onions. Brush vegetable skewer with oil. Bacon does not require any brushing. Take chicken livers off as soon as bacon is crisp and brown, drain well. Take vegetables off as soon as lightly browned. Tomato wedges can be added to mushrooms and onions.

8. Alternate cubes of eggplant, seasoned heavily with black pepper and wrapped in bacon, with cherry tomatoes. Broil until bacon is crisp and serve with mustard sauce, mustard mixed with sour cream or mayonnaise to taste.

9. Start bacon strip on skewer, add small white canned onion. Zigzag back through bacon, add another onion and so on. Serve with warm maple syrup.

10. Alternate pineapple chunks and chunks of peeled bananas, wrapped in bacon, and broil until bacon is crisp. Serve with meat skewers, giving each guest a meat and a fruit skewer.

11. Alternate ham slices wrapped around canned artichoke hearts with black olives. Brush with butter and serve with tartar sauce.

12. Alternate cubes of liver with white onions and tomato quarters. Brush with seasoned butter to which a pinch of ground cinnamon has been added. Dust with paprika and broil until liver is lightly browned.

OUTDOOR GRILLED CORN I AND II

Variation I

8–12 tender young ears of unhusked corn

½ cup butter
1 clove garlic, crushed
salt and pepper

Pull husks back from corn. Take off the silk. Dip ears in butter to which garlic and seasonings have been added and pull husks back over corn. Place on grill. Cover with a heavy clean cloth wrung out in water and let corn steam for 4 minutes. Turn ears once, replacing cloth. Sprinkle on more water if necessary and steam 6 minutes.

Variation II

Wrap husked corn in bacon strips. Use small tender young ears and broil over coals until bacon is crisp. Serve with a little garlic butter.

GRILLED LAMB CHOPS I AND II

Variation I

8 1-inch-thick lamb chops, loin or rib   1 garlic clove, crushed
½ cup oil for brushing   salt
                  1 teaspoon dried oregano

Place chops on grill about 3 inches from source of heat. Brush with oil, to which garlic and salt have been added. Grill about 5 minutes, brushing frequently with garlic butter. Turn and grill second side, brushing frequently with remaining butter. Sprinkle with oregano and serve with grilled onions.

Variation II

Prepare chops as above and brush with butter, to which 1 teaspoon mild curry powder has been added instead of the garlic. Serve chops prepared in this way with Minute Rice, chutney and grated coconut.

CHARCOAL-BROILED LOBSTERS

4 1¼-pound lobsters   1 lemon, quartered
½ pound butter, melted   salt and pepper

Split lobsters by laying them, back up, on a wooden board. Insert long sharp knife into the cross at back of neck where it meets body shell (or carapace) and cut down in one quick sharp motion. Cut down through the tail, open and remove stomach and intestinal vein. Brush generously with butter, place in hinged wire rack and broil, flesh side down, for 2 minutes. Turn, pour over more butter and broil 8 minutes longer or take from coals when meat is white and opaque. Split claws and serve with remaining melted butter and lemon wedges.

OUTDOOR BROILED MEATS

Much depends on heat of fire, cut of meat and your own taste in rareness of meat. It is quite impossible to give an accurate broiling chart, but the following one should be a guide. It is for rare meat, as all charcoal-broiled meats should be. If you want a charred exterior and a well done interior you will have dry, hard meat.

Broil a 1-inch-thick porterhouse, T-bone, tenderloin or sirloin steak for 3 to 4 minutes on each side.

Broil a 1¼-inch-thick steak as above for 4 to 5 minutes on each side.

Broil a 1½-inch-thick steak as above for 5 to 6 minutes on each side. And that is the end of Instant Epicureanism. Anybody with more time can naturally buy a thicker steak.

The Instant Epicure has to have a friend or wife or houseman (Instant Epicures not only can but should be rich) who lays the fires and prepares the coals.

Broil lamb steaks just as you do beef steaks, but sprinkle well with oregano and put a pat of butter on each steak after turning it. You can broil onion slices, sprinkled with Parmesan, and lay them on top of the lamb steaks, in fact there are all sorts of things you can do about a lamb steak, but the thing you mustn't do is broil it until it is well done. Lamb must be pink inside.

Broil ¾-inch-thick chops for 2 to 3 minutes on each side.

Broil 1-inch-thick chops for 3 to 4 minutes on each side.

Broil 1½-inch-thick chops for 4 to 5 minutes on each side.

Broil a precooked ¾- to 1-inch-thick ham steak for 4 to 5 minutes per side. Brush with butter before broiling and baste every 2 minutes with butter. Serve with broiled fruit and your preferred ham sauce.

Broil hamburgers (making 4 slightly flattened hamburgers out of 1 pound ground beef) for 2 to 3 minutes on each side or to taste. Serve them as soon as outside is browned. If you dredge with paprika they will brown faster and so give you a rarer hamburger. Variation: Shape into 8 thin pieces and sandwich together with a little piece of ice in center (or butter or Roquefort cheese). Pinch into firm flattened hamburgers and broil as above. Interior will remain rarer and juicier with the ice.

BLUE STEAK

1 1½-inch-thick steak, sirloin, porterhouse or T-bone	salt and pepper
1 garlic clove, split	1 4-ounce wedge Roquefort cheese, softened

Rub both sides of steak with garlic clove and discard garlic. Broil steak on greased grill 2½ to 3 inches from hot coals. Broil until brown (about 5 minutes), season with salt and freshly ground black pepper. Turn with tongs and season second side. Spread top with Roquefort and broil until done, about 4 to 5 more minutes. Serve at once. This is for rare steak. Increase on each side for medium rare. You can test steak by cutting a slit next to bone with a very sharp knife. Serve with grilled garlic bread and watercress salad.

POMMES DEHORS

2 packages frozen French-fried
    potatoes
1 package frozen French-fried onion
    rings

¼ teaspoon each dried parsley,
    chives, chervil and tarragon
2 tablespoons butter
salt and pepper

Open frozen packages and arrange them next to each other, putting the onions in the center, on heavy foil. Sprinkle with herbs and season well. Close the foil with a double fold and place over outdoor grill. Package should be about 3 inches from coals. Turn the package every 2 minutes for 8 minutes. Open top, dot on butter and serve.

OUTDOOR GRILLED FISH STEAKS

Fish should never be overgrilled, as it becomes dry. When it is opaque and flakes easily (when tested with a fork) it is done. Always serve immediately with plenty of butter or a sauce.

Grill any fish steak, swordfish, salmon, etc., over medium heat (about 325° F.) according to thickness of steaks. The average 1-inch fish steak should grill 3 to 5 minutes on each side. If the steak is 1½ inches thick it should grill 4 to 6 minutes on each side.

Fish fillets or small split fish should grill from 3 to 5 minutes on each side. For example:

4 1-inch-thick salmon steaks
2 lemons
¼ cup butter
flour for dredging

salt, pepper and paprika
2 tablespoons chopped onion
4 sprigs parsley, ground through
    Mouli

On or before grilling, brush both sides of fish steaks with juice of 1 lemon. Quarter the second lemon and grind onion and parsley.

Just before grilling, dredge fish steaks lightly with flour, season with salt and pepper and sprinkle generously with paprika. Grill 3 inches from coals with a few "dots" of butter on each steak. Turn with tongs after about 3 minutes. Place a larger piece of butter on each steak and grill about 2 minutes. Divide remaining butter over steaks. Add chopped onion and parsley and grill 1 or 2 minutes longer. Serve immediately with lemon wedges.

ELECTRIC BROILER FISH STEAKS

Follow above directions exactly, placing fish steaks on foil-lined broiler shelf. Push into top position and broil (about 3 inches from heat unit) in the same manner as on outdoor grill, turning once with tongs.

A note regarding whole fish broiled in the in-or-outdoor grill. If you want to speed up cooking time, cut 4 incisions on each side of the fish. Do not cut through to the bone. Brush generously with butter and broil as suggested. The incisions should run diagonally across side of fish.

BROILED TROUT IN ELECTRIC BROILER

2 packages frozen rainbow trout,
    thawed (4 trout)

½ cup butter
salt and pepper
1 lemon, quartered

Heat broiler. Spread 1 tablespoon butter into cavity of each trout. Season in and outside and dot with butter on one side.

Arrange trout on broiler rack and place as close to heating unit as possible. Broil 4 minutes or until skin is lightly browned. Turn carefully with tongs, dot with remaining butter and broil 4 minutes longer. Serve at once with lemon wedges and canned whole white potatoes, heated with butter and chopped parsley. Cucumber salad is an excellent accompaniment for broiled trout.

OUTDOOR GRILLED TROUT

2 packages frozen rainbow trout,   1 pound sliced bacon
    thawed (4 trout)   1 lemon. quartered
                salt and pepper

Season trout and wrap completely in bacon strips. Leave head and tail exposed and secure bacon with wooden picks. Place wrapped fish in a hinged wire rack and cook on the barbecue grill about 3 inches from coals until bacon is crisp. Turn rack frequently to brown bacon evenly. Serve immediately with lemon wedges and coleslaw.

GRILLED MACKEREL

Grilling mackerel takes about 4 minutes to a side, but they require a long soaking in salt water before the short grilling. If you have time to buy them the day before you want to serve them, prepare them immediately and set in refrigerator until just before grilling.

Cut off heads. Dry fish with a damp cloth, split open and flatten them out completely. Lay them in a shallow pan and sprinkle them with 1 tablespoon salt and ½ teaspoon black pepper. Squeeze 1 lemon over them and add just enough water to cover.

Rinse before grilling, sprinkle with seasonings and arrange in a hinged wire rack.

Grill 4 minutes to a side and serve with grilled tomatoes and bacon, green salad and one of the foil-wrapped grilled breads.

CHAPTER XII   *Beverages*

T HIS IS no place for an erudite chapter on wines, but, as in the
Meat chapter, we stress the fact that the less loving care you are able
to give the preparation of food, the better the quality has to be. So
with the beverages, the modest little rosé has to be ice cold in order
to be palatable and if it isn't you had better open your best Burgundy. The inexpensive white wine has to be disguised in a complicated punch or Bowle or it had better be a good Rhine wine.

When there is only enough time to draw a cork, then be sure
you draw it out of a good bottle of wine and be sure you draw it
the moment you get home, before you take off your coat, so that
the wine can "breathe" while you scurry around. All this, of course,
is for red wine. Your white wine or champagne, which should have
been in the refrigerator since yesterday or in your liquor store's
refrigerator, should only be opened at the moment of serving.

At one time red wines were served only with red meat, game and
some cheeses. Now they have become so popular that they are served
with most meats and are the accepted dinner wines, irrespective of
the menu. Actually you should serve white wines with chicken,

fish, veal and lamb and red wines with beef, game, duck, goose and game birds. White wine with pork, red wine with smoked meats. There are some lamb and veal dishes which are good with red wine, others which are still best with white. Champagnes can be served with any course, although they were once served only with dessert. They are, of course, the perfect late-supper wines.

The consumption of alcohol in the average American home used to stop where the Europeans started their drinking: at the dinner table. After dinner when the average European again stopped his drinking the American resumed his with a highball or a long drink. The cocktail before dinner and the highball after dinner were the accepted rule, while Europeans went straight to the table, drank their wines with their food and usually stopped right there. A cognac or bitters might follow, but wine with dinner was the important thing and anything after dinner was taken more as an aid to digestion than as a deterrent.

Since Americans have taken to the European enjoyment of wine, they have not given up their before-and-after-dinner drinking, with the result that a well-meant dinner party can bring about a conglomeration of potables and eatables that would lay any European low, especially since cooking with wine has come into great favor. Mixtures of alcohol are thus brought about which are not always the last word in sensible living.

As a host or hostess, it is wise to serve combinations which go well together. The guest so often says (next day), "I was all right until I had that Drambuie," or "that Strega," or he deplores the fact that he had Martinis, a soup that was practically all sherry, red wine, champagne, and then, of all things, a dessert saturated with rum or kirsch and after that several B and Bs. Sometimes hosts are venturesome and want their guests to try such deadly poisons (when consumed at the wrong time and in the wrong quantity) as slivovitz or Fiori del Alpi, otherwise known as Fiori del Morti.

Beverages should be, in fact, soothing, entertaining, interesting or stimulating. They should warm and mellow the feelings, not aggravate the indigestion. Every guest should look back on the evening before with happy memories and not with the bleary eye of one who has innocently been given the worst possible combinations of ice-cold alcohol, burning-hot fried foods (breaded, of course), thick sauces and whipped cream. Give your guest a chance

—after all, you would never deliberately go out of your way to give him strychnine; why try to do it with fatal combinations?

I am reminded of a charming friend whom I met one day on Madison Avenue. He said he would like to take me to lunch but he had had such a heavy dinner the night before that he wouldn't be able to eat at all that day. He said, with a gesture as though he were slitting his throat, that he was "up to here." I sympathized, and we parted. . . . It took me two full city blocks to remember that I had been his hostess the night before.

Instant Epicures must arrange their beverages well. When there is no time there has to be organization. Since the barrier between kitchen and living rooms has been destroyed, there is no time to search out bottles or do any secret decanting. If it is going to be red wine, put it in its basket in the living room before you go to work. A word here about the wine basket (or wire contraption that takes its place). Red wine has sediment which should not be stirred. In theory you are putting the horizontal bottle from your cool cellar into a horizontal basket so that the sediment remains undisturbed. In fact, you probably bounced the red wine bottle up and down in your arms on the way home from the package store. It would be sheer affectation to put it into a basket after that. Draw out the cork when you get home, as we said before. Put out ice cubes and open the cupboard or whatever serves you as a bar. Set out something that is ready, like salted nuts, and go and mix one of those simple hors d'oeuvres while drinks are being served. Bring in the electric skillet, plug it in and join your guests. Presumably you took the steaks out of the refrigerator and let them "breathe" with the red wine. Serve cheese and fruit with the last of the red wine, serve cognac or a highball later, and feel free to lunch with any of your guests next day.

LAIT DE POULE
(Hen's milk, considered a strengthening drink in France.)
(per person requiring strength)

1 egg yolk

2 tablespoons powdered sugar

1/3 cup boiling water

2–3 tablespoons heavy rum, heated

Beat yolk and sugar until pale and creamy. Continue to beat while gradually adding boiling water and heated rum. Serve at once in heated beaker, and feel your strength returning.

G R O G
(per person)

When we got around in stagecoaches this sort of thing was good to find at the end of an arduous forty miles. Now that we are driving those air-conditioned cars, this sort of thing is good to find at the end of a comfortable forty miles, provided it's winter and cold.

¼ cup rum
¼ cup brandy
2 lumps sugar

1 cup strong tea
2 tablespoons Curaçao
boiling water
2 lemon slices

Heat rum, brandy, sugar, tea and Curaçao. Add boiling water to taste, pour into pewter or silver beakers, add lemon slices and serve as hot as possible.

B L U E   B L A Z E S
(per person)

1 teaspoon sugar
1 teaspoon honey
1 jigger Scotch whisky

1 jigger boiling water
nutmeg
1 spiral of lemon peel

In a silver beaker or pewter mug, stir sugar and honey. Add whisky and water. Sprinkle with nutmeg to taste, add a lemon spiral and ignite. Serve flaming—drink after the flame dies down.

P O U S S E - C A F É   I   A N D   I I
(per person)

Variation I

Equal parts of the following ingredients should be floated on top of each other in a tall narrow glass. They have to be used in the following rotation:

raspberry syrup

maraschino

yellow Chartreuse

brandy

To prepare, pour liqueur very gradually, gently and carefully down the side of the glass to float it on the liqueur already in the glass. Drink all failures* and very soon you won't care whether they float or not. Just so long as you float.

* With each failure your hand will become steadily unsteadier.

Variation II

Follow all directions and warnings as for Pousse-Café I.

(per person)

green Chartreuse

Curaçao

kirsch

brandy

This is the deadlier of the species, but the better, naturally.

C A P U C I N O

4 cups boiling water

instant coffee, to taste

½ cup heavy cream, whipped, or
    4 large squirts whipped cream
    topping

1 tablespoon cocoa powder

granulated sugar to taste

Prepare instant coffee, cover with stiffly whipped cream and before it melts, dust with cocoa. Do this through a fine sieve or with a sprinkler, to make a film of cocoa over the cream.

Pass sugar separately, or let guests first sugar their coffee, then add cream and cocoa.

J A M A I C A N C O F F E E

4 cups strong hot coffee

1 orange

4 tablespoons dark brown sugar

¼ teaspoon cinnamon stick

4 cloves

¾ cup rum, or to taste

With a potato peeler, cut the thin outside rind from one orange and place it in a saucepan with sugar and cinnamon. With a wooden spoon, crush the sugar and cinnamon over the orange rind until it is bruised and some of the oils have been rubbed into the sugar. Add cloves and rum and heat to boiling. Pour hot coffee into the mixture, strain into cups and serve.

ADULT COCOA

4 cups hot sweetened cocoa
¼ teaspoon vanilla
½ pinch salt

4 tablespoons brandy
¼ cup heavy cream, whipped, or
    whipped cream topping

Prepare cocoa according to directions on label, add vanilla and the least salt possible. Add brandy and serve topped with whipped cream.

CINNAMON TEA
(For a change)

4 cups water
1 stick cinnamon

instant tea, to taste
¼ cup Curaçao
sugar to taste

Bring water to boil with cinnamon, pour into cups, add instant tea to taste and about 1 tablespoon Curaçao per cup. Sugar to taste, and naturally drink it as hot as possible. It's a lovely tea to drink at the end of dinner instead of dessert.

The reason the names of drinks are so odd is that they spring from fuzzy minds. You couldn't spend the night concocting a new drink (and drinking all the experiments) and then call it Alcoholic Beverage #222. You'd call it Druid's Dream or Murder on the High Street, too. Or you'd just call it Thunder if you had had the wit to dream up this combination.

THUNDER
(per person)

1 tablespoon sugar	1 jigger brandy
1 egg	1 dash cayenne pepper

Blend or shake well, pour over shaved ice and serve frappé. Thunder is supposed to be served in yellow stemmed glasses—but who, today, has or even wants yellow stemmed glasses? Just drink it out of any glass, large enough to hold your Thunder.

Cocktails

Among this dashing assortment of beverages we come down to earth with six very ordinary cocktail recipes. They are inserted here for the sake of the man who drinks his "on the rocks" and doesn't care what his guests would prefer, and for the single woman who doesn't know how to mix a proper drink. This extremely important phase of her life might be entitled "Cocktails and the Single Woman" and if she takes it properly to heart she won't be single very long.

The single woman and her cocktails fall into three categories. First, the commonest, she prepares a drink tray and then she washes her hands of the whole thing. She simply asks her young man, or old one, to mix the drinks. If she happens to be "going" with a retired bartender this is splendid. If she is not steadily occupied this may mean superb drinks when Rupert is presiding and hideous ones when James is in the driver's seat. In any case it produces irregular drinks and no single woman can afford to serve anything but the best at all times.

The second category mixes the drinks herself and most of her guests know exactly why she is single and why she is going to stay that way. She mixes up a great shakerful of sweet Manhattans or she produces something with lots of syrupy fruit in it. The last category of all is rare. It consists of the few women who can retain their feminine charm and still shake up strong, good, man-sized cocktails. For the single women who want to join this category, here are a few good, straightforward recipes and if you do it right you'll soon give up the single state. After many years the way to a man's heart is still through his stomach, the only difference is that alcohol speeds the journey.

MARTINI

6 parts House of Lords gin, or   1 part Boissier dry vermouth
    the gin of your choice   lots of ice

Stir and serve with a twist of lemon peel.

WHISKY SOURS

In the home of a famous New York neurologist, the time that is spent in drinking whiskey sours is known as the Sour Hour. This has nothing to do with the guests or the host, it's just the lemon juice and the lack of too much sugar.

3 parts blended whisky   2 parts lemon juice
    ½ of 1 part sugar

Shake with lots of ice.

The sugar can be increased to taste or it can be measured at the rate of 1 teaspoon per juice of 1 lemon.

If you've had what is known as "the night before," this makes you feel virtuous (also very well) on what is known as "the morning after." If you continue with the Bloody Marys too long you'll find yourself right back at the night before.

BLOODY MARY

Following proportions are based on a 2-ounce jigger.

4 jiggers vodka   1 dash Tabasco
5 jiggers tomato juice   ½ teaspoon salt, or to taste
2 tablespoons lemon juice   black pepper in a coarse-grinding
3 dashes Worcestershire sauce,   pepper mill
    or to taste

Combine all ingredients in a large shaker. Grind black pepper into the shaker, about four good grindings, or to taste. Shake well and serve.

PERFECT MANHATTANS

2 jiggers blended whisky   ½ jigger sweet vermouth
                ½ jigger dry vermouth

Stir with lots of ice.

NEGRONI

Use a 2-ounce jigger.

3 jiggers gin   1 jigger Campari bitters

Stir in shaker with lots of ice as you would a Martini.

DAIQUIRI

Use a 2-ounce jigger.

2 jiggers white rum   2 tablespoons sugar, or to taste
1 jigger lime juice   2 dashes orange bitters

Shake with lots of ice.

FROZEN DAIQUIRI

1½ cups crushed ice   3 jiggers lemon juice
4 jiggers light rum   1 egg white
3 teaspoons powdered sugar, or   1 pony Curaçao
    to taste

Combine in a blender the ice, rum, sugar, lemon juice and egg white until it has reached consistency of sherbet. Pour into wide champagne glasses and float a little Curaçao on each glass. Drink through short straws.

SANGRÍA

The Spaniards serve this in place of wine with dinner. It is a lovely beverage in Spain and can be equally good here if your wine dealer stocks Spanish Burgundy. This is not the proper moment for a mercantile note, but Spanish Burgundy is inexpensive, and with the addition of soda you can serve this without pocketbook qualms.

1 bottle Spanish Burgundy	1 split club soda
4 teaspoons sugar	1 lemon, sliced
3 ounces brandy (1½ jiggers)	1 orange, sliced

Pour wine into large pitcher, add all other ingredients and stir well. Fill pitcher with ice, stir again and serve. If you have one of those pitchers that keeps the ice separate in a glass container, use it.

ANNO DOMINI 1 7 5 9

1 bottle red wine	2 cups boiling water
12 lumps sugar	½ cup brandy
6 cloves	½ cup Curaçao
1 stick cinnamon, optional	
thinly peeled orange rind	

Peel 1 long curl of rind from orange with a potato peeler. Heat wine, sugar, cloves, cinnamon and orange rind just to a boil, but do not allow to boil. Add boiling water, brandy and Curaçao, pour into cups, glasses or beakers and serve at once. Nutmeg may be sprinkled on top.

CHRISTMAS GLOW

1 bottle red wine	½ cup sugar or to taste
1 tablespoon honey	½ cup brandy
1 sliced lemon	½ cup cherry brandy
	½ cup boiling water

Heat first 4 ingredients and stir until honey is dissolved—do not boil. Add brandies and boiling water and serve in goblets.

MULLED WINE

1 bottle red wine	¾ cup sugar
1½ tablespoons honey	1 cup brandy
½ orange, sliced thin	¼ cup cherry brandy
½ lemon, sliced thin	¾ cup boiling water

top with nutmeg to taste

Heat first 5 ingredients and stir until honey is dissolved—do not boil. Add brandies and boiling water and serve in goblets.

Drinks don't originate in laboratories. They are combinations worked up by thirsty men or they are devised by bartenders or they are born of necessity. When you've just got a little brandy and a little Benedictine in the house what are you going to invent? A B and B, of course.

BENEDICTINE FRAPPÉ

1 quart lemon sherbet	½ cup Benedictine

Blend or stir together and serve immediately in tall glasses.

CRÈME DE MENTHE FRAPPÉ

1 quart lemon sherbet	4–6 tablespoons crème de menthe

Blend or stir together and serve at once in tall glasses. This is also good using orange sherbet and Curaçao.

GREEN MINT FROST

4 ice cubes, crushed	3 jiggers crème de menthe
1 cup frozen lime or lemon sherbet	(4½ ounces)

4 sprigs mint

Blend until frappéed or shake vigorously. Pour into chilled highball glasses and decorate with mint sprigs. Drink through straws.

BANANA BLEND

4 egg yolks

2 bananas, peeled and cut into 1-inch pieces

2 cups cold milk

cocoa powder, cinnamon or nutmeg

Blend all ingredients, pour into cold glasses, sprinkle with cocoa, cinnamon or nutmeg and serve.

OMNIBUS
(per person)

1 dash grenadine

1 jigger kirsch

ice

club soda to taste

Combine grenadine and kirsch, stir, add ice and soda water.

ALEXANDER

2 jiggers gin

2 jiggers crème de cacao

2 jiggers white crème de menthe

½ cup heavy cream

1 cup crushed ice

Blend only until mixed, about 4 seconds, or shake vigorously. Strain into stemmed glasses and serve.

We are constantly told "How to Mix Drinks" or how to be "The Perfect Bartender." We are never given anything on "How to Drink Drinks" or how to be "The Perfect Bar Attendant." It's not hard to learn. First rule is to enjoy it, don't do it quickly and don't do it for effect only. There should be pleasure, relaxation, and, all things considered, there should be a companion or company. There is really very little point in drinking alone unless you are ambitious about becoming a member of the AA.

FISHERMAN'S PRAYER

1 tablespoon sugar	½ cup raspberry syrup
1 tablespoon lemon juice	1 cup rum

Shake all ingredients with ice, pour over ice cubes in tall glasses and fill with soda water. Add fresh fruit and serve with straws.

Suggested Fruits:

> sliced orange
> pineapple chunks
> raspberries
> sliced peaches

WHITE LION
(per person)

chopped ice in tall glass	1 tablespoon Curaçao
1 tablespoon sugar	½ cup rum
1 dash lemon juice	soda water
1 tablespoon raspberry juice	pineapple and strawberries

Half fill glass with ice. Mix next 5 ingredients, pour over ice, add soda water to taste and decorate with fruit slices and berries.

BRANDY CRUSTA
(per person)

2 dashes Angostura bitters	1 jigger cognac
2 dashes maraschino	1 spiral of lemon peel
½ teaspoon lemon juice	½ cup fresh fruit and/or berries
powdered sugar for glasses	

Moisten the edge of a wide, stemmed glass and dip in powdered sugar to make a border of sugar. Arrange fresh fruit and/or berries in glass. Place first 5 ingredients in shaker with chopped ice. Shake well and pour on fruit.

PHILADELPHIA BOATING PUNCH
(per person)

1 dash lemon juice

1 jigger brandy

1 jigger rum

ice

soda water

1 lemon slice

mixed fruits, optional

Mix all ingredients in a tall glass, stir and drink through a straw. If you like, a slice of orange, a chunk of pineapple, a strawberry or cherry may be added.

The real, full, enchanting, exhilarating enjoyment of a Bowle can only come when there is something wonderful to celebrate. Don't try one at the end of a long day at the office. And don't try one without music.

PEACH BOWLE

6 peaches

sugar to taste

2 bottles light red wine or rosé

1 bottle Burgundy

1 bottle champagne

Peel ripe peaches, cut them into slices and sprinkle with sugar. Depending on sweetness of peaches, increase or decrease sugar. Pour rosé over peaches and chill until needed. Add Burgundy and wait 15 minutes, add iced champagne and serve at once. Do not let too much time elapse while chilling, as the peaches turn dark.

ORANGE BOWLE

This name sounds vaguely like a football game.

4 large oranges

1 cup granulated sugar

4 bottles Mosel wine, chilled

1 bottle champagne, chilled

Grate the rind of one of the oranges over the sugar in a punch bowl. Peel all the oranges with a sharp knife, removing the pith, and slice the oranges across into thin slices, removing all pits. Pour 1 bottle Mosel wine over the sugar and grated rind. Drain the orange slices, add them and the remaining wine to bowl. Add champagne and serve.

Index

Abjy L'Amid (soup), 43
Adult Cocoa, 279
Agnellotti (soup), 47
Alexander Cocktail, 285
Algerian Tomatoes, 161
Ambrosia in Haste, 250
American Tomatoes, 158
Anchovy, Anchovies
  Dip, 33
  Sauce for Hot Salmon, 231
  Toulon, 24
Angels on Horseback, 72
Anno Domini 1759, 283
Antiboise Sauce, 222
Antilles Melon, 249
Appetizers, see Hors d'Oeuvres
Apple
  and Endive Salad, 206
  Horseradish Sauce, 226
  Salad, Dutch, 206
  Sauce, 260
  Sauce, Eden, 260
  Soup, 55
Apricot, Apricots
  Fines Bouches, 240
  Purée, 258
  Sauce, Hot, 234
Artichoke
  and Lobster, 22
  Hearts, 147
  Hearts, Salad of, 201
  Ways of Preparing (2), 144
  Whole Hearts in Hollandaise Sauce,
    146
Asparagus
  Taranto, 146
  Ways of preparing (4), 144
Ateca Salad, 193
Avocado, 231
  Cocktail, 23
  Dip, 34
  Dressing, 224

Habana, 23
Sauce, 224

Babas, 241
  au Rhum, 241
Bacon
  Salad, 200
  Wrapped Frankfurters, 266
Baked Bananas, 248
Baked Cheese and Tomato Sand-
    wiches, 95
Baked French Loaf, 186
Baked Tomatoes, 161
Baked Tomatoes, Balkan, 158
Baked Oysters, 70
Baked Pineapple, 250
Baked Sweet Potatoes, 150
Balance (dessert), 246
Balkan Baked Tomatoes, 158
Banana, Bananas
  and Peperoni, 18
  Baked, 248
  Blend, 285
  Flambée, 248
Barbecued Broiler, 134
Batwinja (soup), 56
Beef à la Russe, 117
Beef Sauté, 117
Beefeater Lobster Cocktail, 84
Beet Salad, 193
Beets, 148
Belgian Fruit Pudding, 258
Belle Hélène Salad, 207
Benedictine Frappé, 284
Bermuda Mushrooms, 164
BEVERAGES, 274-288
  Adult Cocoa, 279
  Alexander, 285
  Anno Domini 1759, 283
  Blue Blazes, 277
  Banana Blend, 285
  Brandy
    Adult Cocoa, 279

Crème de Cognac, 253
Crusta, 286
Grog, 277
Philadelphia Boating Punch, 286
Thunder, 280
Brandy Crusta, 286
Capucino, 278
Christmas Glow, 283
Cinnamon Tea, 279
Cognac, *see* Brandy
Cocoa
　Adult, 279
　Capucino, 278
Cocktails, 280
　Alexander, 285
　Bloody Mary, 281
　Daiquiri, 282
　Frozen Daiquiri, 282
　Manhattans, Perfect, 282
　Martini, 281
　Negroni, 282
　Whisky Sour, 281
Coffee
　Capucino, 278
　Jamaican, 278
Crème de Menthe Frappé, 284
Fisherman's Prayer, 286
Gin
　Alexander, 285
　Martini, 281
　Negroni, 282
Green Mint Frost, 284
Grog, 277
Jamaican Coffee, 278
Lait de Poule, 276
Liqueurs
　Alexander, 285
　Crème de Menthe Frappé, 284
　Green Mint Frost, 284
　Omnibus, 285
　Pousse-Café I, 277; II, 278
Mulled Wine, 284
Omnibus, 285
Orange Bowle, 287
Peach Bowle, 287
Philadelphia Boating Punch, 287
Pousse-Café I, 277; II, 278
Rum
　Daiquiri, 282
　Fisherman's Prayer, 286
　Frozen Daiquiri, 282
　Grog, 277
　Lait de Poule, 276
　Philadelphia Boating Punch, 287
　White Lion, 286
Sangría, 283
Tea
　Cinnamon, 279

Grog, 277
Thunder, 280
Whisky
　Blue Blazes, 277
　Perfect Manhattans, 282
　Sour, 281
White Lion, 286
Wine
　Anno Domini 1759, 283
　Christmas Glow, 283
　Mulled, 284
　Orange Bowle, 287
　Peach Bowle, 287
　Sangría, 283
Vodka
　Bloody Mary, 281
Biscuits, Ways of Preparing, 189
Bisque Anita, 40
Blender French Dressing, 211
Blender Mayonnaise I–IV, 211-212
Black Beauty (dessert), 258
Bloody Mary, 281
Blue Blazes, 277
Blue Cheese Dip, 33
Blue Steak, 270
Borsch I and II, 45; III through VI,
　46; in blender, 45
Bouillon, 47
Brandy (*see also* Beverages)
　Crusta, 286
　Lobster Cocktail, 84
　Peaches, Burnt, 254
　Pears, 252
Bread Crumb Sauce, Hot, I, 224; II
　and III, 225
BREAD, 182-189
　Biscuits, oven-ready, ways of pre-
　　paring, 189
　Bread, Breads
　　Bulgar Cheese, 96
　　Curried, 185
　　Holiday, 186
　　Italian, 183
　　Italian Broiled, 183
　　Onion, 187
　　Rye, Hot, 184
　　Seeded, 184
　　Slices, 5 ways of preparing, 187
　Brioche, Toasted, 188
　Cinnamon Toast with Apple Sauce,
　　183
　Loaves
　　French, Baked, 186
　　Rye, Sliced, 188
　　White, Sliced, 187
　Muffins, Herbed, 184
　Pain Retrouvé, 185
　Rolls, Brown-and-Serve, 8 ways of

preparing, 188
Salt Sticks, Caraway, 185
Toast, Cinnamon with Apple Sauce, 183
Broiled Chicken Improvement, 134
Broiled Filet Steaks, 119
Broiled Frogs' Legs, 265
Broiled Italian Bread, 183
Broiled Scallops, 80
Broiled Shrimp, 263
Broiled Shrimp I and II, 264
Broiled Trout, 79
Broiled Trout (Outdoor), 272
Brown-and-Serve Rolls, 8 ways of preparing, 188
Brown Sauce, 221
Brussels Salad, 96
Bulgar Cheese Breads, 96
Bulgarian Cheese Soup, 41
Bulgarian Chicken and Yogurt Soup, 50
Bulgarian Chicken Soup, 54
Bulgarian Sauce for Fish I and II, 231
Bulgarian Yogurt Soup, 42
Burgos Salad, 195
Burnt Brandy Peaches, 254
Butter Crème Fülle (filling), 257
Buttered Rum Peaches, 254

Calf's Liver, 123
and Bacon, 123
Camerani (soup), 48
Candied Fruit and Apple, 251
Candied Sweet Potatoes, 151
Capri Mushrooms, 165
Capucino, 278
Caraway Salt Sticks, 185
Carnival Dip, 32
Caviar, see Hors d'Oeuvres
Celery Seed Dressing, 209
Chad's Shrimp Cocktail, 21
Charcoal-Broiled Lobster, 269
CHEESE, 87-97 (see also Hors d' Oeuvres, Soups and Salads)
Brussels Salad, 96
Bulgar Cheese Breads, 96
Cheese
and Tomato Sandwiches, Baked, 95
Devil, 93
en Brochette, 93
Envelopes, 92
Muff, 93
Quick, 92
Scramble, 98
Slaw I, 96; II, 97
Waffles, 97
Cheeses, 87

Croque-Madame, 95
Croque-Monsieur, 94
Deviled Cheese, 94
Fondue au Vin Blanc, 91
Fondue Neufchâteloise, 92
Freiburg Fondue, 91
Hungarian Toast, 95
Mornay Luncheon Dishes, Twelve, 90
Sunday Cheese, 97
Zuppa Pavese, 48
Cherry, Cherries
Jubilée, 253
Salad, 206
Sauce, Hot, 228
Chicken
and Coconut Soup, 53
and Rice, with Herbs, 181
Consommé, Cold, 51
8-Minute, 135
in Cantaloupe, Cold, 136
in Red Wine, 136
Tetrazzini, 135
Wing Dinner, 138
with Onion Sauce, 136
Chicken Liver Pâté, 16
Chicken Livers
in Sour Cream, 137
with Apple Rings, 137
Denise, 138
Chive Cheese Dip, 32
Christmas Glow, 283
Cinnamon Tea, 279
Cinnamon Toast with Apple Sauce, 183
Clam (see also Fish)
Bisque, 39
Combine, 40
Juice Cocktail, 15
Juice Marinara, 40
Cocktails, see Beverages
Cocktail Frankfurters in Hot Sauce, I, 29; II, 30
Codfish Steaks, 82
Coffee Sauce, 234
Coffee Whip Sauce, 235
Combination Dressing I and II, 209
Consommé
Africaine, 44
Agnès Sorrel, 50
Mikado, 49
Nesselrode, 50
Zephyr, 50
Continental Rice, 180
Coquilles St. Jacques de Bordeaux, 80
Corn, Clam and Shrimp Casserole, 78
Cosmopolitan Mushrooms, 165
Côtelette à la Florentine, 129

Cottage Cheese Relish, 215
Crab Meat, 76
  and Artichoke Hearts, 76
  and Rice Casserole, 180
  and Shrimp Casserole, 77
  Creamed, 76
  Remick, 77
  with Avocado Sauce, 22
Cranberry Apricot Sauce, 228
Canberry Relish, Raw, 216
Cream Cheese and Red Caviar, 28
Cream Cheese Dip, 31
Cream Sauce, Medium, 221
Creamed Crab Meat, 76
Crème Bachique, 243
Crème de Cognac à la Minute, 253
Crème de Kirsch with Black Cherries, 253
Crème de Menthe Frappé, 284
Crème Germinal, 55
Crème Miranda, 53
Crêpes
  Blanchette, 111
  Canarino, 109
  Danish, 111
  Fruit-Filled, 109
  Leonardo, 111
  Suzette, 110
  Trocadéro, 111
Croque-Madame, 95
Croque-Monsieur, 94
Cucumber
  and Zucchini, 154
  au Gratin, 154
  Salad Sauce, 214
  Sauce for Chicken, 228
  Shrimp Soup, Cold, 38
Curried Bread, 185
Curried Eggs, 100
Curried Tomatoes, 158
Curry Mayonnaise, 212

Daiquiri, 282
Danish Crêpes, 111
Danish Salad, 195
Dessert Sauces, 233 (*see also* under Sauces)
DESSERTS, 237-260
  Alaska, Orange, 239; Peach, 240
  Ambrosia in Haste, 250
  Ambrosia, Mixed, 251
  Americana, Tropical, 246
  Apple
    and Candied Fruit, 251
    Sauce, 260
    Sauce, Eden, 250
  Apricots
    Fines Bouches, 240

    Flamed, 240
    Purée, 258
  Babas, 241
    au Rhum, 241
  Bachique, Crème, 243
  Balance, 246
  Bananas
    Baked, 248
    Flambée, 248
  Belgian Fruit Pudding, 258
  Black Beauty, 258
  Brandy Peaches, Burnt, 254
  Bandy Pears, 252
  Butter Crème Fülle, 257
  Buttered Rum Peaches, 254
  Candied Fruit and Apples, 251
  Chaudeau, Wine, 242
  Cherries Jubilée, 253
  Chocolat, Mayonnaise au, 245
  Chocolate Icing, French, 259
  Cream, Raspberry, 259; Strawberry, 259
  Crème Bachique, 243
  Crème de Cognac à la Minute, 253
  Crème de Kirsch with Black Cherries, 253
  Crème Fülle, Butter, 257
  Crème, Peach, 254
  Drybus, 245
  Eden Apple Sauce, 260
  Everest, Pineapple, Baked, 239
  Figs, Jamaica, 248
  Fines Bouches, Apricots, 240
  French Chocolate Icing, 257
  Fruit
    Belgian, Pudding, 258
    Candied, and Apple, 251
    with Sour Cream, 12 Variations, 247
  Grapes, Iced, 252
  Lemon
    Foam, 244
    Ice, and Green Mint, 257
    Mousse, 244
  Mayonnaise au Chocolat, 245
  Melon, Antilles, 249
  Melons, Oporto, 249
  Michel, Zabaione, 243
  Mint, Green, and Lemon Ice, 257
  Mixed Feelings, 250
  Mousse, Lemon, 244; Orange, 245
  Neros, 245
  Nougat, Peach, 255
  Omelette aux Confitures, 257
  Oporto Melons, 249
  Oporto, Port of, 249
  Orange
    Alaska, 239

Dessert, 244
Marmalade Roll, 256
Mousse, 245
Prune Whip, 259
Zabaione, 243
Pancakes, Puffed, 241
Peach
Alaska, 240
Crème, 254
Nougat, 255
Nut, 256
Peaches
and Preserves, 255
Burnt Brandy, 254
Buttered Rum, 254
Honeyed, 254
Hot and Cold, 255
Pears
Brandy, 252
Ginger, 252
Pineapple
Baked, 250
Everest, 239
Port of Oporto, The, 249
Pruneaux au Vin, 251
Prune Whip, Orange, 259
Prunes, Spiced, with Walnuts, 251
Raspberry Cream, 259
Rich Knights, 256
Rum, Buttered, and Peaches, 254
Rum Omelet, 257
Strawberries Mickey, 248
Strawberry Cream, 259
Tropical Americana, 246
Unbalance, 246
Walnuts with Spiced Prunes, 251
Wine Chadeau, 242
Zabaione, 243
Michel, 243
Orange, 243
Deviled Cheese, 94
Dieppe Sole, 79
DIPS, 30
Anchovy, 33
Avocado, 34
Blue Cheese, 33
Carnival, 32
Cheese, Hot, 34
Chive Cheese, 32
Cream Cheese, 31
Watercress, 32
Double Boiler Spanish Eggs, 105
Dressings, Salad, 207
see Salad Dressing
Drinks, *see* Beverages
Drybus (dessert) , 245
Dutch Apple Salad, 206

Eastern Vegetables, 145
Eden Apple Sauce, 260
EGGS, 98-111
Crêpes
Blanchette, 112
Canarino, 109
Danish, 111
Fruit-Filled, 109
Leonardo, 111
Suzette, 110
Trocadéro, 111
Egg, Eggs
and Oyster Fry, 74
Copenhagen, 103
Curried, 110
Double Boiler Spanish, 105
Five-Minute, 100
Fried au Beurre Noir, 99
Genoese, 106
Green, 102
in Black Butter, 106
Mariner's, 106
Mollet, 101
Parmesan, 107
Pomodoro, 106
Salad, 194
Soup, 53
Surprise, 105
Swiss, 100
Terminus,102
Tivoli, 103
Vivex, 103
Omelets, 103
Omelette Normande, 104
Pallatchinken, 110
Cheese, 110
Pancakes, 107
Frutto di Mare, 109
Jonas, 112
Käte's, 112
Thin Crêpes, 108
Tuna, 110
Scrambled Salmon, 104
Tschimbur, 107
Electric Broiler Fish Steaks, 272
Endive Salad, 205
and Apple, 206

Figs and Salami, 17
Filet, Filets, 114
Diana, 115
Florentine, 121
Lyonnaise, 121
Marsala, 116
Marseillaise, 121
Mikado, 121
Nesselrode, 121

Pan-Broiled, Medium or Well Done, 119; Rare, 119
Rossini, 122
FISH, 60-86
Angels on Horseback, 72
Codfish Steaks, 82
Coquilles St. Jacques de Bordeaux, 80
Corn, Clam and Shrimp Casserole, 78
Crab Meat
  and Artichoke Hearts, 76
  and Shrimp Casserole, 77
  Creamed, 76
  Remick, 77
Crabs, Soft-Shell, Amandine, 77
Egg and Oyster Fry, 74
Fish Steaks, 81
Flounder Casserole, 78
  Green, 78
Frogs' Legs, Fried, 86
Frutto di Mare, 109
Halibut Steaks, 82
Lobster
  Beefeater Cocktail, 84
  Brandy Cocktail, 84
  Landeck, 83
  Carol, 83
  Casserole, 85
  Spread, 83
  Thermidor, 85
  with Herbs, 85
Oysters, 69
  and Corn Casserole, 72
  and Egg Fry, 74
  and Tomato Chowder, 75
  Angels on Horseback, 72
  Baked, 70
  Casino, 71
  Gratinée, 75
  Light Fried, 74
  on Anchovy Toast, 73
  Pan-Fried, 73
  Pompadour, 73
  Rockefeller, 71
  Stew, Elmira, 74
  Stew, Pasquale, 75
  Wladimir, 73
Salmon Steaks, 82
Scallops, 79
  Amandine, 80
  in White Wine, 81
Shrimp, 62
  and Crab Bisque, 41
  and Corn Casserole, 65
  and Mushroom Casserole, 67
  Basil, 67
  Casserole, 63

Cocktail or Salad, 66
Curry, 69
de Jonghe, 67
Fried Ground, 64
Hot, in Red Sauce, 64
in Dill Sauce, 68
Japanese Spring, 65
Marinated, 68
Poor, 63
Salad Vertain, 65
Summer Salad, 66
Wiggle, 69
Sole, Dieppe, 79
Swordfish Steaks, 82
Trout, Broiled, 79
Fish Steaks, 81
Fisherman's Prayer, 286
Five-Minute Eggs, 100
Florida Mayonnaise, 224
Flamed Apricots, 240
Flounder Casserole, 78
Foil-Wrapped Frankfurters, 266
Fondue
  au Vin Blanc, 91
  Bourguignonne, 130
  de Veau, 131
  Freiburg, 91
  Neufchâteloise, 92
  Oriental, 131
Frankfurters
  Bacon-Wrapped, 266
  Foil-Wrapped, 266
  with Apple Sauerkraut, Grilled, 126
Fried Eggs au Beurre Noir, 99
Fried Frogs' Legs, 86
Fried Ground Shrimp, 64
Fried Potatoes I and II, 152
Fried Tomatoes, 157
Frozen Daiquiri, 282
Frozen Hors d'Oeuvres, 34
Frozen Vegetables, The, 143
  Artichoke, 2 ways of Preparing, 144
  Asparagus, 4 ways of preparing, 144
  Cauliflower, 2 ways of preparing, 145
  Green Beans, 2 ways of preparing, 145
  Wax Beans, 2 ways of preparing, 145
Fruit
  Filled Crêpes, 109
  Salad, 207
  with Sour Cream, 12 variations, 247
Frutto di Mare, 109

Garden Relish, 216
Garlic Dressing, 213
Gazpacho Andaluz, 58
Genoese Eggs, 106
Génoise Sauce, 223

German Coleslaw, 196
German Supper Salad, 196
Gin, *see* Beverages
Ginger Pears, 252
Ginger Rice, 177
Glazed Beets, 149
Glazed Onions, 153
Gourmet Salad, 193
Grape and Zucchini Salad, 202
Green Eggs, 102
Green Flounder Casserole, 78
Green Mint Frost, 284
Green Mint and Lemon Ice, 257
Greenwich Mayonnaise, 222
Grilled Filet Steaks with Herb Butter, 116
Grilled Frankfurters, 265
  Split, 266
  Whole, 265
Grilled Lamb Chops I and II, 269
Grilled Mackerel, 273
Grilled Onion Slices, 153
Grilled Tomato Slices, 157
Grog, 277
Gulyas Soup, 59

Halibut Steaks, 82
Ham
  and Pineapple Appetizer, 18
  Asparagus Rolls, 127
  Salad, 203
  Soup, 54
  with Artichoke Hearts, 127
Hanover Sauce, 226
Hard Sauce I, II and III, 233; IV, 234
Herbed Muffins, 184
Herbed Mushrooms, 166
Herbed Veal, 129
Herring in Mustard Sauce, 24
Holiday Bread, 186
Honeyed Peaches, 254
Horatio Mayonnaise, 233
HORS D'OEUVRES, 13–35
  Anchovies, Toulon, 24
  Anchovy Dip, 33
  Artichoke and Lobster, 22
  Artichoke Hearts, Italian, 17
  Avocado
    Cocktail, 23
    Dip, 34
    Habana, 23
    Sauce, with Crab Meat, 22
    Sherried, 22
  Beans, Kidney, 16
  Blue Cheese Dip, 32
  Carnival Dip, 32
  Caviar
    and Cream Cheese, Dip, 31
    and Tomatoes, 23
    Red, and Cream Cheese, 28
  Cheese
    and Ham Puffs, 26
    Blue, Dip, 33
    Chive, Dip, 32
    Cream, and Red Caviar, 28
    Cream, Dip, 31
    Dip, Hot, 34
    Drops, Parmesan, 27
    Melted, 27
    Puffs, I and II, 26
    Stuffed Endive, 27
  Chicken Liver Pâté, 16
  Chive Cheese Dip, 32
  Clam Juice Cocktail, 15
  Cream Cheese and Red Caviar, 28
  Cream Cheese Dip, 31
  Dips, 30
  Endive, Cheese-Stuffed, 27
  Figs and Salami, 17
  Frankfurters in Hot Sauce I, 29; II, 30
  Ham and Pineapple, 18
  Herring in Mustard Sauce, 24
  Hors d'Oeuvres, Frozen, 34
  Ketchup Dip, Raw Vegetable, 31
  Kidney Beans, 16
  Liver Pâté I, 18; II, 19
  Liver Sausage and Grapes, 18
  Lobster
    and Artichoke, 22
    Auguste, 21
    Cocktail, 21
  Melon and Prosciutto, 17
  Mushrooms
    Italian, 16
    Stuffed I and II, 28; III, 29
  Mustard Dip, Raw Vegetable, 31
  Peperoni and Bananas, 18
  Sardine Puffs, 25
  Sardine Spread, 25
  Shrimp
    Cocktail I, 20; II, Hot, 20
    Chad's, 21
    Norwegian, 24
  Tomatoes and Caviar, 23
  Tomato Juice Cocktail, 15
  "The Farm" Puffs, 26
  Watercress Dip, 32
Horseradish Apple Sauce, 226
Humberto Salad, 194
Hungarian Mushrooms, 166
Hungarian Toast, 95

Iced Grapes, 252

Instant Mashed Potatoes, I to VI, 149;
    VII to X, 150
Italian Artichoke Hearts, 17
Italian Baked Tomatoes, 156
Italian Bread, 183
Italian Dressing, 210
Italian Mushrooms, 16
Italian Spinach, 148

Jamaica Figs, 248
Jamaican Coffee, 278
Japanese Spring Shrimp, 65
Jonas Pancakes, 112

Kidney Beans, 16
Kidneys in Mustard Sauce I, 124; II,
    125
Käte's Pancakes, 112

Lait de Poule, 276
Leek
    and Clam Soup, 42
    Soup, 43
    Soup Gratinée, 43
Lemon
    Foam, 244
    Ice and Green Mint, 257
    Mayonnaise, 212
    Mousse, 244
Light Fried Oysters, 74
Liqueurs, *see* Beverages
Liver Pâté I, 18; II, 19
Liver Sausage and Grapes, 18
Livournaise Sauce, 232
Lobster
    and Artichoke, 22
    and Lime Rice, 177
    Auguste, 21
    Beefeater Cocktail, 84
    Carol, 83
    Casserole, 85
    Charcoal-Broiled, 269
    Cocktail, 21
    Landeck, 83
    Soup, 39
    Spread, 83
    Thermidor, 85
    with Herbs, 85
Lucerne Toast, 126

Macaroni
    and Tuna Casserole, 173
    in Casserole, 172
Madeira Filets, 116
Madrilène
    Cold, 51
    Costa Brava, 52
    Hot, 52

Maltese Soup, 48
Marinated Shrimp, 68
Mariner's Eggs, 106
Martini, 281
Mayonnaise au Chocolat, 245
MEAT, MEATS, 113-131
    Beef Sauté, 117
    Beef à la Russe, 117
    Côtelette à la Florentine, 129
    Filet Steaks, 114
        Broiled, 119
        Diana, 115
        Florentine, 121
        Grilled, with Herb Butter, 116
        Lyonnaise, 121
        Marseillaise, 121
        Mikado, 121
        Nesselrode, 121
        Pan-Broiled, Medium, 119; Rare,
            119; Well-Done, 119
        Rossini, 122
    Filets Madeira, 116
    Filets Marsala, 115
    Fondue
        Bourguignonne, 130
        de Veau, 131
        Oriental, 131
    Frankfurters, Grilled, with Apple
        Sauerkraut, 126
    Ham Asparagus Rolls, 127
    Ham with Artichoke Hearts, 127
    Kidneys in Mustard Sauce I, 124;
        II, 125
    Lamb Chops, Rosemary, 123
    Liver, Calf's, 123
        in Red Wine, 124
        in Sour Cream, 124
        with Bacon, 123
    Lucerne Toast, 126
    Meat Balls, Russian, 125
    Meat Fondues, The, 130
        Sauces, I and II, 130; III and IV,
            131
    Pan-Broiled Filet Steaks, 119
    Schnitzel, Wiener, 128
    Scallopini à la Marsala, 128
    Scallopini Palerma, 129
    Steak à la Stanley, 122
    Steak au Poivre, 118
        Grenoble, 119
    Steaks, Filet, *see* Filet Steaks
    Steaks, Minute, 117
    Sukiyaki, 122
    Tournedos
        à l'Américaine, 120
        Argenteuil, 120
        Béarnaise, 120
        Choiseul, 120

Maintenon, 121
Vert Pré, 122
Tongue with Horseradish Sauce, 126
Veal Cutlets, 127
Veal, Herbed, 129
Meat Fondues, The, 130
Sauces I and II, 130; III and IV, 131
Melon
and Prosciutto, 17
Antilles, 249
Chicken in Cantaloupe, Cold, 136
Melted Cheese, 27
Mignonette Sauce, 229
Mikado Salad, 195
Mint
Dressing, 213
Relish, 218
Sauce, 227
Sauce for Roast Lamb, 227
Minute Steaks, 117
Mixed Ambrosia, 251
Mixed Feelings (dessert), 250
Monte Carlo Soup, 51
Moscow Sauce, Cold, 225
Mousse, Lemon, 244; Orange, 245
Mulled Wine, 284
Mutton Sauce, 227
Mushroom, Mushrooms, 162
and Tomatoes à l'Arlésienne, 162
Bermuda, 164
Bordelaise, 167
Capri, 165
Cosmopolitan, 165
French, 166
Herbed, 166
Hungarian, 166
Italian, 16
Purée, 163
Satanic, 167
Skewered, 167
Stuffed I and II, 28; III, 29
Washington, 164
Mustard, Hot, 218
Mustard Potatoes I and II, 151

Newburg Consommé, 49
Norwegian Shrimp, 24
Noodles (*see also* Pastas)
Hungarian I, 173; II, 174
with Beef, 171
with Shrimp, 170
Neros (dessert), 245
Negroni, 282

Oeuf au Beurre Noir, 106
Oeufs Mollets, 101
Olive Dressing, 212
Omelets, *see* Eggs

Omelette aux Confitures, 259
Omelette Normande, 104
Omnibus (beverage), 285
Onion
and Cucumber Salad with Sour
Cream Dressing, 203
Bread, 187
Mayonnaise, 211
Orange
Alaska, 239
Bowle, 287
Dessert, 244
Marmalade Roll, 256
Mayonnaise, 223
Mousse, 245
Pancakes, 236
Prune Whip, 259
Sauce for Pancakes, 236
Soup, Cold, 47
Zabaione, 243
OUTDOOR OR PLUG-IN-ANY-
WHERE COOKING, 261-272
Corn, Grilled, I and II, 268
Fish Steaks, Electric Broiler, Grilled,
272
Frankfurters
Bacon-Wrapped, 266
Foil-Wrapped, 266
Grilled, 265
Grilled Split, 266
Grilled Whole, 265
Frogs' Legs, Broiled, 265
Lamb Chops, Grilled, I and II, 269
Lobster, Charcoal-Broiled, 269
Mackerel, Grilled, 273
Meats, Broiled, 269
Oysters, Broiled, 264
Pommes Dehor, 271
Skewers, Quick, 266; 1 to 7, 267; 8
to 12, 268
Steak, Blue, 270
Shrimp, Broiled, I, 263; II, 264
Trout
Broiled, in Electric Broiler, 272
Grilled, 273
Oyster, Oysters, 69
and Corn Casserole, 72
and Mushroom Stew, 38
and Tomato Chowder, 75
Angels on Horseback, 72
Baked, 70
Casino, 71
Egg and, Fry, 74
Fried, Light, 74
Gratinée, 75
Light Fried, 74
on Anchovy Toast, 73
Pan-Fried, 73

Pompadour, 73
Rockefeller, 71
Stew, 39
  Elmira, 74
  Pasquale, 75
  Wladimir, 73

Pain Retrouvé, 185
Pallatchinken, 110
  Cheese, 110
Pan-Broiled Filet Steaks, 119
Pan-Fried Oysters, 73
Pancakes (*see also* Crêpes)
  Jonas, 112
  Käte's, 112
  Puffed, 241
  Thin Crêpes, 108
  Tuna, 110
Paris Salad, 203
Parmesan Cheese Drops, 27
Parmesan Eggs, 107
Parsley Sauce, 229
PASTAS, 168-174
  Macaroni
    and Tuna Casserole, 173
    in Casserole, 172
  Noodles (Fettuccini)
    Hungarian I, 173; II, 174
    with Beef, 171
    with Shrimp, 170
  Spaghetti
    and Chicken Livers, 173
    with Bacon, 172
    with Clams, 171
    with Meat Sauce, 171
    with Mushrooms, 172
  Spätzle, 174
Pastoral Salad, 204
Peach, Peaches
  Alaska, 240
  and Preserves, 255
  Bowle, 287
  Burnt Brandy, 254
  Crème, 254
  Honeyed, 254
  Hot and Cold, 255
  Nougat, 255
  Nut, 256
Peasant Salad, 205
Peperoni and Bananas, 18
Perfect Manhattans, 282
Philadelphia Boating Punch, 287
Pickled Bings, 216
Pickled Mushrooms, 218
Pineapple
  and Ham, 18
  Everest, 239
  Baked, 250

Fried, 217
  Relish I and II, 217
Polish Tomatoes, 160
Pommes Dehor, 271
Pomodoro Eggs, 106
Poor Shrimp, 63
Port of Porto, The (dessert) , 249
Potage Africaine, 43
Potage Carina, 54
Potato Salad
  German Supper, 196
  Sour Cream and Dill, 197
  Under Green Sauce, 198
Potée Bourguignonne, 57
POULTRY, 131-139
  Broiler, Barbecued, 134
  Chicken
    Broiled, Ready-Cooked, 8 ways of
      preparing, 133
    Broiled Improvement, 134
    8-Minute, 135
    in Cantaloupe, Cold, 136
    in Red Wine, 136
    Tetrazzini, 135
    Wing Dinner, 138
    with Onion Sauce, 136
  Chicken Livers
    Denise, 138
    in Sour Cream, 137
    with Apple Rings, 137
  Turkey
    Muffins, Hot, 140
    Stew, 139
    Turkish, 139
Pousse-Café I, 277; II, 278
Prague Soup, 44
Prosciutto and Melon, 17
Provincial Fried Tomatoes, 159
Prune Whip, Orange, 259
Pruneaux au Vin, 251
Puffed Pancakes, 241
Purée Malakoff, 52

Quick, Cheese, 92
Quick Skewers, 266; 1-7, 267; 8-12, 268

Raisin Sauce, 226
Raspberry Cream, 259
Raspberry Sauce, 236
Raw Vegetable Ketchup Dip, 31
Raw Vegetable Mustard Dip, 31
Red Pepper Sauce, 218
Red Potatoes, 151
Red Relish, 216
Red Wine Liver, 124
RELISHES, 215-218
  Cottage Cheese, 215

Fried Pineapple, 217
Garden, 216
Hot Mustard, 218
Mint, 218
Pickled Bings, 216
Pickled Mushrooms, 218
Pineapple I and II, 217
Raw Cranberry, 216
Red, 216
Red Pepper Sauce, 218
Tomato, 215
Ricardo's Salad, 199
RICE, 174, 181
Chicken and Rice with Herbs, 181
Continental Rice, 180
Crab Meat and Rice Casserole, 180
Ginger Rice, 177
Lobster and Lime Rice, 177
Rice
and Lobster Casserole, 181
Sukiyaki, 178
with Beef and Blue Cheese, 179
with Ham, 178
Risi Bisi, 175
Risi e Bisi I, II, and III, 176
Seafood Rice, 179
Rich Knights, 256
Risi Bisi, 175
Risi e Bisi I, II and III, 176
Romaine Salad, 194
Roquefort Dressing I and II, 208; III, 209
Rosemary Lamb Chops, 123
Rum, *see* Beverages
Rum Omelet, 257
Russian Meat Balls, 125
Russian Pea Soup, 44
Russian Spinach Soup, 55
Rye Bread, Hot, 184

SALAD DRESSINGS, 207-214
Blender French, 211
Blender Mayonnaise, 211
Celery Seed, 209
Combination I and II, 209
Cucumber Salad, Sauce for, 214
French, 210
Blender, 211
Spiced, 210
Garlic, 213
Italian, 210
Mayonnaise (*see also* under Sauces)
Blender I, 211; II, III and IV, 212
Curry, 212
Lemon, 212
Onion, 211
Orange, 223
Tartar, 212

Mint, 213
Olive, 212
Roquefort I and II, 208; III, 209
Sour Cream, 214
Cooked, 214
Spanish, 213
SALADS (Salad, Salade), 190-207
Alsacienne, 197
Andrea, 197
Apple and Endive, 206
Apple, Dutch, 206
Artichoke, Hearts of, 201
Ateca, 193
Bacon, 200
Beet, 193
Belle Hélène, 207
Burgos, 195
Catalan, 204
Cheese, Swiss, I, 204; II, 205
Cherry, 206
Coleslaw
Danish, 195
German, 196
Combinations, Ten Simple, 192
Cucumber, Turkish, 202
Cucumber and Onion, 203
Dutch Apple, 206
Egg, 194
Endive, 205
and Apple, 206
Fruit, 207
German Supper, 196
Gourmet's, 193
Grape and Zucchini, 202
Green, Tossed, 199
Ham, 203
Humberto, 194
Mikado, 195
Onion and Cucumber, with Sour Cream Dressing, 203
Paris, 203
Pastoral, 204
Peasant, 205
Potato, Sour Cream and Dill, 197
Potato, Under Green Sauce, 198
Ricardo's, 199
Romaine, 194
Salamanca I, 193; II, 194
Stromboli, 201
Zucchini, 201
and Grape, 202
Salamanca Salad I, 193; II, 194
Salami and Figs, 17
Salmon Steaks, 82
Sangría, 283
Sardine Puffs, 25
Sardine Spread, 25
Satanic Mushrooms, 167

SAUCES, 219-236
  Anchovy for Hot Salmon, 231
  Antiboise, 222
  Apple Horseradish, 226
  Apricot, Hot, 234
  Avocado, 231
  Avocado Dressing, 224
  Bread Crumb, Hot, I, 224; II and
    III, 225
  Brown, 221
  Bulgarian, for Fish, I and II, 231
  Cherry, Hot, 228
  Coffee, 234
  Coffee Whip, 235
  Cranberry Apricot, 228
  Cream, Medium, 221
  Cucumber, for Chicken, 228
  Swedish, 230
  Génoise, 223
  Hollandaise, 232
    Blender Method, 232
  Hanover, 226
  Hard, I, II, and III, 233; IV, 234
  Horseradish, 226
  Ice Cream, I and II, 235
  Livournaise, 232
  Mayonnaise (*see also* under Salad
    Dressings)
    Florida, 224
    Greenwich, 222
    Horatio, 223
    Orange, 223
  Mignonette, 229
  Mint, 227
    for Roast Lamb, 227
  Moscow, 225
  Mutton, 227
  Orange, for Pancakes, 236
  Parsley, 229
  Raisin, 226
  Raspberry, 236
  Seafood Cocktail, 230
  Sherry, 234
  Swedish Cucumber, 230
  Valentine, 223
  Vanilla Ice Cream, I and II, 235
  Walnut Garlic, 227
  Watercress, 230
Sauces, Dessert, 233
Scallion Eggs, 101
Scallopini à la Marsala, 128
Scallopini Palermo, 129
Scallops, 79
  Amandine, 80
  in White Wine, 81
Scrambled Salmon, 104
Seafood Cocktail Sauce, 230
Seafood Rice, 179

Seeded Breads, 184
Sherried Avocado, 22
Sherry Sauce, 234
Shrimp, 62
  and Crab Bisque, 41
  and Corn Casserole, 65
  and Mushroom Casserole, 67
  Basil, 67
  Casserole, 63
  Cocktail I and II, Hot, 20
  Cocktail or Salad, 66
  Curry, 69
  de Jonghe, 67
  Fried Ground, 64
  in Dill Sauce, 68
  in Red Sauce, Hot, 64
  Japanese Spring, 65
  Marinated, 68
  Poor, 63
  Salad Vertain, 65
  Summer Salad, 66
  Wiggle, 69
Simple Salad Combinations, Ten, 192
Skewered Mushrooms, 167
Skewers, Quick, 266; 1-7, 267; 8-12,
  268
Sliced Rye Loaves, 188
Sliced White Loaves, 187
Soft-Shell Crabs, Amandine, 77
Sopa de Ajo, I, 57; II, III, and IV, 58
SOUPS, 36-59 (*see also* Bisque, Bouil-
  lon, Consommé, Crème, Potage and
  Stew)
  Abjy L'Amid, 43
  Africaine, Consommé, 44
  Africaine, Potage, 43
  Agnellotti, 47
  Agnès Sorrel, 50
  Anita, 40
  Apple, 55
  Batwinja, 56
  Borsch, in Blender, 45
  Borsch I and II, 45; III through VI,
    46
  Bouillon, 47
  Bourguignonne, Potée, 57
  Camerani, 48
  Cheese, Bulgarian, 41
  Chicken
    and Coconut, 53
    and Yogurt, Bulgarian, 50
    Bulgarian, 54
    Cold, 51
  Clam, 39
    Combine, 40
    Juice Marinara, 40
  Cucumber Shrimp, Cold, 38
  Czarina, 54

Egg, 53
Gaspacho Andaluz, 58
Germinal, 55
Gulyas, 59
Ham, 54
Leek, 43
  and Clam, 42
  Gratinée, 43
Lobster, 39
Madrilène
  Cold, 51
  Costa Brava, 52
  Hot, 52
Malakoff, 52
Maltese, 48
Mikado, 49
Miranda, 53
Monte Carlo, 51
Nesselrode, 50
Newburgh, 49
Orange, Cold, 47
Oyster, 39
  and Mushroom, 38
Pea, Russian, 44
Prague, 44
Shrimp and Crab, 41
Sopa de Ajo I, 57; II, III and IV, 58
Spinach, 49
  Russian, 55
Strong, 48
Tomato, Iced, 42
Tomato Juice, Hot, 42
Yogurt, Bulgarian, 42
Zephyr, 50
Zuppa Pavese, 48
Sour Cream and Dill Potato Salad, 197
Sour Cream Dressing, 214
  Cooked, 214
Sour Cream Liver, 124
Spaghetti
  and Chicken Livers, 173
  with Bacon, 172
  with Clams, 171
  with Meat Sauce, 171
  with Mushrooms, 172
Spanish Dressing, 213
Spätzle, 174
Spiced Bananas, 153
Spiced French Dressing, 210
Spiced Prunes with Walnuts, 251
Spinach Parmigiana, 147
Spinach Soup, 49
Steak à la Stanley, 122
Steak au Poivre, 118
  Grenoble, 118
Strawberry Cream, 259
Strawberries Mickey, 248
String Beans, Amandine, 146

Stromboli (salad), 201
Strong Soup, 48
Stuffed Mushrooms I and II, 28; III, 29
Sukiyaki, 122
Summer Shrimp Salad, 66
Sunday Cheese, 97
Swedish Cucumber Sauce, 230
Sweet Potatoes, 150
Swiss Eggs, 100
Swiss Cheese Salad I, 204; II, 205
Swordfish Steaks, 82

Taranto Asparagus, 146
Tartar Mayonnaise, 212
"The Farm" Puffs, 26
Thin Pancakes, Crêpes, 108
Thunder (beverage), 280
Toasted Brioche, 188
Tomatoes, Ways of Using, 154
Tomato, Tomatoes
  à la Menagère, 161
  Algerian, 161
  American, 158
  and Cheese Sandwich, Baked, 95
  and Horseradish, 160
  and Mushrooms à l'Arlésienne, 162
  Bulgarian Cheese Soup, 41
  Cream, 162
  Gratinée, 160
  Juice Cocktail, 15
  Juice, Hot, 42
  Mikado Salad, 195
  Rarebit, 159
  Relish, 215
  Sliced, and Caviar, 23
  Soup, Iced, 42
  Tropical, 156
Tongue with Hollandaise Sauce, 126
Tools for Instant Epicureanism, 9–12
Tossed Green Salad, 199
Toulon Anchovies, 24
Tournedos
  à l'Américaine, 120
  Argenteuil, 120
  Béarnaise, 120
  Choiseul, 120
  Maintenon, 121
  Vert Pré, 122
Tropical Americana, 246
Tropical Tomatoes, 156
Tschimbur (eggs), 107
Tuna Pancakes, 110
Turkey Muffins, Hot, 140
Turkey Stew, 139
Turkey, Turkish, 139
Turkish Cucumber Salad, 202
Twelve Mornay Luncheon Dishes, 90

Unbalance (dessert) , 246

Valentine Sauce, 223
Vanilla Ice Cream Sauce I and II, 235
Veal Cutlets, 127
VEGETABLES, 141–167
  Artichoke Hearts, 147
    Ways of Preparing, 144
    Whole Hearts, in Hollandaise
      Sauce, 146
  Asparagus
    Taranto, 146
    Ways of Preparing, 144
  Bananas, Spiced, 153
  Beans
    Green, Ways of Preparing, 145
    String, Amandine, 146
    Wax, Ways of Preparing, 145
  Beets, 148
    Glazed, 149
  Cauliflower, Ways of Preparing, 145
  Cucumber
    and Zucchini, 154
    au Gratin, 154
  Mushrooms
    Bermuda, 164
    Bordelaise, 167
    Capri, 165
    Cosmopolitan, 165
    French, 165
    Herbed, 166
    Hungarian, 166
    Purée, 163
    Satanic, 167
    Skewered, 167
    Washington, 164
  Onion Slices, Grilled, 153
  Onions, Glazed, 153
  Potatoes
    Fried, I and II, 152
    Instant Mashed, 1–6, 149; 7–10,
      150
    Mustard, I and II, 151
    Red, 151
    Sweet, 150
      Baked, 150
      Candied, 151
  Spinach
    French, 148
    Italian, 148
    Parmigiana, 147
  Tomatoes, 154
    à la Menagère, 161
    Algerian, 161
    American, 158
    and Horseradish, 160
    and Mushrooms à l'Arlésienne,
      162
    Baked, Balkan, 158
    Baked Green, 161
    Baked, Italian, 156
    Cheese-Stuffed, 157
    Cream, 162
    Curried, 158
    Fried, 157
      Provincial, 159
    Gratinée, 160
    Polish, 160
    Rarebit, 159
    Slices, Grilled, 157
    Tropical, 156
    Ways of Using, 154
  Vegetables, Eastern, 145
  Vegetables, Frozen, 143
    Artichoke, 2 ways of preparing,
      144
    Asparagus, 4 ways of preparing,
      144
    Cauliflower, 2 ways of preparing,
      145
    Beans, Green, 2 ways of preparing,
      145
    Beans, Wax, 2 ways of preparing,
      145
Vodka, *see* Beverages

Walnut Garlic Sauce, 227
Washington Mushrooms, 164
Watercress Dip, 32
Watercress Sauce, 230
Whole Hearts of Artichoke in Hollandaise Sauce, 146
Wiener Schnitzel, 128
Wine, *see* Beverages
Wine Chaudeau, 242
Whisky, *see* Beverages
Whisky Sour, 281
White Lion, 286

Zabaione, 243
  Michel, 243
  Orange, 243
Zucchini Salad, 201
  Grape and, 202
Zuppa Pavese, 48

A CATALOGUE OF SELECTED DOVER BOOKS
IN ALL FIELDS OF INTEREST

VISUAL ILLUSIONS: THEIR CAUSES, CHARACTERISTICS, AND APPLICATIONS, Matthew Luckiesh. Thorough description and discussion of optical illusion, geometric and perspective, particularly; size and shape distortions, illusions of color, of motion; natural illusions; use of illusion in art and magic, industry, etc. Most useful today with op art, also for classical art. Scores of effects illustrated. Introduction by William H. Ittleson. 100 illustrations. xxi + 252pp.

21530-X Paperbound $2.00

A HANDBOOK OF ANATOMY FOR ART STUDENTS, Arthur Thomson. Thorough, virtually exhaustive coverage of skeletal structure, musculature, etc. Full text, supplemented by anatomical diagrams and drawings and by photographs of undraped figures. Unique in its comparison of male and female forms, pointing out differences of contour, texture, form. 211 figures, 40 drawings, 86 photographs. xx + 459pp. 5⅜ x 8⅜.

21163-0 Paperbound $3.50

150 MASTERPIECES OF DRAWING, Selected by Anthony Toney. Full page reproductions of drawings from the early 16th to the end of the 18th century, all beautifully reproduced: Rembrandt, Michelangelo, Dürer, Fragonard, Urs, Graf, Wouwerman, many others. First-rate browsing book, model book for artists. xviii + 150pp. 8⅜ x 11¼.

21032-4 Paperbound $2.50

THE LATER WORK OF AUBREY BEARDSLEY, Aubrey Beardsley. Exotic, erotic, ironic masterpieces in full maturity: Comedy Ballet, Venus and Tannhauser, Pierrot, Lysistrata, Rape of the Lock, Savoy material, Ali Baba, Volpone, etc. This material revolutionized the art world, and is still powerful, fresh, brilliant. With *The Early Work*, all Beardsley's finest work. 174 plates, 2 in color. xiv + 176pp. 8⅛ x 11.

21817-1 Paperbound $3.75

DRAWINGS OF REMBRANDT, Rembrandt van Rijn. Complete reproduction of fabulously rare edition by Lippmann and Hofstede de Groot, completely reedited, updated, improved by Prof. Seymour Slive, Fogg Museum. Portraits, Biblical sketches, landscapes, Oriental types, nudes, episodes from classical mythology—All Rembrandt's fertile genius. Also selection of drawings by his pupils and followers. "Stunning volumes," *Saturday Review*. 550 illustrations. lxxviii + 552pp. 9⅛ x 12¼.

21485-0, 21486-9 Two volumes, Paperbound $10.00

THE DISASTERS OF WAR, Francisco Goya. One of the masterpieces of Western civilization—83 etchings that record Goya's shattering, bitter reaction to the Napoleonic war that swept through Spain after the insurrection of 1808 and to war in general. Reprint of the first edition, with three additional plates from Boston's Museum of Fine Arts. All plates facsimile size. Introduction by Philip Hofer, Fogg Museum. v + 97pp. 9⅜ x 8¼.

21872-4 Paperbound $2.50

GRAPHIC WORKS OF ODILON REDON. Largest collection of Redon's graphic works ever assembled: 172 lithographs, 28 etchings and engravings, 9 drawings. These include some of his most famous works. All the plates from *Odilon Redon: oeuvre graphique complet*, plus additional plates. New introduction and caption translations by Alfred Werner. 209 illustrations. xxvii + 209pp. 9⅛ x 12¼.

21966-8 Paperbound $4.50

EAST O' THE SUN AND WEST O' THE MOON, George W. Dasent. Considered the best of all translations of these Norwegian folk tales, this collection has been enjoyed by generations of children (and folklorists too). Includes True and Untrue, Why the Sea is Salt, East O' the Sun and West O' the Moon, Why the Bear is Stumpy-Tailed, Boots and the Troll, The Cock and the Hen, Rich Peter the Pedlar, and 52 more. The only edition with all 59 tales. 77 illustrations by Erik Werenskiold and Theodor Kittelsen. xv + 418pp. 22521-6 Paperbound $3.50

GOOPS AND HOW TO BE THEM, Gelett Burgess. Classic of tongue-in-cheek humor, masquerading as etiquette book. 87 verses, twice as many cartoons, show mischievous Goops as they demonstrate to children virtues of table manners, neatness, courtesy, etc. Favorite for generations. viii + 88pp. $6\frac{1}{2}$ x $9\frac{1}{4}$. 22233-0 Paperbound $1.50

ALICE'S ADVENTURES UNDER GROUND, Lewis Carroll. The first version, quite different from the final *Alice in Wonderland,* printed out by Carroll himself with his own illustrations. Complete facsimile of the "million dollar" manuscript Carroll gave to Alice Liddell in 1864. Introduction by Martin Gardner. viii + 96pp. Title and dedication pages in color. 21482-6 Paperbound $1.25

THE BROWNIES, THEIR BOOK, Palmer Cox. Small as mice, cunning as foxes, exuberant and full of mischief, the Brownies go to the zoo, toy shop, seashore, circus, etc., in 24 verse adventures and 266 illustrations. Long a favorite, since their first appearance in St. Nicholas Magazine. xi + 144pp. $6\frac{5}{8}$ x $9\frac{1}{4}$. 21265-3 Paperbound $1.75

SONGS OF CHILDHOOD, Walter De La Mare. Published (under the pseudonym Walter Ramal) when De La Mare was only 29, this charming collection has long been a favorite children's book. A facsimile of the first edition in paper, the 47 poems capture the simplicity of the nursery rhyme and the ballad, including such lyrics as I Met Eve, Tartary, The Silver Penny. vii + 106pp. (USO) 21972-0 Paperbound $1.25

THE COMPLETE NONSENSE OF EDWARD LEAR, Edward Lear. The finest 19th-century humorist-cartoonist in full: all nonsense limericks, zany alphabets, Owl and Pussycat, songs, nonsense botany, and more than 500 illustrations by Lear himself. Edited by Holbrook Jackson. xxix + 287pp. (USO) 20167-8 Paperbound $2.00

BILLY WHISKERS: THE AUTOBIOGRAPHY OF A GOAT, Frances Trego Montgomery. A favorite of children since the early 20th century, here are the escapades of that rambunctious, irresistible and mischievous goat—Billy Whiskers. Much in the spirit of *Peck's Bad Boy,* this is a book that children never tire of reading or hearing. All the original familiar illustrations by W. H. Fry are included: 6 color plates, 18 black and white drawings. 159pp. 22345-0 Paperbound $2.00

MOTHER GOOSE MELODIES. Faithful republication of the fabulously rare Munroe and Francis "copyright 1833" Boston edition—the most important Mother Goose collection, usually referred to as the "original." Familiar rhymes plus many rare ones, with wonderful old woodcut illustrations. Edited by E. F. Bleiler. 128pp. $4\frac{1}{2}$ x $6\frac{3}{8}$. 22577-1 Paperbound $1.00

THE RED FAIRY BOOK, Andrew Lang. Lang's color fairy books have long been children's favorites. This volume includes Rapunzel, Jack and the Bean-stalk and 35 other stories, familiar and unfamiliar. 4 plates, 93 illustrations x + 367pp.
21673-X Paperbound $2.50

THE BLUE FAIRY BOOK, Andrew Lang. Lang's tales come from all countries and all times. Here are 37 tales from Grimm, the Arabian Nights, Greek Mythology, and other fascinating sources. 8 plates, 130 illustrations. xi + 390pp.
21437-0 Paperbound $2.75

HOUSEHOLD STORIES BY THE BROTHERS GRIMM. Classic English-language edition of the well-known tales — Rumpelstiltskin, Snow White, Hansel and Gretel, The Twelve Brothers, Faithful John, Rapunzel, Tom Thumb (52 stories in all). Translated into simple, straightforward English by Lucy Crane. Ornamented with headpieces, vignettes, elaborate decorative initials and a dozen full-page illustrations by Walter Crane. x + 269pp.
21080-4 Paperbound **$2.00**

THE MERRY ADVENTURES OF ROBIN HOOD, Howard Pyle. The finest modern versions of the traditional ballads and tales about the great English outlaw. Howard Pyle's complete prose version, with every word, every illustration of the first edition. Do not confuse this facsimile of the original (1883) with modern editions that change text or illustrations. 23 plates plus many page decorations. xxii + 296pp.
22043-5 Paperbound $2.75

THE STORY OF KING ARTHUR AND HIS KNIGHTS, Howard Pyle. The finest children's version of the life of King Arthur; brilliantly retold by Pyle, with 48 of his most imaginative illustrations. xviii + 313pp. 6⅛ x 9¼.
21445-1 Paperbound $2.50

THE WONDERFUL WIZARD OF OZ, L. Frank Baum. America's finest children's book in facsimile of first edition with all Denslow illustrations in full color. The edition a child should have. Introduction by Martin Gardner. 23 color plates, scores of drawings. iv + 267pp.
20691-2 Paperbound $3.50

THE MARVELOUS LAND OF OZ, L. Frank Baum. The second Oz book, every bit as imaginative as the Wizard. The hero is a boy named Tip, but the Scarecrow and the Tin Woodman are back, as is the Oz magic. 16 color plates, 120 drawings by John R. Neill. 287pp.
20692-0 Paperbound $2.50

THE MAGICAL MONARCH OF MO, L. Frank Baum. Remarkable adventures in a land even stranger than Oz. The best of Baum's books not in the Oz series. 15 color plates and dozens of drawings by Frank Verbeck. xviii + 237pp.
21892-9 Paperbound $2.25

THE BAD CHILD'S BOOK OF BEASTS, MORE BEASTS FOR WORSE CHILDREN, A MORAL ALPHABET, Hilaire Belloc. Three complete humor classics in one volume. Be kind to the frog, and do not call him names . . . and 28 other whimsical animals. Familiar favorites and some not so well known. Illustrated by Basil Blackwell. 156pp.
(USO) 20749-8 Paperbound $1.50

ADVENTURES OF AN AFRICAN SLAVER, Theodore Canot. Edited by Brantz Mayer. A detailed portrayal of slavery and the slave trade, 1820-1840. Canot, an established trader along the African coast, describes the slave economy of the African kingdoms, the treatment of captured negroes, the extensive journeys in the interior to gather slaves, slave revolts and their suppression, harems, bribes, and much more. Full and unabridged republication of 1854 edition. Introduction by Malcom Cowley. 16 illustrations. xvii + 448pp. 22456-2 Paperbound $3.50

MY BONDAGE AND MY FREEDOM, Frederick Douglass. Born and brought up in slavery, Douglass witnessed its horrors and experienced its cruelties, but went on to become one of the most outspoken forces in the American anti-slavery movement. Considered the best of his autobiographies, this book graphically describes the in-human treatment of slaves, its effects on slave owners and slave families, and how Douglass's determination led him to a new life. Unaltered reprint of 1st (1855) edition. xxxii + 464pp. 22457-0 Paperbound $3.50

THE INDIANS' BOOK, recorded and edited by Natalie Curtis. Lore, music, narratives, dozens of drawings by Indians themselves from an authoritative and important survey of native culture among Plains, Southwestern, Lake and Pueblo Indians. Standard work in popular ethnomusicology. 149 songs in full notation. 23 draw-ings, 23 photos. xxxi + 584pp. 6⅝ x 9⅜. 21939-9 Paperbound $5.00

DICTIONARY OF AMERICAN PORTRAITS, edited by Hayward and Blanche Cirker. 4024 portraits of 4000 most important Americans, colonial days to 1905 (with a few important categories, like Presidents, to present). Pioneers, explorers, colonial figures, U. S. officials, politicians, writers, military and naval men, scientists, inven-tors, manufacturers, jurists, actors, historians, educators, notorious figures, Indian chiefs, etc. All authentic contemporary likenesses. The only work of its kind in existence; supplements all biographical sources for libraries. Indispensable to any-one working with American history. 8,000-item classified index, finding lists, other aids. xiv + 756pp. 9¼ x 12¾. 21823-6 Clothbound $30.00

TRITTON'S GUIDE TO BETTER WINE AND BEER MAKING FOR BEGINNERS, S. M. Tritton. All you need to know to make family-sized quantities of over 100 types of grape, fruit, herb and vegetable wines; as well as beers, mead, cider, etc. Com-plete recipes, advice as to equipment, procedures such as fermenting, bottling, and storing wines. Recipes given in British, U. S., and metric measures. Accompanying booklet lists sources in U. S. A. where ingredients may be bought, and additional information. 11 illustrations. 157pp. 5⅝ x 8⅛. 22090-7 **Paperbound $2.00**

GARDENING WITH HERBS FOR FLAVOR AND FRAGRANCE, Helen M. Fox. How to grow herbs in your own garden, how to use them in your cooking (over 55 recipes included), legends and myths associated with each species, uses in medicine, per-fumes, etc.—these are elements of one of the few books written especially for Amer-ican herb fanciers. Guides you step-by-step from soil preparation to harvesting and storage for each type of herb. 12 drawings by Louise Mansfield. xiv + 334pp. 22540-2 Paperbound $2.50

POEMS OF ANNE BRADSTREET, edited with an introduction by Robert Hutchinson. A new selection of poems by America's first poet and perhaps the first significant woman poet in the English language. 48 poems display her development in works of considerable variety—love poems, domestic poems, religious meditations, formal elegies, "quaternions," etc. Notes, bibliography. viii + 222pp.

22160-1 Paperbound $2.50

THREE GOTHIC NOVELS: THE CASTLE OF OTRANTO BY HORACE WALPOLE; VATHEK BY WILLIAM BECKFORD; THE VAMPYRE BY JOHN POLIDORI, WITH FRAGMENT OF A NOVEL BY LORD BYRON, edited by E. F. Bleiler. The first Gothic novel, by Walpole; the finest Oriental tale in English, by Beckford; powerful Romantic supernatural story in versions by Polidori and Byron. All extremely important in history of literature; all still exciting, packed with supernatural thrills, ghosts, haunted castles, magic, etc. xl + 291pp.

21232-7 Paperbound $3.00

THE BEST TALES OF HOFFMANN, E. T. A. Hoffmann. 10 of Hoffmann's most important stories, in modern re-editings of standard translations: Nutcracker and the King of Mice, Signor Formica, Automata, The Sandman, Rath Krespel, The Golden Flowerpot, Master Martin the Cooper, The Mines of Falun, The King's Betrothed, A New Year's Eve Adventure. 7 illustrations by Hoffmann. Edited by E. F. Bleiler. xxxix + 419pp.

21793-0 Paperbound $3.00

GHOST AND HORROR STORIES OF AMBROSE BIERCE, Ambrose Bierce. 23 strikingly modern stories of the horrors latent in the human mind: The Eyes of the Panther, The Damned Thing, An Occurrence at Owl Creek Bridge, An Inhabitant of Carcosa, etc., plus the dream-essay, Visions of the Night. Edited by E. F. Bleiler. xxii + 199pp.

20767-6 Paperbound $2.00

BEST GHOST STORIES OF J. S. LEFANU, J. Sheridan LeFanu. Finest stories by Victorian master often considered greatest supernatural writer of all. Carmilla, Green Tea, The Haunted Baronet, The Familiar, and 12 others. Most never before available in the U. S. A. Edited by E. F. Bleiler. 8 illustrations from Victorian publications. xvii + 467pp.

20415-4 Paperbound $3.00

MATHEMATICAL FOUNDATIONS OF INFORMATION THEORY, A. I. Khinchin. Comprehensive introduction to work of Shannon, McMillan, Feinstein and Khinchin, placing these investigations on a rigorous mathematical basis. Covers entropy concept in probability theory, uniqueness theorem, Shannon's inequality, ergodic sources, the E property, martingale concept, noise, Feinstein's fundamental lemma, Shanon's first and second theorems. Translated by R. A. Silverman and M. D. Friedman. iii + 120pp.

60434-9 Paperbound $2.00

SEVEN SCIENCE FICTION NOVELS, H. G. Wells. The standard collection of the great novels. Complete, unabridged. *First Men in the Moon, Island of Dr. Moreau, War of the Worlds, Food of the Gods, Invisible Man, Time Machine, In the Days of the Comet.* Not only science fiction fans, but every educated person owes it to himself to read these novels. 1015pp. (USO) 20264-X Clothbound $6.00

AGAINST THE GRAIN (A REBOURS), Joris K. Huysmans. Filled with weird images, evidences of a bizarre imagination, exotic experiments with hallucinatory drugs, rich tastes and smells and the diversions of its sybarite hero Duc Jean des Esseintes, this classic novel pushed 19th-century literary decadence to its limits. Full unabridged edition. Do not confuse this with abridged editions generally sold. Introduction by Havelock Ellis. xlix + 206pp. 22190-3 Paperbound $2.50

VARIORUM SHAKESPEARE: HAMLET. Edited by Horace H. Furness; a landmark of American scholarship. Exhaustive footnotes and appendices treat all doubtful words and phrases, as well as suggested critical emendations throughout the play's history. First volume contains editor's own text, collated with all Quartos and Folios. Second volume contains full first Quarto, translations of Shakespeare's sources (Belleforest, and Saxo Grammaticus), Der Bestrafte Brudermord, and many essays on critical and historical points of interest by major authorities of past and present. Includes details of staging and costuming over the years. By far the best edition available for serious students of Shakespeare. Total of xx + 905pp. 21004-9, 21005-7, 2 volumes, Paperbound $7.00

A LIFE OF WILLIAM SHAKESPEARE, Sir Sidney Lee. This is the standard life of Shakespeare, summarizing everything known about Shakespeare and his plays. Incredibly rich in material, broad in coverage, clear and judicious, it has served thousands as the best introduction to Shakespeare. 1931 edition. 9 plates. xxix + 792pp. 21967-4 Paperbound $4.50

MASTERS OF THE DRAMA, John Gassner. Most comprehensive history of the drama in print, covering every tradition from Greeks to modern Europe and America, including India, Far East, etc. Covers more than 800 dramatists, 2000 plays, with biographical material, plot summaries, theatre history, criticism, etc. "Best of its kind in English," *New Republic.* 77 illustrations. xxii + 890pp. 20100-7 Clothbound $10.00

THE EVOLUTION OF THE ENGLISH LANGUAGE, George McKnight. The growth of English, from the 14th century to the present. Unusual, non-technical account presents basic information in very interesting form: sound shifts, change in grammar and syntax, vocabulary growth, similar topics. Abundantly illustrated with quotations. Formerly *Modern English in the Making.* xii + 590pp. 21932-1 Paperbound $3.50

AN ETYMOLOGICAL DICTIONARY OF MODERN ENGLISH, Ernest Weekley. Fullest, richest work of its sort, by foremost British lexicographer. Detailed word histories, including many colloquial and archaic words; extensive quotations. Do not confuse this with the Concise Etymological Dictionary, which is much abridged. Total of xxvii + 830pp. 6½ x 9¼. 21873-2, 21874-0 Two volumes, Paperbound $7.90

FLATLAND: A ROMANCE OF MANY DIMENSIONS, E. A. Abbott. Classic of science-fiction explores ramifications of life in a two-dimensional world, and what happens when a three-dimensional being intrudes. Amusing reading, but also useful as introduction to thought about hyperspace. Introduction by Banesh Hoffmann. 16 illustrations. xx + 103pp. 20001-9 Paperbound $1.00

JOHANN SEBASTIAN BACH, Philipp Spitta. One of the great classics of musicology, this definitive analysis of Bach's music (and life) has never been surpassed. Lucid, nontechnical analyses of hundreds of pieces (30 pages devoted to St. Matthew Passion, 26 to B Minor Mass). Also includes major analysis of 18th-century music. 450 musical examples. 40-page musical supplement. Total of xx + 1799pp.
(EUK) 22278-0, 22279-9 Two volumes, Clothbound $25.00

MOZART AND HIS PIANO CONCERTOS, Cuthbert Girdlestone. The only full-length study of an important area of Mozart's creativity. Provides detailed analyses of all 23 concertos, traces inspirational sources. 417 musical examples. Second edition. 509pp.
21271-8 Paperbound $4.50

THE PERFECT WAGNERITE: A COMMENTARY ON THE NIBLUNG'S RING, George Bernard Shaw. Brilliant and still relevant criticism in remarkable essays on Wagner's Ring cycle, Shaw's ideas on political and social ideology behind the plots, role of Leitmotifs, vocal requisites, etc. Prefaces. xxi + 136pp.
(USO) 21707-8 Paperbound $1.75

DON GIOVANNI, W. A. Mozart. Complete libretto, modern English translation; biographies of composer and librettist; accounts of early performances and critical reaction. Lavishly illustrated. All the material you need to understand and appreciate this great work. Dover Opera Guide and Libretto Series; translated and introduced by Ellen Bleiler. 92 illustrations. 209pp.
21134-7 Paperbound $2.00

BASIC ELECTRICITY, U. S. Bureau of Naval Personel. Originally a training course, best non-technical coverage of basic theory of electricity and its applications. Fundamental concepts, batteries, circuits, conductors and wiring techniques, AC and DC, inductance and capacitance, generators, motors, transformers, magnetic amplifiers, synchros, servomechanisms, etc. Also covers blue-prints, electrical diagrams, etc. Many questions, with answers. 349 illustrations. x + 448pp. 6½ x 9¼.
20973-3 Paperbound $3.50

REPRODUCTION OF SOUND, Edgar Villchur. Thorough coverage for laymen of high fidelity systems, reproducing systems in general, needles, amplifiers, preamps, loudspeakers, feedback, explaining physical background. "A rare talent for making technicalities vividly comprehensible," R. Darrell, *High Fidelity.* 69 figures. iv + 92pp.
21515-6 Paperbound $1.35

HEAR ME TALKIN' TO YA: THE STORY OF JAZZ AS TOLD BY THE MEN WHO MADE IT, Nat Shapiro and Nat Hentoff. Louis Armstrong, Fats Waller, Jo Jones, Clarence Williams, Billy Holiday, Duke Ellington, Jelly Roll Morton and dozens of other jazz greats tell how it was in Chicago's South Side, New Orleans, depression Harlem and the modern West Coast as jazz was born and grew. xvi + 429pp.
21726-4 Paperbound $3.95

FABLES OF AESOP, translated by Sir Roger L'Estrange. A reproduction of the very rare 1931 Paris edition; a selection of the most interesting fables, together with 50 imaginative drawings by Alexander Calder. v + 128pp. 6½x9¼.
21780-9 Paperbound $1.50

CATALOGUE OF DOVER BOOKS

THE ARCHITECTURE OF COUNTRY HOUSES, Andrew J. Downing. Together with Vaux's *Villas and Cottages* this is the basic book for Hudson River Gothic architecture of the middle Victorian period. Full, sound discussions of general aspects of housing, architecture, style, decoration, furnishing, together with scores of detailed house plans, illustrations of specific buildings, accompanied by full text. Perhaps the most influential single American architectural book. 1850 edition. Introduction by J. Stewart Johnson. 321 figures, 34 architectural designs. xvi + 560pp.
22003-6 Paperbound $5.00

LOST EXAMPLES OF COLONIAL ARCHITECTURE, John Mead Howells. Full-page photographs of buildings that have disappeared or been so altered as to be denatured, including many designed by major early American architects. 245 plates. xvii + 248pp. 7⅞ x 10¾.
21143-6 Paperbound $3.50

DOMESTIC ARCHITECTURE OF THE AMERICAN COLONIES AND OF THE EARLY REPUBLIC, Fiske Kimball. Foremost architect and restorer of Williamsburg and Monticello covers nearly 200 homes between 1620-1825. Architectural details, construction, style features, special fixtures, floor plans, etc. Generally considered finest work in its area. 219 illustrations of houses, doorways, windows, capital mantels. xx + 314pp. 7⅞ x 10¾.
21743-4 Paperbound $4.00

EARLY AMERICAN ROOMS: 1650-1858, edited by Russell Hawes Kettell. Tour of 12 rooms, each representative of a different era in American history and each furnished, decorated, designed and occupied in the style of the era. 72 plans and elevations, 8-page color section, etc., show fabrics, wall papers, arrangements, etc. Full descriptive text. xvii + 200pp. of text. 8⅜ x 11¼.
21633-0 Paperbound $5.00

THE FITZWILLIAM VIRGINAL BOOK, edited by J. Fuller Maitland and W. B. Squire. Full modern printing of famous early 17th-century ms. volume of 300 works by Morley, Byrd, Bull, Gibbons, etc. For piano or other modern keyboard instrument; easy to read format. xxxvi + 938pp. 8⅜ x 11.
21068-5, 21069-3 Two volumes, Paperbound $12.00

KEYBOARD MUSIC, Johann Sebastian Bach. Bach Gesellschaft edition. A rich selection of Bach's masterpieces for the harpsichord: the six English Suites, six French Suites, the six Partitas (Clavierübung part I), the Goldberg Variations (Clavierübung part IV), the fifteen Two-Part Inventions and the fifteen Three-Part Sinfonias. Clearly reproduced on large sheets with ample margins; eminently playable. vi + 312pp. 8⅛ x 11.
22360-4 Paperbound $5.00

THE MUSIC OF BACH: AN INTRODUCTION, Charles Sanford Terry. A fine, nontechnical introduction to Bach's music, both instrumental and vocal. Covers organ music, chamber music, passion music, other types. Analyzes themes, developments, innovations. x + 114pp.
21075-8 Paperbound $1.95

BEETHOVEN AND HIS NINE SYMPHONIES, Sir George Grove. Noted British musicologist provides best history, analysis, commentary on symphonies. Very thorough, rigorously accurate; necessary to both advanced student and amateur music lover. 436 musical passages. vii + 407 pp.
20334-4 Paperbound $4.00

A History of Costume, Carl Köhler. Definitive history, based on surviving pieces of clothing primarily, and paintings, statues, etc. secondarily. Highly readable text, supplemented by 594 illustrations of costumes of the ancient Mediterranean peoples, Greece and Rome, the Teutonic prehistoric period; costumes of the Middle Ages, Renaissance, Baroque, 18th and 19th centuries. Clear, measured patterns are provided for many clothing articles. Approach is practical throughout. Enlarged by Emma von Sichart. 464pp.   21030-8 Paperbound $3.50

Oriental Rugs, Antique and Modern, Walter A. Hawley. A complete and authoritative treatise on the Oriental rug—where they are made, by whom and how, designs and symbols, characteristics in detail of the six major groups, how to distinguish them and how to buy them. Detailed technical data is provided on periods, weaves, warps, wefts, textures, sides, ends and knots, although no technical background is required for an understanding. 11 color plates, 80 halftones, 4 maps. vi + 320pp. 6⅛ x 9⅛.   22366-3 Paperbound $5.00

Ten Books on Architecture, Vitruvius. By any standards the most important book on architecture ever written. Early Roman discussion of aesthetics of building, construction methods, orders, sites, and every other aspect of architecture has inspired, instructed architecture for about 2,000 years. Stands behind Palladio, Michelangelo, Bramante, Wren, countless others. Definitive Morris H. Morgan translation. 68 illustrations. xii + 331pp.   20645-9 Paperbound.$3.00

The Four Books of Architecture, Andrea Palladio. Translated into every major Western European language in the two centuries following its publication in 1570, this has been one of the most influential books in the history of architecture. Complete reprint of the 1738 Isaac Ware edition. New introduction by Adolf Placzek, Columbia Univ. 216 plates. xxii + 110pp. of text. 9½ x 12¾.   21308-0 Clothbound $12.50

Sticks and Stones: A Study of American Architecture and Civilization, Lewis Mumford.One of the great classics of American cultural history. American architecture from the medieval-inspired earliest forms to the early 20th century; evolution of structure and style, and reciprocal influences on environment. 21 photographic illustrations. 238pp.   20202-X Paperbound $2.00

The American Builder's Companion, Asher Benjamin. The most widely used early 19th century architectural style and source book, for colonial up into Greek Revival periods. Extensive development of geometry of carpentering, construction of sashes, frames, doors, stairs; plans and elevations of domestic and other buildings. Hundreds of thousands of houses were built according to this book, now invaluable to historians, architects, restorers, etc. 1827 edition. 59 plates. 114pp. 7⅞ x 10¾.   22236-5 Paperbound $4.00

Dutch Houses in the Hudson Valley Before 1776, Helen Wilkinson Reynolds. The standard survey of the Dutch colonial house and outbuildings, with constructional features, decoration, and local history associated with individual homesteads. Introduction by Franklin D. Roosevelt. Map. 150 illustrations. 469pp. 6⅝ x 9¼.   21469-9 Paperbound $5.00

DESIGN BY ACCIDENT; A BOOK OF "ACCIDENTAL EFFECTS" FOR ARTISTS AND DESIGNERS, James F. O'Brien. Create your own unique, striking, imaginative effects by "controlled accident" interaction of materials: paints and lacquers, oil and water based paints, splatter, crackling materials, shatter, similar items. Everything you do will be different; first book on this limitless art, so useful to both fine artist and commercial artist. Full instructions. 192 plates showing "accidents," 8 in color. viii + 215pp. 8⅜ x 11¼. 21942-9 Paperbound $3.75

THE BOOK OF SIGNS, Rudolf Koch. Famed German type designer draws 493 beautiful symbols: religious, mystical, alchemical, imperial, property marks, runes, etc. Remarkable fusion of traditional and modern. Good for suggestions of timelessness, smartness, modernity. Text. vi + 104pp. 6⅛ x 9¼. 20162-7 Paperbound $1.50

HISTORY OF INDIAN AND INDONESIAN ART, Ananda K. Coomaraswamy. An unabridged republication of one of the finest books by a great scholar in Eastern art. Rich in descriptive material, history, social backgrounds; Sunga reliefs, Rajput paintings, Gupta temples, Burmese frescoes, textiles, jewelry, sculpture, etc. 400 photos. viii + 423pp. 6⅜ x 9¾. 21436-2 Paperbound $5.00

PRIMITIVE ART, Franz Boas. America's foremost anthropologist surveys textiles, ceramics, woodcarving, basketry, metalwork, etc.; patterns, technology, creation of symbols, style origins. All areas of world, but very full on Northwest Coast Indians. More than 350 illustrations of baskets, boxes, totem poles, weapons, etc. 378 pp. 20025-6 Paperbound $3.00

THE GENTLEMAN AND CABINET MAKER'S DIRECTOR, Thomas Chippendale. Full reprint (third edition, 1762) of most influential furniture book of all time, by master cabinetmaker. 200 plates, illustrating chairs, sofas, mirrors, tables, cabinets, plus 24 photographs of surviving pieces. Biographical introduction by N. Bienenstock. vi + 249pp. 9⅞ x 12¾. 21601-2 Paperbound $5.00

AMERICAN ANTIQUE FURNITURE, Edgar G. Miller, Jr. The basic coverage of all American furniture before 1840. Individual chapters cover type of furniture—clocks, tables, sideboards, etc.—chronologically, with inexhaustible wealth of data. More than 2100 photographs, all identified, commented on. Essential to all early American collectors. Introduction by H. E. Keyes. vi + 1106pp. 7⅞ x 10¾. 21599-7, 21600-4 Two volumes, Paperbound $11.00

PENNSYLVANIA DUTCH AMERICAN FOLK ART, Henry J. Kauffman. 279 photos, 28 drawings of tulipware, Fraktur script, painted tinware, toys, flowered furniture, quilts, samplers, hex signs, house interiors, etc. Full descriptive text. Excellent for tourist, rewarding for designer, collector. Map. 146pp. 7⅞ x 10¾. 21205-X Paperbound $3.00

EARLY NEW ENGLAND GRAVESTONE RUBBINGS, Edmund V. Gillon, Jr. 43 photographs, 226 carefully reproduced rubbings show heavily symbolic, sometimes macabre early gravestones, up to early 19th century. Remarkable early American primitive art, occasionally strikingly beautiful; always powerful. Text. xxvi + 207pp. 8⅜ x 11¼. 21380-3 Paperbound $4.00

ALPHABETS AND ORNAMENTS, Ernst Lehner. Well-known pictorial source for decorative alphabets, script examples, cartouches, frames, decorative title pages, calligraphic initials, borders, similar material. 14th to 19th century, mostly European. Useful in almost any graphic arts designing, varied styles. 750 illustrations. 256pp. 7 x 10.
21905-4 Paperbound $4.00

PAINTING: A CREATIVE APPROACH, Norman Colquhoun. For the beginner simple guide provides an instructive approach to painting: major stumbling blocks for beginner; overcoming them, technical points; paints and pigments; oil painting; watercolor and other media and color. New section on "plastic" paints. Glossary. Formerly *Paint Your Own Pictures.* 221pp.
22000-1 Paperbound $1.75

THE ENJOYMENT AND USE OF COLOR, Walter Sargent. Explanation of the relations between colors themselves and between colors in nature and art, including hundreds of little-known facts about color values, intensities, effects of high and low illumination, complementary colors. Many practical hints for painters, references to great masters. 7 color plates, 29 illustrations. x + 274pp.
20944-X Paperbound $3.00

THE NOTEBOOKS OF LEONARDO DA VINCI, compiled and edited by Jean Paul Richter. 1566 extracts from original manuscripts reveal the full range of Leonardo's versatile genius: all his writings on painting, sculpture, architecture, anatomy, astronomy, geography, topography, physiology, mining, music, etc., in both Italian and English, with 186 plates of manuscript pages and more than 500 additional drawings. Includes studies for the Last Supper, the lost Sforza monument, and other works. Total of xlvii + 866pp. 7⅞ x 10¾.
22572-0, 22573-9 Two volumes, Paperbound $12.00

MONTGOMERY WARD CATALOGUE OF 1895. Tea gowns, yards of flannel and pillow-case lace, stereoscopes, books of gospel hymns, the New Improved Singer Sewing Machine, side saddles, milk skimmers, straight-edged razors, high-button shoes, spittoons, and on and on . . . listing some 25,000 items, practically all illustrated. Essential to the shoppers of the 1890's, it is our truest record of the spirit of the period. Unaltered reprint of Issue No. 57, Spring and Summer 1895. Introduction by Boris Emmet. Innumerable illustrations. xiii + 624pp. 8½ x 11⅝.
22377-9 Paperbound $8.50

THE CRYSTAL PALACE EXHIBITION ILLUSTRATED CATALOGUE (LONDON, 1851). One of the wonders of the modern world—the Crystal Palace Exhibition in which all the nations of the civilized world exhibited their achievements in the arts and sciences—presented in an equally important illustrated catalogue. More than 1700 items pictured with accompanying text—ceramics, textiles, cast-iron work, carpets, pianos, sleds, razors, wall-papers, billiard tables, beehives, silverware and hundreds of other artifacts—represent the focal point of Victorian culture in the Western World. Probably the largest collection of Victorian decorative art ever assembled— indispensable for antiquarians and designers. Unabridged republication of the Art-Journal Catalogue of the Great Exhibition of 1851, with all terminal essays. New introduction by John Gloag, F.S.A. xxxiv + 426pp. 9 x 12.
22503-8 Paperbound $5.00